THE BRIDE OF
DREAMS

FREDERIK VAN EEDEN

AUTHORIZED TRANSLATION BY MELLIE VON AUW

1st WORLD
LIBRARY
Literary Society

The Bride of Dreams

Frederik van Eeden

© 1st World Library, 2007
PO Box 2211
Fairfield, IA 52556
www.1stworldlibrary.com
First Edition

LCCN: 2007930787

Softcover ISBN: 978-1-4218-4825-9
Hardcover ISBN: 978-1-4218-4728-3
eBook ISBN: 978-1-4218-4922-5

Purchase *"The Bride of Dreams"*
as a traditional bound book at:
www.1stWorldLibrary.com/purchase.asp?ISBN=978-1-4218-4825-9

1st World Library is a literary, educational organization
dedicated to:

- Creating a free internet library of downloadable ebooks

- Hosting writing competitions and offering book publishing
scholarships.

Interested in more 1st World Library books? contact:
literacy@1stworldlibrary.com
Check us out at: www.1stworldlibrary.com

1ˢᵗ World Library Literary Society

Giving Back to the World

"If you want to work on the core problem, it's early school literacy."

- James Barksdale, former CEO of Netscape

"No skill is more crucial to the future of a child, or to a democratic and prosperous society, than literacy."

- Los Angeles Times

"Literacy... means far more than learning how to read and write... The aim is to transmit... knowledge and promote social participation."

- UNESCO

"Literacy is not a luxury, it is a right and a responsibility. If our world is to meet the challenges of the twenty-first century we must harness the energy and creativity of all our citizens."

- President Bill Clinton

"Parents should be encouraged to read to their children, and teachers should be equipped with all available techniques for teaching literacy, so the varying needs and capacities of individual kids can be taken into account."

- Hugh Mackay

I

As one approaches my little city from the sea on a summer's day, one sees only the tall, round clump of trees on the ramparts and, overtopping it, the old bell-tower with its fantastically shaped and ornamented stories and dome-top of deep cobalt blue. The land to either side is barely visible, and the green foliage flooded with pale sunshine seems to drift in the sun-mist on the grayish yellow waters. It is a dreamy little town, that once in Holland's prime had a short-lived illusion of worldly grandeur. Then gaily-rigged vessels embellished with gilded carvings and flaunting flags entered the little harbor, fishing boats, merchant vessels and battle-ships. The inhabitants built fine houses with crow-stepped gables and sculptured façades and collected in them exotic treasures, furniture, plate and china. Cannon stood on the ramparts and the citizens were filled with a sense of their importance and power as people of some authority in the world. They bore an escutcheon and were proud of it, they had their portraits painted in gorgeous attire, they gave the things their terse and pretty names, and they spoke picturesquely and gallantly as befits people leading a flourishing elemental life.

Now all this is long past. The little city no longer lives a life of its own, but quietly follows in the wake of the great world-ship. In the harbor a few fishing smacks, a market ship, a couple of sailing yachts and the steamboat are still anchored. The fine houses are curiosities for the strangers, and the china, the furniture and paintings may be viewed in the museum for a fee.

There is order, and peace, and prosperity too; the streets and houses look clean and well kept. But it is no longer a vigorous personal life; the color and the bloom have faded, the splendor and pageant are gone. It still lives, but as an unimportant part of a greater life. Its charm lies only in the memory of former days. It is lovely through its dream life, through the unreal phantasy of its past. All that constitutes its charm - the dark shadowy canals reflecting the light draw-bridges, the pretty quaintly-lighted streets with the red brick gables, bluish gray stoops, chains and palings, the harbor with the little old tar and rope shops, the tall sombre elm trees on the ramparts - it all possesses only the accidental beauty of the faded. It can no longer, like a young and blooming creature, will to be beautiful. It is beautiful involuntarily, no longer as a piece of human life, but as a piece of nature. And its loveliness is pathetic through the afterglow of a brief blazing up of individual vivid splendor of life.

In this quite sphere, where life now flows on but lazily and reflectively as in a small tributary stream of, the great river, - I live, an old man, for the accomplishment of my last task.

I live obscurely amid the obscure. I do my best to escape notice, and have no notoriety whatsoever, not even as an eccentric.

I associate with the doctor and the notary is expected of me, and I also go to the club. It is known that I have an income and, besides, earn some money from a small nursery on the outskirts of the town, and by giving Italian lessons.

Frederik van Eeden

The rumors regarding my past have all quieted down, and people have grown accustomed to my foreign name - Muralto. They see me regularly taking the same walk along the sea dike to my nursery, and my gray felt hat and my white coat in summery weather are known as peculiarities of the town. When you read this, reader, I shall be buried, respectably and simply, with twelve hired mourners and the coach with black plumes of the second class, and a wreath from the burgomaster's wife, to whom I gave lessons; from the notary, who occasionally earned something through me; and from the orphanage because, as treasurer, I always kept the accounts in order.

This is as I wish it to be. When you read this my living personality may no longer stand in your way. My individual being may no longer engage your attention. I know how this would veil the truth for you. Never has man accepted new and lucid ideas from a contemporary unless he were an avowed and venerated prophet, that is to say, a man corrupted and lost. I will not let myself be corrupted and give myself up as lost, and yet I know that my thoughts are too great to be accepted from free conviction without slavishness by my living fellow-men. Therefore have I peace in this petty world under the heavy burden of my tremendous life. I did not confer it on myself and I have no choice. Were I to speak my mind freely and honestly, I should be either locked up or worshipped. I deserve neither one nor the other; but such is the nature of the people of this age - they cannot reject without hatred nor accept without slavishness. Thus I live in self-restraint and peace among the lowly.

But these pages are the doors of the cap of my suppressed life. Only by these writings do I keep the peace within and master the tumult.

It is a hard struggle; I am weary from it not from arousing, but from restraining my thoughts. For what I write must be clear and orderly and concise. Readers nowadays are impatient and easily bored, and crave excitement. And they are dulled too, and no longer hear so clearly the true ring of sincere conviction. Yet I have peace, for this will be read. It will strike the summits, and the social system of today is still built so that everything slowly spreads from the summits and penetrates to the very lowest layers.

Do you disagree, reader? Do you accept nothing on higher authority, but judge everything independently for yourself?

Then it is just you I need. Then you are on the summit and all the rest of mankind in ranged about or beneath you. All the rest of mankind accepts and believes on authority - but you do not. Then have I also written this expressly and solely for you. How lucky that at last it has fallen into your hands. Allow me to embrace you in thought, dear, precious, freely-judging and independently-thinking reader. You are such a treasure to me, such a find, that for the world I would not let you go or lose you.

Listen then, dear reader, with a little patience and some painstaking on your part. Sweet spoils are not won without exertion! You are sensible enough not to want to judge without having given faithful attention.

I write this for you because you do not want to act without understanding; because you are restless and dissatisfied, a seeker and lover of the unknown; because at last you have turned on your way to look for what so long has gently pushed and driven you; because your eyes are opened wider and are more intent on the prospect toward which everything seems to lead.

I write this for you, the refractory and rebellious who are

Frederik van Eeden

tired of all slavery.

I write this for you, who feel that you have reached maturity and no longer want to be treated as a child, not even by fate.

I write this for you, the proud and the evil; yes, for the wantonly wicked who despises the meek and the just. I write this also for you, the earnestly good who wants to love his enemy, but cannot.

The complaisant and contented, the adjusters and compromisers, the advocates and flatters of God, those who shun anxiety and stop their ears against too blatant a truth - they had better read something else; there are plenty of pleasant and entertaining books for amusement.

And the slaves of reason, who tread in a circle around their stake as far as the cord of their logic reaches, they too cannot be my readers.

Only he who has overcome the word, who has forsaken the idolatry of the "true word" - he can read me with profit and understanding.

Listen, then: I am an old man proclaiming the glory of a new era. I am lonely and forsaken, but nevertheless I have a share in the great human world and the life of the gods.

I sit here serenely in my sombre, cool, old house, with its musty odor of old wood and memories of past generations. I look out upon the harbor and I hear the continuous murmur of the sea-breeze in the tall elms on the dike, and the screams of the gulls speaking of the vast and briny life of the sea. And yet, in the solitude of this quiet, forgotten life, I feel that I am mightier than the mightiest, a match for fate. I rule life; it shall bow to my wishes. I wrestle with the gods, even to the Most High. Sometimes I tremble, when a careless glance, with some semblance of deeper import, from one of the persons about me makes me think that a spark of this seething life within me has been discovered. But no one sees it, happily, nor knows me!

Had I told you this, (is it not so, dear reader, though you be ever so wise?), and I came not in a fiery chariot with a halo of glory and in dazzling raiment, but in my citizen's clothes, then after all you would undoubtedly have shrugged your shoulders and taken me for a poor fool.

But now I am a rich sage, because I write and hold my peace.

You are still a person, dear reader, but I have gone a step beyond - I am dead and no longer a person. Now, now while you are reading this. In this now, that is also now for me. I am no person, but more than that, and therefore can say to you what, from any person, would annoy you.

For you there is left only a still, small book, that meekly submits to being closed up and laid aside - and then again, as patiently as ever, resumes its tranquil message, when opened.

II

My parents were Italian aristocrats and my childhood days in the paternal home in Milan and our country estate near Como loom up vaguely before me in pictures half memories, half dreams. I cannot clearly distinguish what is purely memory and what a dream, or dream-memory, of these olden days. Memory is like tradition; one does not remember the first impression, but only the memory of it, and who knows how much that was already distorted; and so the picture changes from year to year, like a vaguely-told tale.

My childhood days fell towards the middle of the nineteenth century. It was my time of luxury and state. Our home was a palace with a pillared courtyard, wide stairway of stone with statuary, and a marble dolphin spouting water. We had carriages and servants and I wore velvet suits with wide lace collars and colored silk ties. I remember my father at the time as a tall, dark, proud man, most fastidiously groomed and dressed. He had shiny black whiskers and long, thick, wavy and glossy hair that fell over his forehead with an artful curl. He wore tight trousers with gaiters and patent leather shoes that always creaked softly. He had a calm but very decided manner, and impressed me immensely by his gentle way of giving orders and the confidence with which he could make himself obeyed. Only my mother resisted him with a power equally unshakable and equally restrained. As a child I saw this conflict daily and, without appearing to do so or being myself quite conscious of it, gave it much thought.

My mother was a very fair blonde Northern woman whom I heard praised for her great beauty - a fact a child is unable to determine for himself about his own mother. I know that she had large, gray eyes with dark rings underneath, and that it often seemed as though she had wept. Her voice, her complexion, her expression, everything vividly suggested tears to me. And in the silent struggle with my father her resistance was that of an aggrieved, painful, sensitive nature: his was cool, more indifferent and gay, but none the less firm. I never heard them quarrel, but I saw the politely tempered tension in the dignified house, during the stately meals, even as the servants saw it. Yet my father would sometimes hum a tune from an opera and joke and laugh boisterously with his friends; but mother always went about silently and gravely, gliding over the thick carpets like a spectre and, at her best, showing but a wan smile.

We were wealthy and prominent people and my parents felt that very strongly. And when I think about it now, here in my little provincial town in Holland, where I shine my own boots, then after all I feel compassion for the two - for my cool, well-bred father, as well as for my pale, languishing, distinguished mother. For they considered their high position just and righteous, and complete, and did not see in how much it was wanting. My mother did not see how tasteless the fashion was, - her draped and be-ruffled gown in which she thought herself so elegant and stately, - her own physical beauty and natural grace barely saving her from becoming an object of absolute ridicule. And my father did not know how much his traditional power of heredity had already been undermined by the democratic ideas everywhere astir.

Our luxury too was strangely deficient in many respects. I

Frederik van Eeden

have suffered bitter cold in the great chilly palace; at night one might break one's neck on the dark stone stairway; in some parts an ofttimes very foul and disgusting stench prevailed; the servants slept in stuffy hovels; there was a lavatory of which my father was very proud and which had cost enormous sums of money, but where in broad daylight one had to light a candle in order to wash ones hands.

I feel compassion for my proud father when I think of how he collected art treasures and bought paintings by distinguished artists of the time, which he would contemplate for hours through a monocle, and which formed the subject of long intricate critical speculations with his friends - paintings which after all were really only trifling daubs of no value whatever at the present time.

It was a dream of wholly successful social glory dreamed by my Italian parents as confidently as that other dream, dreamed by the Dutch merchants of this little seaport town. And this Italian dream I dreamed with them in perfect soberness. I can still become wholly absorbed in the illusion. I see the purple velvet with the white plume and the large diamond on my mother's hat, - a small, round bonnet, on the thick, blonde hair gathered into a net. I stand by her side in the carriage and feel myself the little prince, the little son of the Contessa - and see the people bowing with profound respect. I breathe the faint, fine perfume of frankincense and lavender exhaling from my mother's clothes. And I recollect my sensation of calm and pride at the meals with the heavy pretentious plate, the great bouquets of roses, the violet hose of the clergy who were our guests, the fragrance of the heavy wine.

And I am touched when I think of the self-delusion of so proud, arbitrary, critical and sceptical a man as my father, who was prejudiced so completely by this illusion of his greatness. He would have looked down scornfully upon the civic pomp of these seventeenth-century Hollanders and yet that was assuredly finer, even as was the older Italian civilization, which my father thought to surpass while he was really living in a state of sad decline.

It is quite comprehensible that in this family feud I sided with my mother, and that my sister, who was older than I, took my father's part. Also that my father would by no means submit to this, and that I very soon began to notice that I myself was the main subject of the strife, which fact did not tend to increase my modesty. It is strange how, as children, we take part in these conflicts, apparently wholly absorbed in our books and games and yet quite aware of the significant glances, the tears and passions hidden before us, the conversations suddenly arrested at our entrance, the artificial tone employed toward us children, the peculiar signs of dreary suspense, of momentous events beyond our ken imminent in the family circle and which we know we must pass without comment. Little as I was, I knew full well that the priests were on my mother's side and that my father fought against a coalition. But with my mother I felt a sense of warmth, gentleness and tenderness, and had already been won over to her side long before I knew what the contest was about. Her beauty, which I heard praised; the deference I saw her met with; her sanctity, which I recognized as a great power, which my father, otherwise yielding to nothing or no one, dared only resist with faltering mockery; the sphere of suffering and tears in which she lived - all this drew my chivalrous heart to her. I considered my father a great man, a giant who dared anything and could get whatever he pleased - but for this very reason would I defend my mother against him. I went to church with her faithfully, and strictly followed her admonitions to piety, and the frivolous jokes which my father sometimes made on that score I proudly and heroically met with profound gravity.

Frederik van Eeden

But this chivalrous conflict was speedily ended. The tension became aggravated so that the banquets ceased and my mother did not appear for days, and only summoned me to her side for a few moments when she would weep passionately and pray with me. Strange gentlemen came for long and secret conferences; and one bleak winter morning, very early, a large coach appeared in which my father and I departed.

Then there began for us two a restless life of wandering that continued for years. We travelled through northern Africa, Asia Minor, through all Europe, through America, and never did we remain in one place so long a time that I could grow fond of it, or feel myself at home there. As if by intentional design or driven by a constant unrest, my father would always break up whenever an abode began to feel homelike to me and I had found some friends in the vicinity, and it was wonderful with what strength of mind he persevered in this irksome, arduous and ofttimes even dangerous life.

We sometimes travelled through half barbarous countries with very primitive means of conveyance. My father had no permanent servant and would not suffer any woman to take charge of me. We were together constantly, night and day, and he did for me all that a mother could have done. He helped me to wash and dress, and even mended my clothes. He gave me lessons, taught me drawing, music, various languages, fencing, swimming and riding; but although I very much desired to, he never permitted me to attend school anywhere. His attention was never for a moment diverted from me, his care for me knew no weakening, and yet we never became really intimate. I felt that the old conflict was being carried on under conditions that were much harder for me. He had parted me from my mother and now that I stood alone, would vanquish me. He surely did not suspect that I would understand it thus and would consciously carry on the strife. But though I did not reason it out, my intuition clearly apprehended his tactics, and I held out more obstinately than ever with all the stubbornness of a child and the strength of mind which I had from himself inherited.

On three types of humanity my father was not to be approached. Firstly, the priests, the black ones, as he called them, whom he hated with all the fierce vehemence of his race; and, in spite of me, he so successfully inculcated into me his own aversion, that I cannot yet unexpectedly behold a priestly robe without a sensation of shuddering as at the sight of a snake. Secondly, the bourgeois, whom he called philistines, - the humbly living, contented, narrow-minded, timid, - whom he did not hate as much as he despised them with fervid scorn. And finally women, whom he neither hated nor despised, but whom he feared with a scoffing dread.

And now, looking back upon my youth from so great a distance, now I understand that it was not only healthy, natural tenderness that drove him to such exaggerated care for me, but bitter, impassioned feelings of opposition and revenge born of mortifying and painful experience. Priests, women and philistines had been too mighty or too cunning for him; now he would at least keep me, his successor in the world, out of their hands. That was the one great satisfaction he still sought in life, more from grudge against his enemies than for love of me.

Besides there were inconsistencies in his character that I am now quite able to explain, but which as a child, seemed very queer and shocking to me. He posed as a free-thinker and took pleasure in ridiculing my ingenuous piety. He called God a great joker, who made sport of men and amused himself at their expense. "But he won't fool me," he would say, "and I promise you that I'll tell him so straight to his

Frederik van Eeden

face if I get the chance of speaking to him hereafter." Only of natural science and nature did he speak with respect. Nature, according to him, was always beautiful and good where man did not spoil her. He called natural science our only security in life, weapon and shield against priestly lies and religious hypocrisy.

And yet my father frequently went to church, also taking me with him. Wherever he went he never failed to visit the temples regardless of the faith they confessed. He was very musical and he would pretend to go chiefly for the sacred music. But in the Catholic churches I also saw him crossing himself with the holy water and even kneeling for hours in prayer before an image of the Blessed Virgin wreathed with flowers and illumined by candles.

This was incomprehensible to me, having as yet no knowledge of the illogical workings of an artistically poetic and musical temperament. But I drew my own conclusions, and it was not surprising that I considered the devout father the true one, and the unbeliever perverted through evil influence. Thus, despite her absence, mother's influence prevailed. My memory had stripped her image of all that was trivial, commonplace and unlovely, and, little by little, with her suffering, her tears, her beauty, her tenderness, she began to shine for me in pure angelic holiness, the subject of my faithful and ardent devotion.

I shall not dwell on my long and arduous wanderings with my father. Indeed, I do not remember much about them. I must have seen many strange and beautiful sights, but they meant little to me. When the soul is young it does not take root in surroundings too vast and does not absorb the beautiful. I have a clearer recollection of certain picture books, of little cosy corners in the rooms we inhabited, of a small pewter can which I had found on the road and from which I would never be parted - not even when I went to bed than of the countries or cities we traversed.

True, I must have absorbed some of the wonderful things about me, for they undoubtedly furnished me with the material of which my dreams, about which I shall tell you further on, were woven. But as a boy I took no pleasure whatever in travelling. I longed for my mother, and for our country house, where I could play with my little sister under the airy open galleries in the rose garden or build dams in the brook. Only the journeying by rail, a novelty at that time, interested me the first few times, and above all the trip across the ocean to America, when Philadelphia and Chicago were only small places, and crossing the ocean by steamboat was still considered a perilous and risky undertaking.

Only of certain moments with lasting significance have I retained a sharper recollection. Thus I remember a miserable day somewhere in Asia Minor. We had both been ill from tainted food, my father and I, and had lain helpless in a most wretched tavern. Meanwhile thieves had stolen all our belongings, and when we wanted to journey on we could get no horses, for the inhabitants feared the thieves and their vengeance should we accuse them. Amidst a troop of dirty, eagerly debating Syrians in a scorching hot street I stood at my father's side peering into his wan face, sallow and drawn from the illness, with glistening streaks of perspiration and an expression of deadly fatigue and stubborn will.

He had a pistol in each hand and repeated a few words of command over and over again, while from the brown, gleaming heads about us came, in sometimes angry, some-times mournful, sometimes mocking tones, loud, but to me unintelligible, replies. I saw the fierce, self-interested, indifferent faces, with the wild eyes, and I realized how narrow was the boundary separating our life from death.

Frederik van Eeden

Still the scorching wild beast odor of the place comes back to me and I hear the sound of a monotonous tune, with fiddling and beating of drums in the distance, and the papery rustling of the palm leaves above our heads. This disagreeable condition must have continued a long while. At that time all mankind, the whole world, seemed hostile and desolate to me.

I knew, indeed, that my father would conquer. He did not want to die, and I had a childlike faith in his tremendous will-power. And so it actually turned out, and I was neither surprised nor glad. The irksome life of wandering continued, and I had a bitter feeling that it was my father who shut me out from the world and made it hostile to me.

We did after all finally procure a guide that day and made a long march on foot along scorching sandy roads, weak and tired as we were, guided only by a half-witted boy, humming and chewing wisps of straw. Then I began to realize what suffering means. My father did not speak, nor would he endure any complaints from me. I bore up against it bravely, as bravely as I could, but I began to ponder much at that time. "How long would I be able to endure this?" I thought. "And why does he do it? If all this folly and hardship served no purpose, we did not have to bear it then. What could he purpose thereby? Will something very pleasant follow? Or will these hardships continue until we die? Is all this God plaguing us, as he says? Why does God do it, and should we let ourselves be tormented so?"

Then, after hours of silent wandering, I put a question:

"Is there justice, father?"

By this I meant, whether for all this footsoreness, this thirst and this exertion, I would be rewarded by proportional pleasure. My father did not reply. He evidently had need of all his energies to walk on.

But when we had finally reached the seaport and had washed ourselves with seawater, he said abruptly: "There is only power!"

That answer did not please me. It was pleasure I wanted. Power could not avail me.

III

Consider well, dear reader, the purpose of these writings. It is not to occupy ourselves with the recital and attendance of thrilling and glowing adventures, but to try to what extent my words can clear up and illumine for you the dark background of these adventures. Illusion is the all-powerful word of the philosophers, with which they seek to destroy the things happening about us. But I have already worn out that word. At times it is in my hands as a foul tattered rag, it has lost its old use for me. I can also say - there is no illusion - there are only known and unknown things, truths revealed and unrevealed, very rapidly moving and very slowly flowing vital realities. And all my life it has been my constant and passionate desire to penetrate from the known to the unknown, from the revealed to the unrevealed, from the fleeting to the lasting, from the swiftly moving to the more slowly flowing - like a swimmer who from the centre of a wild mountain stream struggles toward the quiet waters near the shore. And wherefore this hard struggle? Because the still waters also hold blessings of consolation, of joy, of happiness. There is the pleasure, the real pleasure, that I as a boy expected from justice, the fair wages for trouble and pain, the equivalent reward.

My father did not believe in justice, but he did believe in power. But thus he did exactly what he wished not to do, he let himself be deceived and tried also to deceive me. But even when only a small boy, I would not let myself be cheated by counterfeit coin. "Go along with your power!" I thought. "I want pleasure. What can power or might avail me without pleasure?" I wanted wares for my money, for I believed in justice.

The Dutch merchants, who built my pretty and substantial house, were not very far-sighted fellows and on their hunt for happiness sailed straight into the bog. But they demanded wares for their money, and that was right. Now I, as an old man, live on the beautiful ruins of their glory overgrown with the immature buds of a newer, grander splendor of life; but I have continued to believe in justice, so firmly, that I quite dare to assume the responsibility of expounding this faith to you, dear reader, with all my might. And this faith teaches that you must not let yourself be cheated, and must demand wares for your money. That is - good, righteous, solid wares. We will not let some inane gaieties, some paltry and miserable pleasures, some tinsel be passed off on us as the real golden happiness. This one tries to coax you with tempting food and drink, another with the pleasures of being rich and mighty, still others with the comfort of a good conscience or perhaps with the flattery of honors and the satisfaction of duty fulfilled - or finally with the promise of reward hereafter, a brief on eternity with the privilege for your ghost of making complaint to the magistracy in case the ruler of the universe does not honor them. Nothing in my old age affords me such melancholy amusement as the foolishness of these persons, who deem themselves so wise, especially those practical, rational, matter-of-fact and epicurean persons, who go to such a vast amount of trouble and suffer themselves to be put off with such hackneyed, transitory, unreal, hollow stuff.

And I know not what is worse, the deception of the priests or

Frederik van Eeden

that of the philosophers, who scaling to a height upon a ladder of oratory write a big word upon a piece of paper, flaunting it before you as the legal tender for all your pains. With a beaming countenance the good citizens go home with their strip of paper on which is written, "pure reason," or "will for might," and are as contented as the so-styled freed peoples of Europe liberated by the hosts of the French revolution and honestly paid with worthless assignments.

What my father let me gain for my trouble did not seem to me a fair return, nor could he hold out to me any reasonable prospect of better reward. The diversity of life, the beauty of the world which he obtruded upon me so copiously would, as I approached maturity, have delighted and comforted me. As a lad it vexed and wearied me.

I was a tall lad, a replica of my proud, dark father, as everyone said. I remember the sally of an indignant Parisian street arab, who called after me: "Hey, boy, why so high and mighty?" And in my own country, where one turns more quickly to measures sharper than words, this loftiness brought upon me even fiercer attacks. A country lad imitated my proud bearing and pure Italian, getting for it a slap with a towel which I carried on my way to bathe in the sea. On my return the answer came - a stab in my back which for days forced me to assume a lowlier bearing.

I had early grown accustomed to the attention we attracted wherever we went. The father - always elegantly dressed, with his old-fashioned pompousness and melancholy eyes - and the son - nearly as tall and bearing a striking resemblance to him. Especially for women we were subjects of interest. But my father never seemed to pay any attention to this, nor did I ever see him come into closer contact with any woman.

But to me, long before I could appreciate the beauties of art and of nature, a glance from the eyes of a woman was the most precious of all life had to offer. That I primarily accounted as unalloyed gold outweighing much anguish and trouble.

I will try to be exact and absolutely sincere. I may avail myself of that privilege - old while I write, and dead when I shall be read. I am of a very amorous nature and the thought of friend or sweetheart was always an oasis in the desert of my thoughts. Even amidst the most important cares and duties such thoughts were ever of unspeakably greater interest and importance to me. They were never dull or tedious, never bored me, and were my consolation in times of gloom and discouragement. The pain they brought was also dear to me, and never possessed the loathsome hatefulness of other barren vital pangs.

It is difficult for me to recall when the first beams of this great and chiefest joy of life began to shine more brightly for me, but I cannot have been much over five or six years old. I played the passive part at the time, and it was the girl who chose me as her friend and invited the attention which I right willingly bestowed. But when later I myself went out to seek the joys of love, I thought only of boy friends. And it was a boy, a tall pale Hollander and, as it now seems to me, certainly not a very attractive lad, whom I approached one bright summers eve wandering together in the starlight, with the proposition of eternal friendship. The pale lad possessed what is called common sense and replied that he had too vague a conception of eternity to dare accept this proposal. Later, among women I have seldom met with such conscientious scruples.

Our constant travelling made all these attachments very brief and transitory and, as a child in search of love cares nothing for caste prejudice, they were also very diverse, but therefore none the less intense. I loved a nice brown-eyed and bare-footed Livornian fisher lad, because he was so strong and could row so well, and swim like a fish. And later, when I was bigger, it was a young German travelling salesman who taught me college songs and impressed me with his show of greater worldly wisdom, that won my heart. In these relations I was always the most ardent enthusiast, fervently pining, filled day and night with the subject of my love. And it can still make the blood rise to my wan cheeks when I think of the treasures of devotion that I squandered on these unresponsive beings. But now I know too that I may count myself lucky that they were so unresponsive. For through this wandering life at my father's side I had remained green as grass, and how easily one all too responsive might have turned the young tender instinct, with which the Genius of Humanity has endowed us, forever from its destined course to life-long torture. For we are all, man and woman alike, born with a twofold nature, and the pliant young shoot can so easily be contorted and its rightful growth permanently warped.

The maiden saw in me the lover long before I began to look on her with a lover's eyes. I had, indeed, found the unspeak-able joy of intimacy surpassing and atoning for all, but not yet the peculiar higher joy of an intimacy, with greater disparity, between youth and maid. I thought all intimacy glorious if it was but very fervent, and even entertained some vague notion regarding the great joy of an intimacy and cordiality embracing all, man and woman, young and old. But these moments of revelation and insight were but very brief and buried forthwith under commonplaces.

It must have been between the age of ten and twelve, that looking into the bright eyes of a girl, I first experienced that peculiar and higher bliss, that boy friendship could not give me. This was an event that so engrossed me, that I was oblivious of everything else and walked about like one moving in a dream.

I know not whether it was due to the blood of my fair northern mother, but never could a southern, dark-eyed and black-haired lass fascinate and interest me so vehemently and intensely as a blue-eyed blonde. Especially the English type, the cool, self-possessed, as well as somewhat haughty and coy blonde maiden, slender and yet strong, with wavy hair, attracted my attention and interest with an irresistible power.

Have patience, dear reader, it is a delicate and difficult matter, and I must deliberate well and speak carefully if we would more deeply penetrate the meaning of these things.

When these feelings overtake us as a child, we think it is the personality, that it is Alice or Bertha who interests us so intensely, and that only Alice or only Bertha can inspire such strange and powerful emotions of bliss and desire. And above all that it is just Alice or just Bertha whose more intimate acquaintance is so eminently desirable.

But how is it possible that we retain this illusion, and even live and die in it - pleasant and enviable though it may be - when we know that each feels this same interest in some other and ofttimes even see it transferred from one to another?

Being in love is the desire to fathom a most interesting secret, indispensable to us all. The beloved maiden attracts us, as a ray of light attracts the wanderer in the dark. Yet we know that every creature of her kind can shed this radiance about her, and that it is simply our own accidental receptivity that, among so many thousands, gives to this one creature in particular her attractive power.

Thus I think I can positively say that it was not herself I sought in my beloved, but the reflection of one common light that also shines through other windows as well as through the eyes in which I discovered it. But though my reason must affirm it, my heart comprehends little of this. When I think of her whom I loved last, longest and most devotedly, then she herself, her own personality, is a certainty to me that I would not willingly relinquish for any higher certainty, many years though I have spent in anxious pondering on this subject.

The list of my boy friends is not worth recording. They were puppets wondrously decked out by my fertile imagination, worshipped as heroes for a while with all the ritual of German friendship cult - and later, when in their personal life they showed no resemblance to my ideal expectations, rudely dismantled and cast aside and hated. I can still see a photograph of one of them lying in my washbowl with pierced eyes, curling and charring under the avenging flame of a match.

The last of the series, the young commercial traveller, longest retained his glory. I saw him only about a week in a watering place, and subsequently he was able to maintain his position of hero-friend by a correspondence in which he answered my fervent ingenuousness stammered in poor German with fluent plagiarism from the classics of his romantic fatherland. All went well, until after a few years I met him again and noticed that it was not even a puppet but a skeleton that I had arrayed in a hero's armor. I was furious at him as though he had purposely deceived me - but my anger was unmerited. He had in perfect good faith tried his best to live up to the national traditions of friendship and to keep burning the smouldering fire of his own humble ideal of love.

A friend, who would have paid me in my own coin, who requited what I desired to give him, - as, faithful, as devoted, as passionate, as self-sacrificing, as attentive and solicitous as it was my nature to understand and prove friendship - such a one I never found. And I was unreasonable enough to retain a bitter and scornful feeling toward those who, seeming to give promise of such an exalted friendship, had disappointed me so sorely. I now understand how good it is that at this age such friendships do not exist. Is it not hard enough to extricate ourselves from the seemingly hopeless complications of sexual instincts and relations? Are we not still far from the adjustment of passions, arising much too early and continuing much too long? physical and mental desires, affections misplaced, extinguished and transferred to others? and children who must be fed? Should we desire to add to these problems the complications of strong friend-ships which might perhaps transform and divert our entire nature? Let each, who feels an honest, strong, profound, budding passion for a being of opposite sex sprouting within himself be grateful. The more so if he is not confronted by abysses all too deep, by doors all too closely barred and by deserts all too barren; if in this other soul he can detect feelings somewhat akin to his own. To expect, besides, exalted friendships between those of equal sex is imputing too much power and good will to the Deity in whose hand we live.

For me, then, it was not Alice or Bertha, - but Emmy, and more particularly Emmy Tenders, the daughter of an English-Scotch merchant, who of all human beings seemed to me the most interesting and worth knowing. I really cannot say whether she was pretty or whether others consi-dered her so. She interested me in such strong and intense degree that it never occurred to me to look at her from an æsthetically critical standpoint. I remember that I was interested and surprised when, after I had already known her over a year, I heard an old gentleman referring to her as "that lovely child." It flattered me like a personal compliment, but it sounded wholly new to me.

I know that she was lithe and yet quite robust, that she had light grayish-blue eyes and an abundance of thick blonde hair that framed her face in heavy waves. It is quite impossible for me to say or to give even an intimation of what it was that so attracted me in her. I saw her first in her own home in the company of her mother, a pleasant Scotch lady, and her brothers, sturdy, clever, staid and silent lads. And from the moment I saw her I was drawn to her by a mysterious feeling of attraction, which even now, after more than fifty years, is as inexplicable to me as it then was. She was affectionate toward her mother, treated her brothers like good comrades, and me in a somewhat arch and pleasantly ingenious manner. She said nothing particular, nor did I ever foster the illusion that she had anything very particular to say. But her nature concealed a secret for me that I felt I must approach and fathom at all costs, though I staked my greatest treasure, at the cost of my life would have seemed but a miserably feeble consideration to me.

And mingled with this, thus making it all the more inexplicable, was a feeling of mournfulness, of pity. When I said to myself: "how dear she is!" I pronounced the "dear" with a mingled feeling of tender pain and fervent pity.

What could be the meaning of this? She seemed entirely well and happy and led a pleasant life, with good parents, cordial family relations, luxuries, many outdoor pleasures, ball games, tea-parties, boat excursions, dances - everything that could make an English girl of our time happy.

And yet when I thought of her playful ways, her dear, young supple limbs, her thick, wavy, blonde hair, which she would push back now and then with both her hands, the tears welled up in my eyes from sheer compassion.

See, reader, after all it is just as well that for the beginning, nothing comes of these great friendships. They merely divert us. One would think that love meant the intellectual communion of spirits. But that is nonsense. What an intellectual giant one would have had to be to offer Goethe or Dante a worthy friendship. Yet Gemma Donati and Christiane Vulpius were their mates, their equals in power, before whom they willingly bowed and humbled themselves. Every sweet woman conceals a secret of life that outweighs the wisdom of the greatest man, and for which he would willingly barter all his treasures and yet count it too small a price.

Let us be patient, dear reader, and proceed carefully. My time of love is past and yet the matter is as much of a mystery to me as ever. But it is the work on which we are all employed, and I hold that first the love between man and woman must be better regulated and understood before we can proceed to friendship.

Now I turn the jewel of my love-life a point about and contemplate another facet as if to discover the hidden form of the crystal.

Emmy Tenders was the first woman who, when I had grown from youth to manhood, at once, absolutely, and completely won me without effort on her part. She was the first woman I eagerly sought, though it was with the deepest reverence and a shrinking fervor. But, as I said before, probably ten years previous to this girls had sought me, detecting the prospective man in me before I had myself become aware of him.

This had indeed flattered me and, as I have confessed, I had also found in the glance from the eyes of some one of them promise of higher joy than my boy friendships could give me - but with a peculiar obstinacy inexplicable to myself, I had always repelled these approaches. Without acting in obedience to boyish tradition, to whose influence I was never subjected on account of my nomadic life, my own feeling made me see something childish and unworthy in the association with girls and women, while on the other hand I exalted my boy friendships as nobler and manlier.

But oh! the subtle and effective manner in which this avenged itself on me. When later my time of seeking had come, and I was assailed and driven by overwhelming passions, it then appeared that I had retained the memory of these little adventures of childhood days with irritating exactness, and there mingled with it a bitter feeling of regret for the lost opportunities. The kiss blown me from a window in Naples, the extraordinary, more than motherly cares of the hotel chambermaid in Vienna, the roses pressed into my hands on the street by a young Spanish girl somewhere in the south of France, the embrace and the kiss on my cheek which I once suddenly felt in a dark garden where I stood listening to some music and which I - oh, obstinate simpleton that I was! - scornfully and indignantly repelled - how often and with what teasing tenacity have they haunted me in my dreamy days and sleepless nights, when the icy crust of boyish pride had long been melted, but the girls had also grown proportionally more chary of their favors. And even now with half a century intervening, I cannot watch this subtle game of mutual hide-and-seek without a smile, and I recognize some truth in my father's opinion that many a time it must indeed also afford amusement to the Unseen One who secretly directs the figures of this graceful dance.

Remember, dear reader, that up to the time I met Emmy

Tenders, I was green as grass. It had never occurred to me to seek for any connection between the wondrously blissful emotions of intimacy that continually occupied me - and certain physical sensations which only alarmed me because I thought them unhealthy. And yet I consider this very connection well-nigh the most mysterious and interesting of all the enigmas of life. And perhaps, as I, you too have always felt when reading the writings of the great and distinguished lovers among mankind, a certain want of exactness, which led me to exclaim: "But how did you deal with that question?"

My father fared in this matter like the man who dropped his glasses in a dark room and when, after much hesitation and deliberation he very carefully set down his foot, stepped precisely on the glass. He had tried to bring me up with such extraordinary care and wisdom, and now failed for that very reason. He encouraged my boyish scorn of girls and courting and did not oppose my partiality for boy friendships. The terrible risk I thereby ran of warping my sound and natural instinct and thus making myself unhappy for life, he did not seem to see, and when the time came to enlighten me in this regard he neglected to do so. My very sensitive prudishness concerning everything pertaining to my body he, rightly and to my gratitude, respected as long as possible.

But when it became clear to him that I was seized with a glowing passion for Emmy Tenders - and he must indeed have been very deaf and blind not to notice my very apparent confusion and perplexity, my air of abstraction, my brightening at everything that suggested her, my pallor, my nocturnal wanderings abroad and my agonies of weeping in bed - he considered the time for my final enlightenment come.

Between two sensitive, proud and refined natures like my

father and myself, this was a most painful and most difficult task. But he performed it with his customary undaunted determination. I have never spent a more uncomfortable hour in my life. My father had brought books and prints for better demonstration; he dared not look at me and mumbled a good deal under his breath in a hollow voice. Beads of perspiration stood on his brow.

When he had left the room, nervous and embarrassed as a child who has done wrong, my first thought was: a revolver. I was crushed and wanted to end my life. But the secret, - the secret itself bound me to life. The strange, attractive, mysterious, repulsive secret fascinated me too much to leave it.

Insensible with pain and humiliation, I went to my room. And there, before I could help it, the name "Emmy" rose to my lips. I shivered, crying out the name once more, now like a despairing shriek of distress. Then I fell down upon my bed and wept as though I would weep out my very heart.

IV

The type of men which my father called philistines has this common characteristic, that for all wonders and mysteries they forthwith find a convenient explanation. Does the truth not fit it exactly? Then they do as did the Kaffir, who receiving as a present a much too narrow pair of shoes, solved the difficulty by undauntedly chopping off his toes and then, greatly delighted, went out walking in the precious gift.

This time it was my father himself who pretended to see nothing strange or mysterious in my deeply agitated state of mind. The substance of the matter he had now explained to me scientifically, biologically, physiologically and anatomically; to this nothing need be added nor did it leave anything unexplained.

My disgust, my profound horror and dejection at this simple increase of knowledge which, as every new acquisition of knowledge, should have delighted and edified me - Yes! for that there was no room in his explanation, as little as for his own embarrassment while imparting it. And therefore, without any sentimentality, these toes must be lopped off so that the boot would fit.

Reader, do not imagine that I demand of you deep regard and

Frederik van Eeden

veneration for the great foolish boy who lay helplessly weeping because of that strange difference between men and flowers that with the former carries so much discord into their most important vital function.

I myself now softly laugh at my self of fifty years ago, not scornfully, but with gentle irony - sympathetically. I pat the boy on the shoulder and admonish him kindly: "Quiet, laddie, be not so dismayed. We are a strange mingling of ape and angel. But try, as quickly as possible, to reconcile yourself to this, then everything becomes quite bearable. Do you think this same thing would have caused like consternation to Emmy Tenders, if the knowledge but came to her in the right way, that is to say the way of reverent love, and deep devotion? She is indeed wiser. And had you learned it as a poet and lover and not as a philistine then you too would not have found it so appalling."

But all this, dear reader, does not alter the mysterious and distressing truth, and one cannot make disharmony bearable by denying it. So much is certain that my father's assertion, declaring my horror wholly unreasonable, affected me like an attempt at lopping off my toes to make the boot fit. I resisted passionately, maintaining an inexorable separation between my noble and lofty sentiments for Emmy and the low and vile things my father had disclosed to me, and thus wandered hastily and eagerly on the dangerous path whose course branches out but once - one road leading to fanaticism and the other to dissolute cynicism.

This was my father's work. But I have never reproached him for it with feelings of bitter resentment. Why not? Can we pronounce sentence, reader, in a suit whereof the most important facts still lie in impenetrable darkness?

From my unimpassioned tribunal here in the dreamy and

forgotten little town, I hold acquittal for all who have strayed and gone to ruin in Cupid's flowery and thorny labyrinth. For assuredly it is not of human designing.

That there is guilt I cannot deny. Every ill has a father and a mother, and for once and all, we are accustomed to calling these parents sin and guilt. But I follow the genealogical tree of these strange and tender woes beyond Adam and Eve or the Pithecantropus Erectus, even should I then have to launch my accusations at Powers which from generation to generation have imprinted in us the belief in their inviolability.

And now observe what makes the matter still more strange and illogical. I am not only of a very amorous but also of a very sensual nature. Together with my strong susceptibility to the joys of soul communion there went the mighty overpowering impulse of propagation. Before the contact of these two currents had been brought about in such a painful manner the low, dark, physical instinct had filled me with a continual though not very distressing restlessness and with doubt concerning my health. The splendid equilibrium of my other functions, that has maintained itself to this day, always outweighed this doubt.

But when the secret was half explained it became all the more absorbing and enticing and so occupied my thoughts that, even now an old man, I wonder again and again that a human brain can ponder over such comparatively simple facts ad infinitum, without having them lose their interest, and without really arriving at any conclusion.

Physicians would speak of pathological conditions and of libido sexualis. But I would point out to you, dear reader, that though there may be very good and noble men among physicians, every physician of our day without exception, in so much as he would be called a physician, is at the same time also a philistine. With their explanations and their fine words for things that are beyond their comprehension because their science is still unpoetical and unphilosophical, they do not serve us in the least.

And how could one of these present-day sages reasonably explain to me that in a noble and lofty human type such as I, certainly not without some right, dared call myself, the very strong working of an impulse common to all animals was coupled with an exaggerated sensitiveness for its ignoble character? Were this impulse good and beautiful and in no part ignoble, whence then my aversion? - were it really low and unworthy, whence its presence, so impertinent and overpowering, in a refined and highly cultured member of the human race?

And if any would speak here of exceptions and strange freaks of nature, should we not immediately bar his lips with a series of names all shining in the history of mankind? Are we not acquainted with Sophocles' very significant sigh of relief at being delivered from this plague by his years? Is it without a deeper meaning that Dante on the summit of the mount of redemption lets his dearest and most honored poets do penance for this very weakness - Arnaut de Verigord, Guittons of Arezzo and also Guido Guinicello his father and the father of all those -

che mai

rime d'amore usar dolci e leggiadre.

Did it stand differently with Dante himself, with Shelley, Byron, Heine, Goethe?

My father's deed arose from an imagined sense of duty, but

had wholly different consequences than he probably expected. He must surely have thought that now, knowing what it implied, I would either steer straight for matrimony or renounce my boyish love. He had satisfactorily torn to pieces the veil of illusion that something loftier and more mysterious than common propagation was concerned here - woman's witchery which he knew and from which he wished to shield me. He also expected my confidence and my appeal for advice in difficulties and dangers of a kindred nature.

But behold, I remained as ardently devoted and valiantly true to Emmy as ever. I felt a desire to shield her with my life against the baseness of this world and let my body serve her as a bridge across the earthly pool of mire. And higher than ever, I held her image above every profaning thought. I considered it a sacrilege to think of her as one of the thousand females about me and to confound my love with the wooing and wedding of the rest of the world.

But with that, the passions suddenly awakened by my father, fed by a vivid imagination and now craving recognition and liberty, were not stilled. The slumbering hounds were aroused and clamored for food. And as I had not the slightest intention of granting them what my father pointed out as their natural and lawful portion, but what, as something sacred and holy, I was determined to keep from their devouring jaws cost what it would, they sought other food and threatened to destroy me.

"But what would you do about it, old hermit?" the young reader will ask; "what do you consider a model solution of the question?"

I would do nothing about it, young reader!

The old Muralto is not called to draw up for you a scheme of life. He only shoves his little lamp ahead as far as he can reach into the darkness. For the confusion and the rubbish thus brought to light he is not responsible and each must see for himself how he finds his way through.

The hounds want food, that is certain. And, whether intentionally or not, some day they will be awakened; from that, too, there is no escaping. Blessed is he who can forthwith offer them their proper prey. And woe to him who thinks that, without danger to himself, he can let them starve to death or seek for booty unbridled!

And would you retain the confidence of your children do not threaten to mutilate the feet of their sensibilities for the sake of a narrow theory. I myself at least, after what I had experienced, would sooner have gone to the nearest police agent for intimate advice, than back to my father.

Emmy's home was situated in London on the Thames. The smooth emerald-green, well-trimmed lawn with the multi-colored flower-borders, and the blue porcelain vases, extended to the water, and there on summer afternoons the family sat on the cane chairs partaking of tea, feeding the swans swimming by, and watching the gay traffic, - the multitude of graceful little crafts with fashionably dressed men and women in softly blending tones of green, violet, pink and white, the muscular gig-rowers in training, shooting by with a regular swish of oars and followed by shouting friends on horseback; the competitors in a swimming match making their way amidst all this tumult cheered on every side; the luxuriant houseboats floating by, full of flowers and happy people, from which echoed strains of music and a flood of light emanated at night.

I lived in the suburbs with my father, and when I mingled with the bright, merry, fair and innocent human world, then all my father had told me seemed but an ugly fairy-tale.

But London is a strange and, for a person of my temperament, a most dangerous city. The glamour of angelic human purity is so successfully assumed there that it makes itself all the more glaringly and horribly manifest, and exercises a more exciting influence, when the black demon suddenly leers at us from behind the veil.

Not only Emmy Tenders, but every woman of her type and race, every cultured English woman, possessed for me something lofty, something holy and irreproachable. The women of other countries still bore some resemblance to the female animal; there I could still conceive and imagine this fatal humiliation; but an English woman seemed so pure, so noble, so chaste and yet so candidly innocent that her mere presence sufficed to drive away all impure thoughts. And of all English women, Emmy Tenders was indeed the sweetest and purest. When I saw her again all anxiety and horror vanished. I was completely happy and also thankful that no revolver had been within my reach in that dark moment following the revelation. That summer's afternoon by the Thames amid the merry family group some vague conception dawned in me that Emmy's wondrous power would have made pure all that appeared ugly and vile to me, if only the revelation had come to me through her.

But it seems indeed that the English rely too much upon the cleansing power of innocence in their woman. And it is curious how public opinion among this prudish nation will permit exhibitions of unabashed flirtation which would be publicly tolerated in probably no other part of Europe and certainly not in Asia or Africa. In the light, graceful little boat I glided over the sparkling river amid the tender summer's bloom which clothed everything with a charm of fairyland and facing me, on the silken cushions, sat my beloved, in her white dress, holding the cords of the rudder. And to the left and right, under the shadowing branches of the drooping willows, my now wide-opened eyes saw pairs of lovers, each in their own boat, in affectionate attitudes that greatly embarrassed and distressed me. Emmy did not seem to see them or appeared to be wholly undisturbed thereby. Then it occurred to me that I myself must be to blame here and that a peculiar inborn depravity made the natural appear so hideous to me and obtrude itself so plainly on my view. And all the more I honored and admired the pure creature the bright mirror of whose soul the impure breath of the world could not dim, and to whom the human love-life seemed as natural, common and unexciting as to the naturalist or ancient philosopher.

The old hermit and philosopher Muralto would here remark, that the young poetic lover Muralto was a long distance from the sage. It has indeed occurred to the old man, though seldom, thank heaven, despite his many years, that he could regard the human love-life like a naturalist or an old satiated philosopher without the pleasing distress, the sweet excitement of former days - yet he did not feel better and wiser at such times, but deeply mourned a precious loss. I may err, reader, but consider the words of experience!

And in these same ardent days of first true love the giant city exposed herself to my now enlightened eyes in all her disharmony. And I, who in wanton Paris had passed as an innocent child through a hotbed of sensuality and a hailstorm of seduction, on a single twilight eve in London had four or five encounters the particulars of which remained in my memory as barbed arrows remain imbedded in the flesh, smarting and itching and burning like the thorny fibres of cactus or sweetbriar seed with which one has come into too close contact.

When the women of my country, of a Latin race, cast away their pride and, from need or indifference, make the game of love their profession, they still retain a natural and charming glamour and play the sorry game with a certain grace and conviction as a poor homage to the lofty secret which they must needs desecrate.

But the English or German woman who lays aside her chastity - God be gracious to these bunglers! - casts off her modesty as downrightly as though she were glad that she need not carry it longer - no! let us say as though the greater depth of her fall resulted also in a more absolute hopelessness of ever arising again. Cold, businesslike and practical, they carry on their profession and regard the human love-life as unmoved and unexcited as a naturalist or an old philosopher.

But just this class distinction, this sharp and dreadful contrast between the pure English woman, so nobly represented in my queenly love, and the creatures who, fifty years ago and probably to the present day, toward twilight haunted the fine London parks and in the most unabashed manner reminded me of the recently received fatherly disclosures - just this stirred the newly aroused passions within me to an untamable uproar. The tormented hungry dogs raged blindly.

Was the noble creature that filled my heart too good for them - well: they would then procure for themselves other food. Eat they would, though it were hideous carrion! The tormented dogs became wolves, became hyenas.

Let this not arouse your indignation, dear reader. I gladly believe that your beasties never caused you much trouble, that they were willingly satisfied with lettuce leaves, or would probably also fast at will, or submit contentedly to the matrimonial leash. Possibly they were marmots. But did you yourself rear this tractable race? Then count not yours the honor nor mine the shame, but accord both to that unknown Breeder who followed the genealogical tables and selected the mothers and fathers, uniting them with delicate discernment and hidden design. The pasturing of docile cattle involves no honor or glory, and I choose to render account of my pasturage to him alone who knew, better than I, what he did when he entrusted me with the savage drove.

Neither let it surprise you that my love for Emmy could not drive away the impure images and destroy their power of attraction. The reconciliation of ape and angel that our human nature demands had, thanks to my father's bungling match-making, gone fatally wrong. A hopeless separation had arisen, the angel seemed inaccessible and the beast sought his own wild paths. My thoughts would suffer no desecration of Emmy's sacredness. But the fatherly lesson had startled up in me a seething swarm of thoughts as difficult to direct or drive away as a roomful of flies. I could scarcely keep them off the one white lily in my chamber, what wonder then that the stinking carrion brought from the nocturnal London parks was black with them?

V

Emmy was nineteen years old when I made her acquaintance, and I was sixteen, but fully developed at that age, as is not unusual in my country. For three years I courted her, steadfastly, but in a curiously capricious and inconsistent way, with all the changes of an all-daring and naught-fearing devotion, wildly-blazing happiness, sudden shyness and trembling shrinking, violent dismay, self-reproach, deep self-contempt - all this being caused by the confusion and the strife in the intimate household of my soul.

Emmy was, as I can now say without partiality, a good, dear, natural and simple child, born to make an excellent and loving housewife and consort.

How often I imagine that I, the patriarch of to-day, with my present knowledge, would have stepped between the two and easily steered the two little boats into safe currents on a joint and prosperous journey. So little would have been needed, a little hint, a loving word of direction, a gentle stay - and everything would have been well. But these are idle and tormenting after-thoughts, perhaps quite erroneous too.

I was not so undesirable a suitor, even though I was three years her junior. Emmy's parents were liberal-minded, like most English people not insensible to rank and title, and would surely not have precluded the young noble Italian from their family, even though he had been brought up in the Catholic faith.

Thus the amiable child complacently bore with my stormy adoration, less hidden by me than is customary among the English, schooled in self-restraint; she waited patiently; gently, almost imperceptibly, encouraging me the while until I should be old enough to dare press my suit more urgently. It sometimes seemed to me as though a girl was much less curious and surprised, and, from out a hidden well, much sooner and better informed concerning the course of the coming mysteries than a boy. She does not think about it and would not be able to express it, and yet she knows everything at the right time, as though the body had thought for her.

Though our travelling life continued still, my father stopped oftener and longer in London than in any other place, as though yielding to the unpronounced pressure of his son. Perhaps this time he purposely wished to submit me to the flames, my reserve hiding from him the true state of my heart and my thoughts.

And when, after our first meeting, we were again on our way, it was Emmy who gave the first timid sign to enter into correspondence. On St. Valentine's day, the significance of which I knew full well, a colored scrap-picture arrived, representing a rosy woman's hand with elegantly curved finger tips offering a bouquet of blue forget-me-nots. The source from whence it came was evident enough to me, and I, awkward churl, was rude enough to send her a rapturous letter of thanks for it, which of course met with a very cool rejection and denial.

At long as I was away from London I had comparative

peace. I thought about my beloved, wrote to her and of her in my diary and studied the subjects which my father, who wished to make a diplomat of me, appointed. I spent the winter with him in Berlin, but there I noticed nothing of the London scandal, though I fully realized that something of the sort could not well be missing in the big city. All my thoughts of love, the pure and beautiful as well as its base desecration, swarmed about the great, gray, smoke-darkened and fog-bound city across the sea.

Just as the elements of our sensually visible being, the cells of the body, manifest a peculiar life and independent nature, so the elements of our invisible being - the desires and passions - seem to be beings with a peculiar nature. They are like animals and children, hearkening to the voice that first called them, following the habits first taught them, curiously stubborn in the errors grown habitual to them in youth, and with a strange tendency toward the lower, as though falling through the influence of a gravitation.

I had my "low" and my "lofty" times, as I called them. Sometimes for weeks and months my thoughts would be pure and tranquil: then they would be again suddenly aroused by some trifling cause - sometimes mental: a newspaper article, a conversation overheard - sometimes physical: a little fête, carrying on their harassing and tormenting game, constantly repeating and circling around the same facts and words, throughout entire sleepless nights, gnawing and picking at these never satiating subjects, so offensive and yet so attractive, as a dog gnaws at an old whitened bone.

Especially in a time of dejection and gloom, when the world offered me no flower of outward beauty, the imagination immediately sought comfort in that which was always exciting, always charming and intriguing, and never satiated or vexed me. Neither study nor physical exercise had the power to restrain the arbitrary course of the thoughts; the mind possessed no weapons against them.

A feverish suspense beset me when it became certain that I was to see Emmy again. A clear apprehension had already been born in me that only her presence, her encouragement, her devotion could redeem me. And when I saw her cordially bowing from the carriage that awaited us at the suburban station on a bright, sunny May day, and went to meet her trembling and dizzy with emotion, and seeing nothing of the great world about me save her hair, golden in the sunlight, the white dress, the broad-brimmed straw hat and the shining eyes - I really believed that I was saved, and I no longer wavered in my heart and was positively determined that I actually wanted her for my wife, no matter what a saint she might be and how unworthy I.

Thus everything might have come out right, but things do not run so smoothly in this world. I was seventeen and Emmy twenty. There still followed weeks, long months - melancholy moods returned again, discouragements - there were also walks through the dusky parks. And the hungry dogs continued to whine and to howl and the thought-flies continued to buzz and to defile themselves. Man may be reasonable and patient; he has natures to control, apparently for his own good, that are neither reasonable nor patient; that themselves never rest and demand guidance from a spirit, that does need rest; that always want to have their own way, and yet sink fatally downward if the government of the mind leaves them unguarded. And these are given us by nature, as we are told, the same nature which according to my father is always good if man does not spoil her.

So as not to disturb you by exciting your imagination, dear reader, which might make the driving of your own team more troublesome to you, I shall mention no particulars of my struggle and my defeat. This precaution of an old man need not hurt you.

I fell under the joint influence of the following things: the fatally arisen rupture between corporal and spiritual desires, - the sharp contrast between English purity and English lewdness that, with its incomprehensible contradiction, has as exciting an effect as the dog in the duck-yard, who decoys the inquisitive ducks into the mouth of the strangler, - and finally the accursed self-contempt that makes one say: "There's nothing lost with me anyway."

With his attention so steadily fixed upon me, my father could not remain without suspicion. He came to my room one morning, installed himself there, and said:

"I hope, Vico mio, that you have remained and will remain a nobleman in all things."

When we Italians perceive that someone would enter upon a friendly conversation with us, we look upon it as an invitation to set up together and complete a small work of art, and we gladly give it an attentive hearing and zealously assist with careful application, so that something good and fine be brought forth. When I hear two Hollanders carrying on a conversation, it sounds more like children of a village school repeating their penal task, careless, slipshod, unwilling and embarrassed - if only they get it over with.

"My father," I answered, "I believe I know quite well how you wish a nobleman to be, but perhaps I do not know how he should comport himself in everything. Do you refer to any particular circumstance, or are you speaking generally?"

"If you recognize generally that a nobleman must avoid all intimate intercourse with ignoble persons, Vico, - the particular instances that I have in mind are therein included."

"That is plain, father. But yet I have something more to ask. First this: do you call it intimate intercourse where the spirit on either side remains at an infinite distance? And then this: can a nobleman have ignoble desires?"

I saw my father start painfully. Slowly and eyeing me sharply, he said:

"I fear, Vico, that I must speak plainly here, too. To the first I make this reply: It is certain that we have a body, but of a spirit that can separate itself from this body we know nothing and have no single proof. And as concerns the second question: natural desires are never ignoble as long as they remain in the natural channels."

"Without agreeing to the first," I replied, "I shall let it rest, because our natures are too different, and we do not understand each other anyway. But your answer to the second gives me much to ask. If a desire in me is natural and thus not ignoble, how then can it drive me to ignoble things? Are all natural desires good in all men? And how do I distinguish between natural and noble desires and unnatural and ignoble desires?"

"Have you no power of discrimination for that, Vico?" my father asked.

"If I use my discrimination, father, I call ignoble what my father calls natural."

My father arrested the conversation a moment to reflect. Then he realized that in order not to lose more ground, he must turn from the general to the particular.

"Let us beware, son, lest we become entangled in words. I have happily established that we both have an aversion from the vile and low. Take care then, that is all I wished to say, that you do not come into contact with it."

"But the vile and low in me desires contact with the vile and low in others," said I, bitterly.

My father grew impatient and said:

"I don't believe in this baseness and vileness in you. The popes surely talked you into that when you were a child. I understand that you have to deal with desires and passions that are absolutely not unnatural or bad, but very common at your age. But do not seek relief from them with unworthy, licentious persons. Of the great danger I have already warned you, have I not? Do not forget that in a few moments you can, through defilement, devastate your entire life."

"I do not forget that, father."

"Very well, but you should also be too proud to trouble yourself about such low-graded creatures."

"I would gladly have reason to be proud. But what is passing on in me is well suited to keep me humble. Can you deliver me from all this lowness and ugliness? You yourself have aroused it in me."

"I?" my father called, frowning angrily.

"By your scientific explanations. Before that time I had comparative peace. Now I am desperate, like a captive and tormented cat. It will end badly with me, father, that is certain. I foresee it, and can do nothing to prevent it. I can put out my eyes and chop off my hands, but I cannot control my thoughts and drive away these visions. That is beyond human power. I shall go to the bad, that is certain, and then the sooner the better. There's not so much lost with me."

With an anxious, painful eagerness my father listened to these first outspoken words. Then he said with a little laugh, half pitying, half scornful:

"One thing is plain to me now, my boy, that you must get married soon. Well, happily you need not seek long or fear a refusal. You can get of the very finest that wears a petticoat. Don't be bashful, Vico! You have a noble name, pure blood, a handsome face, and a fine, strong, healthy body. I shall supply the money. Be calm, my boy, you can have what you want for the asking."

I got up, deeply indignant. I believe that I laughed a theatrical laugh.

"Most decidedly your meaning is that I should make use of a pure and holy being, whose name I am not worthy to pronounce, as a safety valve, a preservative, a drain for my own foul and low passions. I assure you that, had it not been my father who had spoken such words to me, I would have challenged the man."

My father attempted a pitying smile, but it was artificial and painful:

"Good heavens, Vico! what exaggerated, impossible, fanatical nonsense! Then were all mothers who bore children drains for their husbands? Do be calm and reasonable, lad! You are not unworthy, your passions are not foul and low, whoever got that into your head? Your mother, surely, and her black friends. It's terrible how a mother can early poison the thoughts of her child."

"If one of my parents poisoned my thoughts, then it was not my mother. I realize my unworthiness through my own consciousness, not through outside persuasion. But my father cannot understand that, because he is a stranger to my deepest and most sacred feelings. Even though your advice had been good, father, your manner of expressing it would already have repelled me. But, moreover, your advice is idle. An English girl of twenty does not marry a young man of seventeen, and in three years from now I'll be lost anyway, hopelessly lost. I foresee that positively. And oh! what does it matter? It's only I, after all!" Scornfully shrugging my shoulders, I ran about the room. My father lifted both hands to his forehead and stared into vacancy with a look full of gloom, long-nurtured wrath and desperation. I still remember that look and wonder that I was not more painfully struck by it at the time. After a while he got up, sighed, and with the words, "We shall see!" he walked out of the room.

Again the poor man had brought about the contrary of what he wished to attain. One impression, above all, I retained from the conversation - it was that my mother would surely understand me and perhaps save me. I knew that she still lived and I also knew the name of our country seat. For the first time since our departure from home the thought of writing to her entered my mind. Amid many tears I composed a long, passionate letter to her that night, in which I told of all my tortures, my raptures, my struggles, my wondrous love and my deep self-degradation and self-contempt. I gave no facts, for young, sensitive, passionate letter writers seldom do, but prefer keeping to general terms. Nor did I employ a single religious expression, because I had really completely forgotten the brief maternal education, and simply translated elemental feeling of the heart into language most current to me.

"Help me, dearest mother," I wrote. "Help me. I know that

you alone can do it. I have never forgotten you, and every day and night have thought of you. I still see you as distinctly as though I had left you only yesterday. I am a strange and terrible riddle to myself, and father, alas! cannot understand me. He speaks of nature that is always good, and says that my desires are natural and therefore good. But to me these desires seem ugly and despicable and the nature that drives me to them not at all good. He cannot understand this. Nature torments and tortures me. And no matter how I battle I see no deliverance. And at the same time, I adore a wondrous being, an angel of purity. And my father says that I must transfer the desires which I consider despicable to this sacred beloved. And that is a terrible thought to me. I love her with a passionate, boundless love, but I tremble to touch her with my impure lips. I harbor thoughts that would make me die of shame in her presence. And with my sordid depravities I am fit only for the low creatures, just as unhappy as I, whom I see running about here and who address me occasionally. Tell me, dearest mother, is there still help for me, is there still redemption? What is that nature of which my father speaks? Is it a thing or a thinking being, and how can it be good, always good, and bring me into such terrible straits and make me so unhappy?"

In this strain I wrote many pages and sent them off at a venture without much hope. And for two weeks I vainly went to the post-office every day, toward the last without the least hope.

But the answer came after all and I hid myself with it in my room, securely bolted, and with trembling hands I tore the envelope and kissed the paper and for a long time could not read for the tears that streamed from my eyes.

And when the contents, like a warm flood of tender benediction, seemed to pour itself out over my benumbed and tormented heart, of course I cried and kissed all the more and with greater fervor. We Italians are always a little, what here in my small town would be called, theatrical and affected, even though we be wholly without witnesses.

Frederik van Eeden

VI

I am proud of it that so many years ago I already addressed to my mother the question which, as far as I know, the best philosophers have never put to themselves with sufficient stress. Even those who by preference call themselves natural philosophers, thus those who have offered their lives to the service of Nature, who have sacrificed everything to understand her, who never speak of her without reverence and admiration and never cease praising her beauty, her bounty and the peace she bestows upon her scholars and admirers - even they, with amazing carelessness, forget to apprise us whether they consider her dead or living, a being or a thing, a thinking, feeling, clearly conscious and responsible Deity, or a blind, senseless force; and finally to teach us how we can persist in our praise and homage in the face of so much torture, so many monstrous faults, so much relentless cruelty.

Nature worship is the religion which unobserved makes the most proselytes nowadays. Even the druggist of my little town, who is a clever botanist, has gradually renounced his slack Protestantism for an ardent and devout nature worship. When he accompanies me to my nursery occasionally, on his search for plants, he can be stirred to truly southern enthusiasm at the sight of insects, birds, plants, trees, meadows, - all the wonders of his adored "Nature." His Bible had to make place for a periodical entitled "Living Nature," but dead nature - the clouds, the sea and the stars - inspires in him no slighter enthusiasm. This is all very lovable, but I often find it quite difficult not to cause the good man embarrassment by asking him where he considers that his beloved Nature ends and something else begins. Whether he counts man and their products also as a part of nature, and if so, why his admiration should make a sudden turn before the slums of Amsterdam; and if not, or only partly, what peculiar something it then is that has created so curious a product as man, and yet should be the opponent and enemy of, and debarred from, the great good and beautiful unity of all other things.

Yes, yes, dear reader, I know that men do a great deal of thoughtless babbling, and in a vague and careless way prate of Mother Nature, and beautiful Nature and human nature, and so on and so forth, without even knowing or distinguishing with the slightest degree of exactness what they really say or mean. But yet there have also been those among my fellows and good friends, like my amiable comrade Spinoza, and my greatly beloved friend Goethe, who did not care in the least for hollow phrases and also well-nigh constantly thought about these things, and who yet never proved with sufficient force men's right to praise Nature as much as they do, to bring all that is knowable into her domain and yet to judge of some of her products, as let us say: baboons, tyrants, grand inquisitors, drunkards, philistines, modern buildings and bad verses, in an ethically and aesthetically disapproving sense and, moreover, to call this opinion natural.

See then, the answer I received from my mother was quite as plausible to a young mind. She really seemed to have a nail for every hole and a hole for every nail.

"Nature, my dear son," she wrote, "is blind and subject to

Frederik van Eeden

sin. Through a Divine decree which we cannot penetrate she has been delivered over to Satan. But to offset nature there is the miracle. That is the wonder of Divine grace, through which we can find redemption from sin. The blood of Christ is the medium of redemption, and nothing more is required of us than to believe in Christ and in the redeeming power of his blood. Then the Miracle of Grace shall be performed in us and none can fall so deeply into sin, but faith in Christ can bring him salvation, and powerfully as nature works toward corruption, the miracle has wrought things

'a che natura

non scaldo ferro mai, ne batta incude.'"

The letter whereof this is a fragment made a profound impression on me. In the first place it came as a tangible, living token of the mother, so greatly venerated and adored - well-nigh as a departed saint; then, too, it awakened old, tender, childish feelings by the familiar tones of piety, which now struck my more experienced ears as something entirely new. And with the eager enthusiasm natural to me I thankfully and reverently accepted each of these proffered thoughts, fitting and arranging them until they seemed exactly to fill the gap which I had discovered in my spiritual life.

Exactly! Nature's trend is downward through the influence of Satan who draws us. This was just what I had felt. On the other side is God, who also draws us - but upward. That, too, I had felt. Thus at times nature is left to its own desires and Satan free to allure. Why? You must not ask. Divine decree. To a certain extent this is perhaps transferring the difficulty, but once thus firmly pronounced, - the door shuts unhesitatingly - the spirit becomes reconciled to it. Of course, something impenetrable may remain!

And now the salvation: Christ.

It was the first time this word was brought into the field of my vision, like a new plant that I saw sprouting in the garden of my life. Now, after fifty years, it is not yet full grown, but gives promise of blossom and fruit. Marvellous are the transformations it has undergone.

First I seemed to hear a word devoid of sense, and knew not what to do with it. A man, a God, a human-God, a Divine Man - all well and good, but what was that to me? Words, words. Satan who drew me downward I had felt, God who drew me upward I had felt. Of Christ I felt nothing. The assurance that he had lived, died and was risen again, did not affect me as long as he remained imperceptible to me.

Now I had gained the impression that Emmy knew more of him. It was customary in her family to offer morning prayers, and when I heard her pronounce the words: "Jesus Christ, our Lord," she did it with such expressive fervor that I could not doubt but that she positively knew whereof she spoke. At the time I had not yet learned the creative power of the suggested word.

So, in the course of a merry morning gallop, I, queer suitor that I was, began to theologize with the dear girl and asked her squarely: "Emmy, who is Christ?"

Now in my artlessness I had thought that anyone questioned by an earnest and not indifferent person, about a good acquaintance and dear friend, would manifest pleasure and gladly and heartily give the desired information. But Emmy seemed exceedingly surprised and even alarmed, as though the question did not at all please her, but more evidently distressed her.

"Don't you know that?" she said in a somewhat sullen and reserved tone of voice. "I thought you were religious."

"I surely am, Emmy, but that is why I want to know more of him."

"But aren't you Catholics taught that?" Emmy asked.

"To be sure, Emmy, but that does not satisfy me. It tells me nothing. I also want to feel that Christ is and what he is."

"Do you wish to turn Protestant?

"That makes no difference to me. I only do not want to use words without knowing what they mean. When you say, 'Jesus Christ, our Lord,' it seems as though you really knew what you meant with it."

"Of course I know!" said Emmy, the least bit crossly.

"Can't you make it clear to me, then?"

To my continued astonishment Emmy seemed to think this an unpleasant topic of conversation. It seemed as though she wanted to get it over with. She began, as though unwillingly, about God who had been born a man, had died for our sins, had risen again.

"No, Emmy, all that means nothing to me. It may all be very true, but what good is that to me now? If he died, well then, he is dead -"

"He is risen again," Emmy said quickly and almost angrily.

"Then he never died either; then it's folly to speak of dying. Is death still death when you know you will rise again directly? I'm willing to be killed three times a day then; no one is so much afraid of the bit of pain. Thus Christ still lives, - very well! then I ask: How do I become aware of that? By what am I apprised of it? What is he really then, and whereby should I know him if I saw him?"

"You must believe in him," Emmy said, still more or less crossly.

The verb "to believe" that Emmy used has an auxiliary with less favorable meaning. In English "to make believe" is in other words to impose on a person's credulity. It was as though this thought had made me suspicious and I began to surmise that Emmy's anxiety and anger were akin to that of the schoolgirl who is praised for a composition which she has copied from another. But surely it was in perfect good faith that the dear girl thought to believe what people had made her believe. As with everyone under suggestive influence, her deceived personality, without being clearly conscious of it, repelled any critical pressure that might bring to light the unreality of the imprinted image. How sorely I tormented the artless maiden at the time with my naive and inexorably insistent questioning! And how glad she was when at last I abandoned the Christ question and began to talk of tennis and croquet!

Although unformulated, yet this conversation positively revealed to me that Emmy in truth knew nothing of Christ, but used the word on her parents' and society's authority, and as a corresponding reality possessed nothing but a vague, fleeting phantom of a good and beautiful man with long hair and pointed beard, who was dead and yet living, - a man and yet God, existing everywhere and nowhere, and who on account of all these contradictory qualities is probably most easily known and addressed in pictures and images, which cannot and need not resemble him, with words that are

Frederik van Eeden

pleasantly ingratiating through the familiar tones of precious associations.

But I had readily adopted from my father his scorn for this kind of faith in imprinted unrealities and suggested images, and I still retain it as the greatest treasure he left to me, covering all his sin toward me.

Surely there is no illusion - there are only grades of reality; and what we call phantasmagorias are merely very fleeting realities, created by man, in comparison to the eternal and immutable realities which we apprehend with our soul and our senses, and which must be of higher origin. But we will not give to human creations honors alone due to the Divine, and will not pronounce hollow words nor adore suggested phantoms.

Thus the Christ idea of the maternal gift had as yet no value for me - but even so I was rich with the ideas of God and Satan as the causes of this sad discord and confusion in my soul. Now all that was necessary was to fight Satan and to call on God for aid. Mother's advice had been: "Pray and chastise and subdue the flesh." I tried it immediately with trusting ardor, and behold! 't was true - it really helped. I hardly dared believe it myself, it seemed almost too good.

I prayed night and morning in my own, original, upright way, to the power which I felt as an uplifting influence, calling it God.

I imposed penalties upon myself, denying myself wine and delicate food, bathing a great deal in ice-cold water, clothing myself insufficiently, making forced marches on foot, and when Satan again seemed to be getting the upper hand, even sleeping beside my bed on the hard floor. For that I would rather go up with God than down with Satan - well I of that I was most positively convinced. It is strange with what blind arrogance man can consider himself an exception in this regard, as though anyone on earth would enjoy and prefer descending into the deep with Satan than ascending with God on high. And it may be called even stranger that I went to all this trouble, the while the maternal wisdom deemed salvation possible only through a miracle, which I, certainly, could not compel, and by faith in Christ which, though I honestly desired to, I could not awaken in myself.

The little fish did not see that by these evolutions it had even now entered the encircling meshes of the net which would land it into the same suggested faith from which it had once before turned away in alarm.

For the evolutions helped, there was no doubt about that. I soon felt more cheerful, braver, and above all, purer and stronger. Satan, if not absolutely routed, yet seemed to be considerably intimidated. I rowed, played cricket and croquet, studied, rode horseback, went walking in the country, not in the dangerous parks. I did not consider the infamy of my fall wiped out and maintained a respectful aloofness from my beloved, as one unworthy of her. But I saw her often and worshipped and adored her to my heart's content, without thinking far ahead.

This success was not the result of a miracle, nor of faith in Christ, but probably of the glad shock produced by mother's letter and of a strong auto-suggestion. But it seemed to confirm her wisdom and thus prepared the susceptibility to deeper suggestions.

During these exercises of virtue Satan's image through its countervailing influence became ever clearer to me. The crafty, evil power, whose existence I had officially recognized by my declaration of war, was obviously flattered and manifested itself with stronger reality. At the time I did not yet know that suggestion can engender reality, and that all actions are also auto-suggestions.

Satan retreated, hid himself, surreptitiously arose again, awaited his chance, taking advantage of unguarded and weak moments, and in one word demeaned himself as a very live and sagacious Satan.

His cleverest artifice consisted in finally taking advantage of my excess of virtue. After a few weeks of self-torture, over-fatigue, scant food, little sleep and insufficient clothing, I naturally fell ill, and the kind Tenders family would not hear of it that I should be tended elsewhere than in their own home.

Behold Satan's splendid chance, which he turned to excellent account. He kept still as a mouse; no impure thoughts, no visions, no troublesome dreams annoyed me. The hungry dogs which I had now come to look upon as Satan's faithful domestic pets were hushed, first by the auto-suggestion, subsequently by my illness, and finally by the promise clearly betrayed in my actions, that I would grant them nobler prey. Indeed, though I did not acknowledge it to myself, to what else could it lead - these daily more tender and ardent relations between the desperately enamored and speedily recuperating patient and the dear nurse, assuredly not insensitive to his adoration? The flame of martyrdom was swiftly quenched with beef tea, soft-boiled eggs and sweet malaga wine, and I could not possibly recognize Satan's voice in these gentle commands to self-indulgence, nor could I think to honor God by disobedience to such a charming mistress.

What a time! what a time! all the way from my nursery to my house I have been smiling in anticipation of my afternoon hours of literary activities, smiling and smiling in sweet remembrance. The children by the wayside got nickels instead of pennies, and the fisherman who lay caulking his boat hauled up on shore in the little harbor peered out from under the scow with an attentive expression as though he would say: "Well, bless my heart, and if the old gentleman ain't gone and got a jag on this morning!"

I am indeed blissfully intoxicated with the heady aroma of these long past days of young love! the sound of her approaching footsteps in the morning, the rustling of her gown before I beheld her, as she came to bring me some dainty which she had concocted for my regalement. And the merry little chats, when she would at first sit on the chair beside my bed, but later perchance also on the edge of the bed. And once at the very end, when I was to get up the following day, and thanked her for all her loving care, she bent over me, and before either of us really knew what we were about - so it seemed to me at least, perhaps her consciousness was clearer - we had kissed each other on the lips. And the blessed tears I shed when she had gone, - for the undeserved grace of this happiness, which yet never could endure, - these are things, are they not, dear reader? which we usually look upon as the very highest summits of our earthly joys, that still shine most radiantly when our sun is near its setting. But know then too that joy and bliss are of more imperishable matter than rock and glacier, and that very sublime beauty is more clearly perceived from a distance. Long ago, I have observed that most happiness can be valued best when it lies a certain distance behind us, and one must grow old to taste the full flavor of beauty at the very moment of perception.

There still followed a few lovely days of glorious summer weather, which I spent in a hammock stretched above the smooth green turf between the oaks. I saw the round sun shadows upon the grass, the sparkling, gently flowing Thames, the white swans, the gaily crowded boats, the kindly, happy people about me, and in their midst, as the sunny kernel of joy, the wavy, golden hair of her whom I loved best, and who only lent the true radiance to all this summer glory. I read Heine and listened to Schumann, and I breathed the subtle penetrating fragrance of the linden blossoms, the wonderful fragrance full of poignant melancholy and sweet longing that does not touch our senses ere love has deeply nestled in our Heart. I had travelled through so many lands and yet had never smelled the perfume of the linden blossoms, so that it was as though the great linden tree had become fragrant through Emmy's wondrous power just as she made the golden summer sun truly to shine.

But then I was restored to health and the lovely, lazy life was ended. And Emmy, mindful of our last rather unsatisfactory conversation on horseback and perhaps also to offer an antidote for Heine, brought me a small New Testament as a parting gift, which I gratefully and reverently pressed to my heart and began to peruse diligently.

VII

Now the crafty devil held me securely in his meshes and could display himself without having the terrified little fish swim away. My body, now strong again and refreshed, wanted Emmy for my wife in the ordinary, human, time-honored way. It made this known with undeniable distinctness, without concerning itself in the least about my exalted scruples. Women can still cherish the illusion that kisses and embraces have no deeper significance; a man is more distinctly warned; and I really think it not at all kindly of the great and noted lovers that they so often profess ignorance in that respect, thus misleading the reader.

Satan could grin perfidiously now at the fix I was in. The shame of my unworthiness could, perhaps, have been wiped out with the help of Emmy's magnanimous forgiveness. Such an absolution is not unusual in the world of romance, and quite the rule in the actual world. But the body absolutely would not bear of postponement, and though circumstances were ever so favorable to me, yet modesty and convention, yes, even practical common sense, demanded a few years more of waiting.

A few years - how lightly these periods are set and written down in the love stories, from the time of father Jacob's seven years - and how terribly different is their significance

Frederik van Eeden

for the man of different temperament.

The Old Testament shepherd lad may perhaps have borne it in good stead - but if we try to be frank, dear reader, what then may we suppose that such periods hide for the man of modern civilization, of wrong, of corruption, of unworthy transactions between the moral, ideal and natural reality?

When but recently come to England, I had read the statement in one of Thackeray's books that possibly there might be pure women, but certainly no pure man, and with youthful arrogance I had sworn a solemn oath that I would make him out a liar. This was the first of the fine set of broken, patched and mended oaths with which the quarrelling household of my soul was gradually fitted out. And one would think that the ambition for the collecting of this precious and breakable bric-à-brac should not be so generally praised and encouraged. I, at least, have had to pay dearly for this hobby, and with melancholy, struggles, self-torment, self-reproach and continuous worry it has embittered the best years and the most beautiful emotions of my life. And if now, in the end, I, at least, saw the way clear, dear reader! - but truly! if I should have to begin again, from the very beginning, I should not know yet bow to act better. I would surely never make promises again - but what I once pronounced impure and unworthy, I still call it so. And that I was, nevertheless, drawn into it through my own nature, like a rebellious cat, I still consider equally disgraceful and unjust. But how I could have prevented it I do not know yet, for I fought like a hero, and after all I was not one of the weakest; - yes! I was stronger even than the greater majority.

But this I know, that with all this worry I would not besides give to remorse a place in my house, and I advise you, dear reader, relentlessly to throw this guest out of your door. I would certainly continue to be as rebellious and unforgiving toward the vile and unworthy, - but if there is consciousness of sin and sense of guilt to bear, I know now who is justly ready and willing to bear with us and to ease this burden for us poor toilers.

The constitution of society and the precepts of convention are moreover so badly qualified to ease the struggle, because society and moral law manifest so little comprehension of the true nature of our difficulties. Where I felt no danger whatsoever, there were strong walls of strict convention; and where I knew positively that I would succumb, the world offered no defence.

With one of Emmy's friends or another innocent girl or woman, no matter how lovely and attractive, one might without danger have sent me off on a journey and have left us together for days and weeks without witnesses, and not a shadow of eroticism or impure thought would have arisen in me. With Emmy herself, her innocence and my own scruples and respect were a better safeguard than all moral laws. But as soon as I detected in a woman, totally strange and indifferent to me, ugly even and repulsive, this peculiar weakness, usually paired with good nature, which indicated in an almost imperceptible manner that the parting wall of modesty would fall at my first assault, I already felt myself lost from the beginning in spite of all conventional restrictions.

I sometimes vainly endeavored to imagine how ugly a woman would have to be to make me repel her advances with stony coolness. Every woman, the least attractive even, could make me stumble, simply by humbling herself. As by an excess of chivalry, I could not refuse a woman's request nor even await it. It was as though I must prevent her casting off her modesty at all costs by my own debasement; that is to say, as long as she desired only my body and not my heart.

My heart remained out of shot range behind the walls of my true love for Emmy.

When physical desires and spiritual sensibilities are once severed one from the other, they never grow entirely together again and possibilities of sad confusion remain throughout life. In spite of my pure and passionate love for Emmy, my bodily desires could be excited to madness by the first woman that came along seeming inclined to let the veil of modesty drop before me. And while, with - the exception of Emmy, the most beautiful, sweetest and noblest women did not exercise the slightest alluring power over me and Emmy's guileless trust in me and her absolute want of jealousy in that respect were entirely justified, a coarse, low-born, sensual and good-natured woman could seduce me to things that neither Emmy nor any of the persons who knew me would have deemed possible. Thus you see, dear reader, how highly necessary it is to regulate the strange connection between ape and angel in valid and permanent fashion, from childhood up, for the two have such different conceptions of good and beautiful that it will not do to leave to each his freedom in one narrow, fragile house.

For all the rest, I was constitutionally strong and well balanced in soul and body. Of disease I know little, and that breaking down of the bond between the visible and invisible part of our nature that people call nervous troubles nowadays was ever strange to me.

And this was the most perplexing and confounding circum-stance in my difficulties, that when the ape had finally had his way, he rewarded me for it by a feeling of physical refreshment and comfort, by a consciousness of renewed and invigorated life, a clearing of thought, an increased activity and capacity for enjoyment.

All this agrees very badly - does it not? with the traditional punishment that should follow upon the misdeed. Perhaps it even seems to you in flagrant conflict with the moral world order. I cannot help it, but it was as I have told you, and you can only save the honor of tradition, as I did at the time, by declaring it all a most contemptible artifice of Satan. But conscience is not hushed by this explanation. On the contrary, who would maintain a real, live devil must have a conscience for him to gnaw. Pure and elemental it need not be; he is satisfied - with any cheap group-fabrication, and the torments remain the same.

My life in these years was one long, secret struggle, the fierceness of which only my father suspected, without being able to do anything to help me, poor man - for he really suffered under it with me because his life task was at stake.

In his helplessness he even seriously considered and covertly proposed our following the example of certain aristocratic English families where, as he declared he knew positively, a pretty servant girl was engaged to keep the son of the house from worse excesses, until the time for a respectable marriage had arrived and the girl was sent home with a liberal remuneration.

But the mere allusion roused me to indignant passion, little as I was entitled to such pride. How shall we account for it, that every reminder of what man recognizes as degrading in his love life is never more unbearable, never more painful than between parent and child?

My life and my being in these years was like the struggling of two powers in deadly dispute, rising and falling between heaven and earth, between clouds and sea - the eagle of ideal sublimity and the snake of earthly brutishness.

Frederik van Eeden

"Feather and scale inextricably blended."

For me, in an outwardly calm and care-free life, an anxious and terrible struggle with

"Many a check

And many a change, a dark and wild turmoil."

The distress, the shame, the self-contempt, the despair resulting therefrom made my behavior toward Emmy so strange, so uneven and capricious that she often felt hurt by it, and so was careful to draw back a little more.

Before long I had a rival: a young English officer, equally handsome, equally good to look at and strongly built as I, but somewhat calmer, somewhat more measured and somewhat more assured of his own right and virtue. For these qualities he was hateful to me, but with secret bitterness I recognized his superior rights, because I took him for a pure man.

In my country, in Spain, in France, also in Germany, men, even those calling themselves well bred, are often caddish enough to make coarse sexual jokes toward comparative strangers and to assume a freer tone when no women are present. Such behavior could make me furious and I always answered it with mocking non-comprehension. And at the same time it tormented me, that anyone knowing my thoughts and habits would call me a hypocrite for this reason. But my disgust for such coarsenesses was strong and sincere, and I valued it in my English friends that they seemed to feel the same as I in this respect.

My rival, Captain Truant, was polite and correct in everything and toward me he was cordial and pleasant, but he could not quite hide that he looked upon me as an Italian, that is to say, a man of lower race and backward civilization. I realized that he would think it very unsuitable and a great pity to have a sweet, well-bred blonde English girl like Emmy throw herself away upon a dark foreign type. True, I had money and a duke's title, but there are also Japanese, Turkish and Persian noblemen, who are therefore not yet a match for a pretty cultured English maiden. So without any mental scruples, with the calm conviction of the Englishman that his actions are perfectly justified, Harry Truant came between us two with a stanch, even, steady wooing. And what immediately struck me with distressing clearness was the greater ease with which Emmy and Harry understood each other. They were at home in each other's world and immediately understood each other's ways, each other's tastes, each other's humors. Perhaps in the beginning my exoticism had been to my advantage through the incentive of the strange and new. But my incomprehensible caprices, my strange, sometimes passionate, sometimes utterly reserved behavior had wearied and frightened Emmy for some time. And I saw that the more familiar and wonted ways of her thoroughly English countryman did her good and were more agreeable to her. I saw all this with bitter resignation; I thought that I was receiving my rightful deserts.

Yet the dear girl would not lightly have cast me off for another. It had never come to an actual proposal and she might consider herself free. But she was scrupulous enough to feel herself bound even by an unconfessed affection, by the intimacy of our conversations and by the one kiss. I realized this and in grieved and hopeless self-sacrifice, wished to put a stop to it.

"I know quite well what is going on, Emmy," I said one night as we sat together at the river's edge. "I only want to tell you that you must not consider yourself bound to me. You are free?"

She looked at me a while, irresolutely and with a sorrowful expression. Then she said, gently shaking her head:

"What does ail you, Vico? What is it that is lurking in your mind that you behave so strangely toward me?"

Her gently compassionate voice, the ardent confidential tone, the dear expression of her face, were more than I could bear. I felt the tears coming and clenched my fists. It was no use. I had to get up and went on a little further, leaning my head and hand against the rough bark of a tree, by force restraining my sobs, when I felt a gentle hand upon my shoulder.

"Vico!" she said.

But with a nervous jerk I shook her hand off my shoulder and in a choking voice said:

"Do not touch me. I am not worthy of you." The hand dropped and I realized that she became somewhat cooler and more cautious. Of course she began to suspect something very bad.

"Can't you tell me, Vico?" she asked, not unkindly but much more severely.

"No, Emmy. Never! - Think that I love you as no one else can ever love you. . . . But I am not worthy of you, and I want you to be happy. I shall stand in your way no longer. Do not trouble yourself about what will become of me."

"Poor boy!" said Emmy earnestly and tenderly. "Is it really something so insurmountable?"

"Absolutely insurmountable, Emmy. Think of it no more,

God bless you!"

"God bless you, Vico!" said Emmy, following me with a look half sorrowful, half resigned.

More resigned than I liked to see.

Such farewells have taken place before and have also often been followed by reconciliations, yes, by several farewells and reconciliations. But here there was not the mutual equality of vehement passion, and not the singleness of purpose that, overriding all scruples, wins by perseverance. My rival made swift and prosperous use of the advantage afforded him.

I avoided Emmy's house, but still occasionally visited the club which Captain Truant also frequented. And a few weeks later I saw him enter there one evening and receive the congratulations of his friends. I realized what this meant and with a paralyzed, icy feeling I remained seated, staring at the paper which I pretended to read.

But the lucky fellow stepped up to me, he was not noble enough to wish to spare me.

Among those who noisily greeted and congratulated him there was also an officer, nicknamed "the gallant capting" by the others, an insignificant, blustering little fellow with a monocle, for whom I felt a particular aversion, because he, although ever himself the dupe, when he had drunk a good measure, would now and then with his brutal volubility and English jokes successfully turn the laugh on me, the stranger. Loudly laughing and talking to Harry he came and stood close beside me.

"And how about Dina, now?" the braggart asked Truant.

"Hush! hush, man!" said Truant. "A little discretion, if you please!"

But the tipsy fop would not be shut up so quickly.

"Will you give me authority to fill the vacant place, Harry? As lawfully authorized comforter?"

"All right! All right!" said Harry Truant, to get rid of him.

But I had distinctly heard and comprehended everything. Or rather I only comprehended that by a word of authority I had suddenly obtained permission to do exactly what my body desired. The tormented body, desperate from the long struggle of serpent and eagle, now desired vengeance and destruction. The room, the gas lights, the chairs, everything in an agreeable, even pleasant fashion began to fade, to float, to wheel about—and with the silent murderous resolution that in like circumstances had characterized my forefathers of the masculine line, I clutched Harry Truant by the throat.

If these memoirs were to find an English or American publisher, it would be politic to announce here that the Englishman with his practised boxing fists with ease doubled up the Italian and knocked him into a corner, unconscious. Anything short of that the public of Rudyard Kipling would not stand for, of course. Yet I prefer to state the truth: that Harry Truant and Vico Muralto dealt each other some ugly blows that night, but without deadly consequences, and that they were with difficulty separated by those present. The challenge for a duel, as conflicting with the laws and morals of his country, was not accepted by the English officer, which at the time greatly vexed me and stamped him in my eyes as the very soul of cowardice and dishonor, but which to-day I not only excuse, but highly respect.

That same year Harry and Emmy went to India as husband and wife. Vico and his father entered upon their last journey together.

VIII

In my youth people sometimes called me a poet, and though they employed the term vaguely and at random, yet it was not wholly unjustified. For I am a destroyer of suggestion, a shatterer of the group, a wanderer from the herd, an idol-hater, but also a searcher for joy, beauty and bliss, a lover of reality; and all these are characteristics of a poet.

But making verses did not suit me. Let me call it unwilling-ness; then you may speak of the impotence, and perhaps, even so, we are both saying the same thing. I honor and admire the great singers, but I myself have always felt a barrier when I wished to metamorphose my personal and intimate emotions into separate entities and into public property. I felt as though I must kill them first, before administering this cure, as Medea did with her father-in-law Æson, - and that I could not do.

I was equally impotent to create imaginary characters, which in their own way revealed my sorrows, my weaknesses, my follies and my virtues, forming new personalities with independent life: as my dear friend Goethe created Werther, Faust, Egmont and Tasso.

I realize that it must have been a great delight and conso-lation and also a strong proof of humility and love, an admirable emulation of the Divine Creator and enriching of the human world. But I myself could never attempt it.

My great grief seemed to me too sacred and too intimate to put it into little verses and send these out into the world as singing birds, to my own relief and the delight and edification of all.

Moreover I found it humiliating to make my own nature into a mask and in a well-sustained rôle let it aspire for human applause; as is the custom of my young friend Nietzsche, who lances such vehement tirades against actors and comedians, but does not seem to perceive how much he himself, like all poets, is an histrionic artist.

Here also I decidedly lacked the truly humble love of mankind that must have moved my surely not less proud friends, Shelley and Goethe. In the bard and the actor I always seemed to see the courtier.

Ariosto had his Alfonso d'Este and Goethe his Carl August.

And the great bards of freedom of the past century, Shelley, Byron, Hugo? Ali! Were they not courtiers of King Demos?

I am not an enemy of King Demos, and I know that his earthly realm is at hand. May he replace and rule all kings until King Christ rules supreme among men. I wish him prosperity and glory, as Diogenes, I imagine, must have wished to Alexander. But to be his courtier, I always lacked the necessary self-denial, and to rebel against him, like friend Nietzsche, there again I had too much realization of his worth and power. So that, impotent to be a lord and unwilling to be a courtier, I was driven into this forgotten nook. And here, to keep body and soul together, I must be something of an actor after all now, and play the philistine

Frederik van Eeden

part, though it be vi coactus and not for human applause; while I, a lowly slave, nevertheless through my quiet mental activity enjoy the highest freedom in my chains, proclaiming to King Demos the weakness and instability of his power, because he shall not himself ascend the throne without the help of tyrants and shall be driven off by a yet more mighty and righteous Lord. And even for this Lord I am still a critical and fault-finding subject, but I think these are the ones he prefers.

In these first days of profound sorrow I strove with even greater effort to know who this Christ was who redeemed us or could redeem us, and I wrote to my mother about it and read diligently in Emmy's precious gift.

My mother wrote me long prolix letters in reply, which I read attentively and reverently, unwilling to admit that they really had nothing more to tell me. They were the same things - the miracle of grace, the redemption through the blood of Jesus - repeated over and over again in all sorts of new inversions and combinations, so that it seemed a miracle already that with so few notes one could make so much music. My father was well aware of these letters and furtively regarded me half scornfully, half disturbed, as I sat deciphering them patiently and with earnest devotion to the last syllable. That it was all over with Emmy was a relief to him, but all the more anxiously he watched this animated correspondence and the increase of the maternal influence; especially as I should shortly attain my majority.

We had gone to Holland on our last trip to the little seaside resort on the North Sea with its unpronounceable name, and thus I for the first time tarried in that strange little nook of Europe, that was to become the seat of my voluntary hermitage, amid that curious little nation, which of all nations probably displays the most profound mingling of lovable and detestable qualities. On this first visit with my father I saw nothing of the people and little of the country. But I saw the coast of the North Sea and there I learned to love the sea more than when I sailed her. On that sandy coast we became intimate, the sea and I, there she took me to her bosom and we communed heart to heart, whispering the most intimate secrets into each other's ears. There the sea became for me a being with a soul - as everything is, though we do not perceive it - and there her aspects and her voice acquired a meaning, as all that we call lifeless has a meaning.

And on this first visit I went with my father to see the works of Rembrandt, with some doubt and unbelief and prejudice, as befits Italian patriots. And then with my newly awakened vision of the life of all things, I saw that this man did with all the living and the dead about him what the coast of the North Sea had done for me with the sea: - he showed the meaning and the mysterious life of everything, be it living or be it dead so to speak. And he showed how living men aside from their own personal life lead yet another, vaster world-life without themselves knowing it. And he pictured this world-life as something beautiful and grand, even though the people and the things were in themselves ugly.

And this was such a revelation, such a boon for my early matured soul that I absolutely would not believe that this man, who could do what none of my greatest countrymen had been able to do, was a perfectly commonplace Hollander. But I regarded him like some strange god, by chance incarnate here, and I revered him above all the saints in the calendar. Yes, I wished in a vague sort of way that he might prove to be Christ, for then I, should know what to believe. For it may be very fine to manifest, as Giotto and Fra Angelico, and Rafael and Titian, how beautiful human nature is and can be imagined; but yet there is more comfort and salvation in revealing how in the unlovely, mean and ugly the divine life dwells, and is beautiful and can be seen as beautiful even by us poor human beings. Yes, even though it were ever so imperfect, as in many a canvas that seems to me like an anxious and desperate struggle to bring out something at least of the everlasting beauty, - it was there, it was visible, perchance a faint ray in a dark, dreary cloud of ugliness, and the great task was again accomplished, the great consolation offered.

And finally I visited with my father the little village where Spinoza led his quiet philistine's life, and patiently bored the hole through which the confined thoughts could find an outlet. And when I saw the little house and the quiet, peaceful landscape and heard of the lonely, sober, chaste life of this equanimous and devout Jew, I desired for myself no better lot than to be able to follow his example as soon as possible.

It has taken a little longer than I thought at the time; stronger and more continued rubbing with the rough world was necessary to charge my soul with such high potency that, as his, it would emit bright sparks in isolation. But now it has come about after all, and I would not contradict you if you said that it was Rembrandt and Spinoza who drew me to the regions sanctified by their labors for the fulfilment of my life's task, had not this meditative dwelling sphere been already dear to me for other reasons.

On the day I came of age a letter from my mother arrived in which she reminded me that I was now free to go my own ways, and moreover informed me that on her journey from the north she would stop in Holland and hoped that she might at last clasp me in her arms again.

It was a momentous day for me when at last I was to see again my saint, adored so many years in the holy, dusky light of memory. My heart beat and my hands trembled as I stood behind the sleek hotel porter in front of the closed door of the apartment and heard the voice - soft, languidly cordial - inviting me to enter.

There she stood, tall, straight, the same face with the light gray eyes with the deep rings under them, but much paler now, and the once blonde hair showing silvery white beneath the black lace veil. She was dressed in black and white with a great silver crucifix on a black chain. I fell upon my knees before her, kissing her hands. She kissed me on the brow and lifted me up. I trembled with emotion when I felt her cool, soft lips, and saw her face, with the delicate pale violet and amber tints and the fine countless little lines crossing one another, so near my own. And I breathed the old familiar perfume of frankincense and lavender and felt her pure breath upon my brow. It was a moment of consecration. Even had she not been my mother, I should have felt awe and veneration for this stately and distinguished woman with her expression of long and patiently endured affliction, her fresh, well-preserved old age, her solemn, dignified garb and the peculiar sphere of purity and chastity that seemed to surround her. All my shame and humiliation came to my mind and threatened to relieve itself in a flood of tears. I longed to confess, to reveal all the ugliness and foulness in my soul, so that she should purify it through her power.

Woman in the last period of her life, when maternity slips away from her, can, if she well understands her new position and with wisdom sustains it, become a new human creature clothed with a higher dignity. Man in the fulness of his years still ever remains the male, and the lover. Woman is directed toward another sexless position and fulfils a new part not of minor importance. Thus I conceived it, when I saw my mother, and I comprehended now why some nations so greatly revered the power of priestesses and sibyls or feared

Frederik van Eeden

the power of witches. I felt the influence of an unknown potency, a natural consecration that could forgive, purify, bless, absolve and prophesy wholly according to priestly prerogative, but stronger here where God and Nature ordained it than where human authority officially and formally conferred it.

My impulsive nature would undoubtedly have driven me to make a full confession even at this first meeting, had I not soon become aware of another person in the room. For a moment I thought of my sister, but then I remembered that my sister had taken the veil. This was a pretty young woman whose beauty, quite differently than with Emmy, I immediately saw and appreciated. She had large, dark, serious and gentle eyes, a fresh white complexion and dark glossy hair that was brought down low over the temples, braided and twisted to a knot in back. She was also dressed in black with a white lace collar and a gold breast pin in which were enclosed some brown plaits of hair. She stood at the window somewhat shy and embarrassed while I greeted my mother, but I saw her eyes shining with kindly satisfaction that she had been allowed to witness this scene.

My mother told me that this was Lucia del Bono, her faithful friend and adopted daughter. And I could notice that Lucia's veneration for my mother was almost as deep as mine, and also that the two women had talked about me a great deal and that this meeting was an important event not for the elder one alone.

In the unbearable grief for my lost love these visits to my mother and her beautiful, sympathetic companion now became my greatest solace and it was not long before I saw from my father's dark and suspicious glances, from his listless and discouraged air, which suddenly made the still vigorous man appear aged, and from his almost invariably silent and tightly compressed lips, that he realized what was going on.

He did not ask, and I did not speak. But we both felt that we had been seized by an irresistible current which was sweeping us toward an inevitable catastrophe.

IX

Holland may be described as a painting whereof the frame constitutes the most impressive part. It is a fit dwelling place for the hermit who from inward meditation amid hazy meadows, dreamy cows, and peaceful little towns can easily turn to the contemplation of the greatest revelations of the gods - the vast heavens, the clouds and the sea. But toward the people he must learn to assume the attitude of the ancient hermit toward the spiders and rats in his cell. Sometimes they are annoying and disagreeable; sometimes too, in their revelations of life, instructive and interesting. I live on good terms with the inhabitants of this quiet little town because I never let them see how I think of them, and never show myself as I really am. To this attitude, which, with sharper insight, they would consider haughty conceit, I owe my reputation as a modest and respectable man. Were I humble enough to treat them as my equals by being natural with them, they would then call me a conceited ass and a cad.

But on one point we understand each other, on the subject of the water, the sea and the sport of sailing. If I kept a horse and rode to my nursery in the morning they would consider me a fool and I should surely never have become treasurer of the orphanage. But the fact that I have a yacht and frequently show them what storms she can weather, raises me in their esteem. Only the sea can arouse in these little shrivelled souls a dim shadow of the old boldness and beauty of life.

True, most of them are too much attached to their miserable little lives to risk them solely for the sake of stirring emotions without compelling need, and they prefer to let me go on my reckless expeditions alone or accompanied by the well-paid fisher lad. But they do not laugh at my reckless-ness, and at the club I notice that they regard the old gentleman with a certain amount of respect when he returns again from one of these sailing expeditions, which many a young seaman would refuse to undertake even for the sake of profit, and does not even brag or boast of it, but only slightly smiles at the exclamations of respectful amazement. Thus they honor physical courage, which is nothing more than muscular strength and a craving for the pleasing excitement of danger, while the moral courage to reveal to them the true nature of my thoughts and feelings they would punish with such sharp and malicious ill-will that in order to retain my peace of mind and pursue my life's task undisturbed, I think I should not challenge it and prefer to deceive them.

It was my father who made me a slave to the intoxication of the thrilling suspense of sailing out amidst whistling winds, seething foam, immense surging waves round about, fallow driving clouds above, the tugging taut rope in one hand, the straining tiller in the other, the eye travelling from sail to horizon, from pennant to ocean, the boat trembling the while from the waves breaking against her bow, and amid this tumult weighing the chances for a safe homecoming, total submersion or the breaking of the rigging. It was then he felt happiest; it deadened his melancholy, as biting on wood deadens a gnawing toothache. And he found in me a willing pupil, eager as I was for violent emotions and tortured by self-contempt, wild passions and all the pangs of lost love-joys.

Frederik van Eeden

In Holland, too my father had immediately hired a boat to sail the ocean, and the Scheveningen seamen had quite some trouble to make him understand that the North Sea was not an Italian gulf or lake and in rough weather would not permit of any rash enterprises in small sailboats. Yet after a few weeks, be managed to attain his object and I followed him gladly.

One afternoon we had sailed out, dressed in our oilskins, and the skipper who, submerged to the waist, had pushed us off the shore through the breakers, had warned us to be back within two hours, for at that time the ebb-tide set in and, with the fresh north breeze, the strong current would make it difficult for us to land. My father had nodded as though he were thinking of something else and had long ago penetrated and computed the caprices of the gray and formidable North Sea.

For an hour we sailed on silently, as was frequently our wont, my father holding the rudder. The coast had dwindled to a faint luminous line above which like a thin white mist hung the foam of the breakers. I lay on the deck, glanced toward land and horizon - then at my watch, and said:

"Come about; father, it's time." He did not seem to hear, and I turned toward him repeating: "It's time! come about!" Then I saw that be did not want to hear. He had hauled the mainsail in closely, luffing sharply, the sheet tightly drawn, and was staring fixedly and straight ahead under the large yellow sou'-wester. His eyes had the hard grim expression of old people who after a long life of struggle still fight for the bit of breath left them, or of indulged and long-tortured invalids, or of the starved or shipwrecked who no longer have feeling for anyone or anything but their own distress. Between his close-cropped gray whiskers and his tightly pressed lips I saw - what before I had never noticed - two sallow lines deeply furrowing his cheeks. All at once I felt a pity, such as I had never felt for him before - as though the realization of all the grief which he had suffered under my very eyes now suddenly penetrated my consciousness.

"What ails you, father?" I asked. He began talking away regardlessly as though there were no wind and no waves about him.

"You said three years ago that by this time you would be lost. I think you are right. You are."

"No, father, I think I was mistaken. I am beginning to see salvation."

"You do not see salvation, Vico, you see ruin. I understand it very well. Your mother has you again in her clutches. She is a harpy; do you know the monsters? Part woman, part vulture. They suck away half your healthy life-blood and replace it with gall. Melancholy and gloom are her idols. Suffering, pain, grief, trouble, bitterness - these are the archangels in her heaven. She makes sorrow her object of worship, and she pictures her God as a hideous corpse hanging on a cross with pierced bands and feet, covered with blood, wounds, scars, sores, matter, dirt and spittle, - the more horrible the better. And that attracts the dull masses exactly as the colored prints of murders and barbarians depicted in the papers. Was there ever more devilish error?"

"And if salvation can only be bought with pain, father? If all this suffering was the price of redemption for our sins?"

"Jew!" my father snapped at me with glittering eyes, his mouth drawn disdainfully in unutterable contempt! "Jew! where did you learn this bartering morality? Buy! Buy! everything can be bought! If you are but willing to pay, you can go anywhere, even to heaven. Salvation can be bought for a slaughtered human being. A fixed price and dirt cheap! - Salvation for all mankind for the corpse of a single Jew. What a bargain! and God is Shylock, be holds to his bond! his bond! Blood is the fixed price, nothing can change that. If not the blood of sinners then let it be the blood of my son. Thus reads the contract:

'My bond! My bond!

My deeds upon my head! I crave the law!

The penalty and forfeit of my bond!'

"Do you know, Vico, why the Jews are hated so everywhere? It is instinctive resentment because the world feels that it has been infected with the Jewish poison. The priesthood, the black vermin, is a Jewish Germanic bastard brood. They have made a Jew of God himself and they will make one of you too. And that my son! my child, the heir!"

The suffering on my father's face was terrible to see. Tears began to flow from his fixed eyes.

I tried to calm him. "Do come about, father! - it's over time!"

"We'll go on a while yet," he said with a ghastly affected airiness, and I sat there with the blood freezing in my veins, fearing he was going mad. All at once he burst out again.

"The blood of his son! the blood of his son! to buy off sin with which he himself had burdened us - his own debts thrust on us and accepted by us against our will and pleasure, and this acceptance paid for with the blood of his own child. What a Jew! What a sly, heartless usurer! Did you make these debts, Vico? - value received? What did you get for it?

What did you get for this hereditary sin? Hereditary sin! Ha! ha! ha! hereditary sin! what an invention! - Hereditary debt! What a crafty, bartering Jew one must be to invent such an idea."

Once more I made an attempt, and standing upright at the mast I cried vigorously:

"Come about, father! - about!"

But he called back with even greater vehemence:

"Go ahead, I tell you!"

And then whilst I looked about over the sea and considered what to do:

"I tell you, Vico, there is life and there is death. And we must live as long as we can. But it must be real life too. Death is no life. The life of most men is a slow miserable death. There is no honor and no merit in maintaining a life that should more truly be called death. A bloodless, enervated, foul, rotten life. It is a shame that men do not yet know how to live, and even greater shame that they know still less how to die. I wanted to have you live. But I did not succeed and now I shall teach you to die. - Are you afraid?"

Then something began to stir and rise up in my soul, like a snake goaded forth from her cavern. I, too, began to forget the wind and the waves about me. True, I felt a tingling down my back to my very finger tips. Yet I was not a coward and I spoke firmly:

"I am not afraid, father. I believe I shall know quite as well as you how to die if it should be necessary, even without your teaching me. But I won't be murdered, not even by my father."

The tears from the fixed, now red-rimmed eyes began to flow more abundantly.

"Vico!" he cried in a much softer, trembling voice: "Will you be true to me then? Will you let yourself be saved? Will you save your precious life and your reason? Will you abjure this accursed harpy? Will you escape the sinister band?"

But I was irritated and excited and proudly replied: "I shall save myself, I shall be true to whomever I find worthy. I do not respect the man that curses my mother."

Then his face changed horribly, he lifted up his trembling right hand, thereby awkwardly knocking off the canvas cap from his head so that the damp gray hair fluttered. He made Jesus' sign of doom in Michel Angelo's last judgment, screaming loudly meanwhile:

"Then I curse you, do you hear! I curse you, Lodovico Muralto. Your father curses you!"

I had enough of Old Testament sentiments left in me not to be indifferent to such an imprecation!

I started, but tried my very utmost to see in him only the raving, irresponsible maniac. At the same time the thought flashed across my mind that he himself must also have been infected by Jewish ideas, that he should clutch at these weapons, more sounding than wounding. But I said nothing, walked up to him and from behind his hand attempted to grasp the tiller. "About!" I cried.

"Very well! about!" my father cried fiercely, and with that be wrenched the tiller out of my hand and pulled it violently toward himself, so that instead of sailing before the wind it struck us directly on the beam with mainsail closely hauled and sheet fixed.

Even had I desired death as eagerly as he did at the time, yet now I would instinctively have resisted. Seamanship teaches scorn of death but still greater scorn for bad man?uvring. "Blockhead!" I cried out, hastily cutting the taut rope so that the sail fluttered out into the wind like a half-escaped bird. But the boat had shipped so much water that I could not right her again and in a moment she was entirely swamped. I climbed to the high side stretching out my hand to my father. But he gave me one look of bitter scorn, shook his head and let himself sink, freeing his hand with a wild jerk from a loop in the rigging.

After this, I drifted about four hours. We had been missed and the life-boat had been sent out after us, but for a long time was unable to find me, as the dusk had begun to fall. Finally I was picked up by a fisherman who signalled for the life-boat to come and get me. I had lost consciousness and when I awoke it was night and I found myself in bed hearkening to the soft voices of two women in the room. I thought I was in Italy with my mother and my nurse in our house at Milan, so eloquent of the past were the old familiar sharp sss and rr sounds of these soft Italian whisperings. But soon I recognized the Dutch hotel furnishings, Lucia, and beneath the black lace veil the silvery hair of my venerable mother.

X

When for four hours, wet and benumbed upon a wave-swept piece of wood, with nothing round about but the sea and falling night, one has fought for the maintenance of a thing, one begins to consider that thing important after all, even though before it was ever so indifferent to us.

I had never valued my life so highly; but after I had once been incited to a stubborn, desperate but successful resistance against the attempt of robbing me of it, it had become dearer to me. Now I was determined to know everything there is to be known concerning the value of this hard-won treasure.

Why did I make this tremendous effort? What do I gain by it? And all these others, none of whom, forsooth, praise life as so glorious and desirable a joy, what induces them to cling to it so frantically at the cost of so much pain and trouble?

My father had taught me, and no one, not even my mother and the priests denied it, that we are reasonable beings who ought to act reasonably. To exert oneself for something undesirable, I consider, and everyone with me considers, unreasonable. If it is a Jewish idea to do or to give naught for naught - well, you may label me Jew then. That was also my idea of justice. And then I felt myself more of a Jew than the

Jew, Spinoza, who says that one should love God without expecting love in return. My inborn passion for sober truth was stirred to opposition by these words. I did not believe that this feeling could be true, not even in Spinoza. He must merely have imagined it because he wished to be different from the grasping Jews and Hollanders of his age. Right remains right. Love demands love in return, - and life must be good for something if we are willing to suffer and struggle for it. I could be as liberal and generous as the best of Italians, but the highest striving in all nature is for balance, and he who lets himself be pushed off his chair disturbs the balance instead of preserving it, and he who throws his own cabbages to his neighbor's hogs fosters laziness and injustice.

"Yes! now my life has been saved, dear mother," I said on the first day of my recovery. "But at the cost of much trouble and distress. Father and I parted the while he cursed me and I denounced him as a 'blockhead.' I am not superstitious, but these are not comforting memories. I defied his curse, I resisted him and retained my life. But for what? Who tells me that he was not right and that it had not been better for me to die?"

"God has willed it so, my boy. I fear that for your unhappy father there is no salvation; he died cursing and without repentance. But God has preserved you so that you should live for him."

"Preserved me to live for him? Does he need me then? The creator of the sun and the fixed stars, the milky way and the nebulae? Needs me? How is that, mother?"

"He wished to preserve you through his merciful love. You need him. Therefore you must live for him."

"If I need him, mother, then he must live for me and not I for him. How can anyone who needs help himself live for another? God is surely not in need of help. But I -"

"You must love him with all your heart and all your soul. You must be ready to offer all to him. You must be willing to bear life and to suffer for him. You have received everything from him. Joy and sorrow - it must all be equally dear to you because it comes from him."

"Dear mother, then I must surely have received my reason and my tastes from him too. And when my father gave me a watch and a compass I trusted that these things would point right. And when God gives me reason and tastes, must I then suppose that these point wrong? Wherefore did I receive them then? My reason calls it nonsensical to lead a wretched and miserable life, even for the sake of the Almighty Creator of Heaven and Earth. How can this be pleasing to a supreme being? What can it matter to him? And my taste calls happiness desirable and sorrow reprehensible, whether it come from one or from another. Sugar is sweet though it come from the devil, and quinine is bitter though it come from God. I cannot taste it differently."

"And is the bitter not just what you need to heal you, Vico?"

"Is it less bitter, therefore? And should I even thank the Almighty for first letting me get sick, which is unpleasant enough already, and moreover giving a bitter taste to the medicine which he made necessary? He has made me so that I feel glad and thankful for whatever gives happiness and tastes sweet, but not for affliction and bitterness."

"That is your pride, Vico! Your father instilled that into you. Learn to love God! Lay away your pride. Learn to love God humbly and through love thankfully to accept the bitter from him."

"Listen, mother. I might say now: Yes! yes! I can repeat it all after you exactly and persuade myself that I feel it all too. But then I would lie. And God has made me so that I would rather not lie if I can help it. I know no reason why I should be thankful to God for afflictions or should call the bitter sweet and the ugly beautiful. If he is my creator then he is also responsible for the desires and feelings of his creature."

"What I tell you, Vico, is something you cannot understand except through the light of grace. You must be born again through faith. You reason now as all who trust to their human understanding. I can only pray that his grace will be poured out over you. And for the sake of your mother, who loves you so, you surely do not wish to shut your heart and blind yourself to the true light? You surely will want to hear what the church teaches and want to obey and accept what older and wiser people, through love, tell and advise you."

"My heart is open to every light, mother. I am willing to hear and to consider everything. But though I would ever so gladly, I cannot obey and accept unless what I am told and advised seems acceptable to me."

"May God break your self-conceit!" my mother sighed.

What I have written here is an average and collective type of many hundreds of conversations which I had with my mother during the ten years following. With the indefatigable zeal of flies incessantly buzzing up and down and striking against a window pane, we two tenacious and autocratic persons tried to thrust upon one another our own peculiar individuality. My mother with a more aggressive love, I more on the defensive, but in my self-assertion, none the less militant. Possessed by the universal conceit of the reasonableness of our feelings and convictions, neither one of us noticed that this was simply a struggle between two natures whereof one was trying to subject the other. And accustomed as almost all the human herd to the idolatry of the true word, we both imagined that by merely talking, talking we could finally make the word which we ourselves considered true the idol of our fellow-man too, like two missionaries of different faith holding up their symbol before one another until one of the two falls on his knees.

And the mother now said that it was the father's education that made me refractory, just as the father had thought to oppose the maternal influence: as though they continued the old feud about me and through me.

The four hours of anxious suspense on the capsized boat, my father's curse ringing in my ears, his grim sinking face before my eyes, had struck such a deep gash into my young and tender soul that at first I would awaken every morning from a dream, in which the whole thing was lived through again, crying for help in a voice hoarse from screaming as I had cried so long across the lonely dusky sea. Only very gradually did these evil memory dreams cease, and till late in my life they would recur whenever my power of resistance was weakened.

These dreams acted upon me like warnings, repeating the stern lesson of the terrible event. "You have repelled your father and chosen your mother's side. You have rejected his ideas and thereby driven him to death. And what if he had been right now? Are you sure that your mother deserved this sacrifice? Are you sure that your life was worth saving? What have you - really - of that life which you so desperately defended? By your defiance you have taken a heavy responsibility upon yourself. You must now seek this assurance: the assurance that your father was in the wrong and that you are doing right by continuing to live and adhering to your mother."

These were the warnings that beset me every morning when the morning light had once more dispelled the fearful vision. In vain I sounded the depths of my soul - to find whence issued these compelling and distressing thoughts. A power dwelt within me which seemed to possess a mighty voice, and a strong coercive force when I did not want to listen. And I soon observed that this power increased in proportion as I felt weaker and more discouraged. Was it the voice of the herd, which my father had taught me to despise, but which he no more than I could infallibly distinguish from his own voice? Who was this speaker, this tyrant?

There existed a bridge of heartiness and affection between my mother and myself which always remained practicable even when the flood of controversy raged highest. When it seemed as though we would never understand each other, we would simply stay the structure of our phrases and without détour approach one another through the ever open door of our love, without troubling ourselves about logic or consistency.

And Lucia was much less averse to theology than Emmy. Supplied by my mother with shining words of authority and bombastic arguments, and no less anxious than my mother herself to let the son participate in the joy of her conviction, she eagerly granted any request for engaging in deep conversation. We did not go walking alone together, as this did not agree with her principles of education, but when we three were together the origin and prospect of our life was discussed more, and with greater fervor, than anywhere probably in all the little seaside town, perchance in all the little land.

And it is good that people do not act as reasonably as they imagine, otherwise we should see all mankind engaged in such conversations: they would forget to reap the harvest, to start the trains, to keep the fires of the factories going.

For it is strange to see everyone making the greatest efforts and wearing himself out and hardly anyone trying to render account to himself of the why and wherefore. Especially the so-called thoughtful people cut a strange figure, as usually they all disagree, or only agree about their own ignorance; and yet they go on living complacently without earnestly persevering in their efforts of reaching a conclusion. They all pretend to believe in the true word, but they do not manifest much faith in their idol, because words concerning the most important truths have but little power to attract them. It is good so, for otherwise, from sheer uncertainty, the entire machinery would come to a standstill and the truly free, such as you, dear reader, and I, would find no opportunity to gather the leading truths for them, and, wrapped in glowing formula, so dexterously to throw them before their feet that they perceive them and pick them up as their own discoveries.

Lucia del Bono was not only a beautiful, but also a bright, clever and, as my mother assured me, good and noble Italian woman. She had lost her parents, and my mother who had taken her into her home as her adopted daughter, was her saint, her oracle. Whatever mother did was good, whatever mother said was true, what mother wished was the nearest to God's will of anything we could know. And soon I perceived that, among other things, mother had long wished Lucia to become my wife. Through Emmy's loss and through the unchanging persistence of my passions, Satan's voracious pets, I however considered myself peculiarly fitted for a monastery, if I could only once reconcile myself to the doctrines suitable to such a life.

"After all, there is no other way of salvation for me" - I once said to my mother when I was alone with her on the hotel veranda. "Now I may indeed have holy resolves again and make solemn promises, but I look reality too squarely in the face to believe, myself, in these promises. I can never love a woman more truly and more fervently than Emmy, - and even this love was not strong enough to shield me from the temptations of the low and the vile. If I remain in the world, I shall nowhere escape temptation. I have seen enough to know that there is temptation everywhere for one like myself. It is bitter and humiliating, particularly for one with a proud and haughty nature, and who does not like to turn away from an enemy. I feel myself a match for men and would be willing to fight an overpowering majority, but God has left me defenceless in the hands of women."

To this mother replied: "There is no life more splendid and lofty than that of the monk who denies and suppresses all the lower, worldly and transitory feelings in order to let the eternal develop the more freely. But it requires a good deal to consecrate yourself wholly to Jesus, Vico dear. If only you are strong enough for that!"

"No, mother! I want to do it just because I am not strong enough to resist the world and my fleshly desires. I must be in an absolutely pure environment and lead an abstemious life, only then will I remain good. I have tried it for three weeks. But then I fell ill and was nursed and petted by kind hands and then Satan again had me in his power."

"You can fall ill in a monastery too, Vico. And Satan will not leave you in peace there either. Think of how even the saints were tormented by demons and temptations."

"Ali, mother, what I have read about that, and seen on paintings, proves that they do not know my temptations. Did you imagine that I would succumb to the pretty ladies who troubled Antonius of Padua? They are much too pretty, too poetic, I should say. With them I would feel ashamed. And all those monsters and demons, as Teniers paints them, they would not frighten me in the least. I know them well from my dreams. They give you a fright, but you can easily drive them away, much more easily than -"

"Than what, Vico?" my mother asked. But before I could conquer my strong disinclination to give an idea of the true nature of my visitants, Lucia came out of her room.

"What do you say to this, little daughter!" my mother said with grave, almost embarrassed mien, "Vico wants to enter the priesthood."

It was curious to mark the change of expression on Lucia's face. With a peculiar wide, shining look, her great dark eyes travelled from mother to me, but she cleverly concealed that it was a painful surprise. She could not suppress a deep blush, however, and when she felt it and realized that it could not help betraying an all too deep and painful interest, the blush of shame became yet deeper.

"That is fine!" she said in a voice solemn with emotion.

"If Christ will only accept me," I said; "according to you two I am still half a heathen."

"Oh, he will surely accept you! he will be good to you!" said Lucia, in a tone which betrayed more certainty concerning the being of whom she spoke than Emmy's "Jesus Christ our Lord."

"How do you know that so surely, Lucia?" I asked, immediately attentive. "Do you know him so well? Can you explain to me what he is?"

"Do I know him?" she cried out passionately, with a little comprehensive smile at mother. "What shall I reply, mother? He asks whether we know the dear Lord Jesus."

"What would you yourself reply, Vico, if she asked you whether you knew me, your mother?"

I was silent, and thoughtfully regarded the two women, so obviously convinced. Then Lucia said: "I know him much better, Vico, than you know your mother, for you have not had her near you for very long, nor is she with you all the time. But my Jesus never leaves me. I have always had him near me as long as I can remember day and night."

I said nothing, but looked at her encouragingly, intimating that she should go on and tell me more of Jesus. And she did it gladly, - far more eagerly than Emmy, - and though it was not all clearly and absolutely lucidly expressed, not entirely connected and too long, to repeat it all to you here, yet it was captivating and instructive and, to me, implied the existence of a firm and neither weak nor transitory reality.

Suggestion is a very convenient word with a meaning easily adaptable to all sorts of explanations; but if there were no bounds and no end to this explaining by suggestion, we might as well rub out from our suggested slate of life, with a suggested sponge, the whole beautiful world of clear and eternal realities. No, the Christ of Lucia and my mother was no suggested fancy, but a living reality.

But what was he?

Of the Bible the two women knew very little. My mother, despite her Northern origin, had had an Italian Catholic education as well as Lucia. In this, for valid reasons, the Bible is forbidden. They did not speak much of the life of Jesus as an historical person, nor of his adventures, nor of his teachings. It was his suffering, his martyrdom, and his death that to them seemed to be above all deserving of meditation.

And if I had not known it - if the Nazarene of whom the New Testament narrates had borne another name, it might perhaps never have occurred to me to identify him with the Deity worshipped by my mother.

But now that I must needs assume that all information regarding the being, personally wholly unknown to me, that so occupied the lives of these two women and of millions of human beings besides, was to be found in these ancient writings, the English translation of which, contrary to my mother's wishes, I faithfully kept - now I began to read with renewed and even closer attention.

But I found nothing to give me light. I found a very beautiful and touching narrative full of dramatic power, written by the hand of a master, but to its detriment four times retold with embellishments and obvious falsifications. And the hero of this narrative was a very human mortal, more delicate, more sensitive and nearer akin to us than Hiob: just as bold in the flight of his thought, just as fanatic and even immoderate in his declarations, and certainly less strong, less resolute, his character less unmoved by the lot threatening him than the mighty hero of the older drama. I was deeply stirred by the reading of this wonderful creation, by the thoroughly human truth of his struggle, his disappointments, waverings and weaknesses, his courage and self-denial, his alternately proud and discouraged bearing, his very explainable self-deception, caused by the influence of his childish followers and worshippers, his fatal and truly tragic ending, not desired but foreboded, and manfully not evaded, - immutable necessary result of human weakness in human heroic strength.

But what did all this have to do with the wonderful reality in which my mother and millions with her found all their joy and their security, with which, through which, for which, in which they lived as fish live in the water?

I found nothing but a little outward resemblance, the name, the death he suffered. But for the rest it seemed to me that they might as well have named any other hero of tragedy - Prometheus for example - as the mighty and loving being that, even now, directed all their steps and shed light upon their path.

And through many careful and attentive conversations with the fair Lucia, in the presence of my mother, who was for her the living fountain from which she gratefully drew when her wisdom threatened to forsake her, I became convinced that had Lucia been taught that the divine reality she felt in herself was named Spinoza, because Spinoza was a God, incarnate in human form, who had lived in Rynsburg as a man, had proclaimed many words of living wisdom and therefore suffered scorn and contempt and finally, after a life of simplicity and chastity, had died in loneliness and poverty for our salvation - the pious maiden would just as readily have accepted it and would have found exactly as much strength, happiness and contentment in it.

Do not lose patience, my reader, because I tell you such commonplace things. Of course as an independently thinking and observing person, you know all this just as well as I. But for the herd it is all new, absolutely new. And it will still be so when you read this and I am dead and for many, many years after. Do not forget that we too belong to the herd, you and I, and that an accurate comprehension of our relations

Frederik van Eeden

does not exclude a loving understanding and a wise affection. There is joy in my pride only because it rests on an immutable estimation of worth. I know that the herd thinks and feels slavishly and I do not, and that it is therefore necessarily subject to me; but my joy would rot and wither in my pride, did I not know the comforting and refreshing humility, the humility that by patient deeds of love unites me to the herd, and gives me full measure of comfort in this faithful, sincere and patient record for the good of all, so that I have found peace, tranquillity of mind and a foretaste of bliss in the utmost spiritual loneliness, in this dead life.

There is neither contentment nor happiness in unshared wisdom. Therefore I make bold once more to speak plainly of such commonplace things. If we would build our towers higher and higher, we must seek to broaden the foundations, otherwise we topple over with our individual wisdom just as we had imagined heaven attained. The herd does not need our leading more urgently than we its following.

True, it must have been a great and ingenious Jew, who, now more than eighteen hundred years ago, wisely responding to the cry of anguish from his enslaved countrymen for a redeemer, as king, as Christ, pointed out to them the new man, the meek, the "Chrestus," with whom the whole earth felt herself pregnant.

No one can have known the divine reality, which so many millions have called Christ, so profoundly, and have felt it more clearly living in himself than he, when flown from his subdued and desolate country to Alexandria, be created the mighty and tragic heroic figure and chose the name that for so many centuries was to be accepted by mankind, as the personification and epithet of this same reality.

But I charge him gravely that with Jewish fearfulness he

withdrew his own person from the struggle in which he let his hero perish, and suffered or even wished his noble and true work of art to be changed into a false piece of history. What might have gladdened and elevated poor suffering and blinded humanity as a wonderful masterpiece of art, like the book of Hiob, or the Iliad, or Prometheus Vinctus, or the Athene of the Parthenon, or the Zeus of Olympus, showing how man in the creations of the artist rises highest above personal pettiness and weakness, how the genius in fiction creates the highest perfection, such as has never been seen in flesh and blood, - has now, as an invented historical occurrence, driven the whole world to the rudest falsifications of truth and impossible efforts of imitation.

The glorious shapes of Phidias, more beautiful than any living human race has ever actually been, have still brought us joy and inspiration after a miserable barbaric Christian world bad mutilated and neglected them, - but the beautiful figure of Jesus, which as a work of art might have been immortal and beneficent, embellished with Pauline metaphysics and mixed in the Byzantine sorcerer's pot with Egyptian and Chaldean hodgepodge, has become an evil spirit for wretched human kind.

For eighteen hundred years the world has been the dupe of this marvellous dramatic genius and his work, changed in a fatal hour from fiction to history. I know no stronger proof for the existence of a malicious devil who takes pleasure in our amusing errors.

And many a night, when it is warm and the sea calm and the doves coo in the softly whispering elms on the city walls, I wander out of my quiet little city and gaze over the smooth extent of water, musing for hours on the beauty and the joy that would now reign on earth if, unprejudiced and unconfounded, men had asked what God it was that so mightily

revealed himself in them and urged them with such perceptible will and pressure, and spoke in so audible a voice: if
they had earnestly and attentively hearkened to the constant
whisperings and warnings of their deep true nature, if they
had borne and learned to follow the bridle of this faithful
warner in their own soul, who strongly desires and alone has
power to give us peace, - instead of worshipping the true
word, and looking for outward signs and miracles, and
through the beautiful creations of a human genius letting
themselves be seduced to human deification, to stupid
imitation, to fanaticism, to falsification of word and reality,
to a sickly pursuit of pain, glorification of poverty, fear of
knowledge, scorn of the world, hatred of beauty, poor stray
sheep!

Then the great and good works of Greeks and Romans, of
Indians and Saracens would have been thoughtfully carried
on, art preserved, knowledge esteemed, - and the garden of
peace made verdant with clear springs of beauty from these
two pure fountains. While now, alas! again and again, in
thousands of hearts, the true Christ must die the bitter death
upon the cross because the truest word that he inspired one
of his dearest favorites to utter was besmirched by a flat lie,
and his most beautiful poetical image destroyed by a grossly
sensuous error.

But be of good cheer, my reader; the devil made a good
move, but shall lose the game nevertheless. The falsehood
poison has soon spent itself, and the powers of the sick
increase. No longer do the shepherdless dogs drive the flock
asunder in a hundred different directions. You live, my
reader, and hear the voice of me, the dead, - and as though
heralded forth by trumpets, you learn that the crucified in
you and in me is also victoriously and gloriously risen again.

XI

It was three weeks before the body of my father was found. A stormy nor-wester had thrown it high up on shore at the foot of the dunes not far from the mouth of the Rhine, and a clam-digger came to claim the promised reward. My mother went there with me and prayed a long time by the side of the body. I did too, in my own way; that is to say, with a constant reservation, as one might write a letter to someone whose address one was not sure of. Nevertheless every prayer is a suggestion in which through words of invocation one creates an image of a Deity and through forcibly uttered exhortations and protestations changes one's own soul. Is there in any act greater possibility for self-deception? As a child and youth, it is still possible to observe oneself praying and to continue in the belief that one is acting worthily and honestly. But for a man, self-observation during this act usually also carries with it shame at the game that he is playing and the pose that he assumes.

The body lay in a coffin, already closed, in a tiny church of the fisher village, and it seemed as though my father's surviving spirit mocked me for the trifling words with which I, foolish boy, thought to reach and to move the soul of clouds and sea, of sun and stars. How childish the burning candles and the chanting voice of the priest seemed, with the roaring of the wind over the reed-covered sand hills, and the

　　　　　Frederik van Eeden

glowing eye with which the setting sun looked upon her earth from across the sea.

When the funeral was over, we decided to leave Holland for my native country. There, in Rome, I would, if anywhere, find my way back to the mother church. Solemn, talking little, full of expectation, and usually deep in thought, I travelled swiftly across the continent in the company of the two women. Italy, that I had not seen for many years, lured me with a thousand sweet memories, with the combined charm of the wonderland of sun and beauty which it is to all Northerners, and of the world of dear childish moods, whose deceiving sweetness increases with distance and length of separation, and can make even the most barren country gleam as a place of refuge and consolation. With a little more experience of life I might have considered beforehand that the real Italy could not fulfil all the blessed promises of the imaginary Italy. At the beginning they did indeed all seem to be realized. It commenced with sunshine, and the vintage - golden light upon browning foliage, merry country folk and song; a gleam of a better world after the dull and solemn North: a glorious sensation of being at home among people who like myself dared to say something graceful and to do something wanton; the beloved flexible and vigorous sounds of my mother tongue, and the great joy of the people's craving for beauty and elegance down into the very lowest circles: roughness and wildness not without a certain dignity, not simply rude and coarse as with the Northern barbarians: a poor lad in rags who sings something on the street that penetrates my inmost soul. Ah! how little the rude among this Dutch people can do or say that penetrates my soul! If my reason did not tell me, what then could convince my heart that they and I are beings of a kind?

I cannot dwell here on the charm with which my native land stirred my emotions when I beheld it again. It has nothing to do with the task and the duty that I fulfil in these writings. Hundreds of writers can delight you with subtle sensuous fancies and can comfort you for a moment with beautiful visions, warming the cold indolent spirit by colorful, glowing or gracefully woven words. My task is to give lasting consolation through the unsensual force of unchanging thought, so that you will know a point of rest in all sorrows and can taste every pleasure with calmer attention.

In Rome my disillusionment came with the rainy days of winter. Then all at once it penetrated my consciousness from every side, like a cold draft through broken window panes - the realization that something was still wanting here, that in the North had been attained: an established order of institutions, a general moral integrity. The half-forgotten shadows of my childhood, hidden behind the beautiful, came to view, called forth by kindred miseries. We had to live comparatively simply, and my dignified old mother, as well as I, had to climb the four chilly, dimly lighted, stony flights to our apartment, where it was cold and uncomfortable too. To let Lucia go about alone in Rome, like an English girl in London, was simply out of the question. I myself had to be very much on my guard against suspicious persons who whisperingly accosted me with foul proposals. And a stroll through the section San Lorenzo on a bleak December day, where I saw, how my poor people, kept in ignorance and filth, manfully battle against suffering and misery, made me feel that Italy, when her glorious sunlight fades, is still ever the land of the "sofferenza" and still deserves the cry of lamentation:

"Ahi, selva Italia! di dolore ostello!"

This sorrowful word never leaves me; often do I sigh it through the stillness of my gloomily respectable house, the abode of the old Dutch merchants; and then too perchance I

Frederik van Eeden

scream it out into the gale on the open sea-dike where my petty fellow citizens cannot hear it.

In this gray, beclouded, chilly land, where the bleak, restless wind bends low and razes to the ground everything that standing alone would lift up its head, less rude anguish is suffered nevertheless than among the sunny, luxuriant, blue-skied hills of my beautiful native land.

But this does not imply that the Italians should envy this so much more methodical, cleanly and prosperous nation. For glowing life and blooming beauty fare still more madly among the Hollanders, and sharp anguish is more salutary to man, and preferred by the genitive soul of humanity, than the unfelt evil of ugliness, of dullness and of the great and beautiful passions stifled by fear. Everywhere in the present world a minority sensitive to beauty exists among a great horde of cads. But in no country is the minority nobler, but smaller also, and the horde more caddish than in Holland - and in imagination I often see the Neapolitan tramp and loafer stand out as a prince or nobleman among the inmates of a Dutch village inn, or hall for more respectable entertainment. But your purse and your life are safer and the average standard of middle-class respectability higher here below the sea level than in most countries above.

The first ones that I sought in my native land were the priests, whom my father had always made me shun. My mother's sentimental wisdom did not satisfy the wants of my reason, and she herself thought that I should be easily and swiftly convinced of what, to her, seemed so evidently true, if I but heard someone versed in the eloquence and the logical argumentative power which her intuitive knowledge lacked.

But ah me! we were sadly mistaken there, my mother and I.

Her position and rank enabled her to refer me to the very best address; and none less than one of the most powerful and influential prelates of the age, an intimate of the Vatican and a political celebrity, was to guide me, youthful errant, back into the path of salvation. I was much impressed by his great name, and in the beginning I also could not withhold myself from the suggestion that goes out from each one into whose hands the herd has pressed the magic rose of deference and subjugation. But neither his environment, - a gloomy apartment tastelessly furnished in bourgeois style, - nor his outward appearance, a bony, half jovial, half cautiously cunning, more or less boorish face upon a heavy unwieldy body, was adapted to strengthen my illusion. He was very genial, talkative, good-natured, and made a little kindly intended speech to which I sat and listened with the conviction that I must be making a confused, distressed and foolish appearance.

Subsequently he committed me to the care of one of his younger disciples, a pale, seemingly timid, but, as was soon manifest, very strong-willed, ambitious young priest, who scrutinized me with well-nigh impertinent searchingness, like a doctor his patient.

I did not let my mother notice the tremendous shock that I experienced at this first visit, as she betrayed her hopeful expectation by a painful agitation. For her sake, too, I went on and moved in the circles which I could not really believe quite so bad as my father had pictured them. But I could not carry it through very long. Even on the street I would shudder with repulsion when I saw the insignificant, coarse, often positively unpleasant and villainous faces peering out from under the rough, black felt hats. It was as though they bore upon their foreheads the mark of guilt for the misery in which my poor people were toiling. And no sooner had I gained sufficient knowledge of the sentiments, the desires,

Frederik van Eeden

the ideas that peopled the spiritual world of the young man appointed as my shepherd, then I knew once for all that his labor would be vain.

He was not an insignificant man, the young priest, nor was he an ignoble character. At the time I learned, in one moment, to conceive for him a deadly hatred and contempt. But these are some of our Italian extravagances. I expected and longed for a hero to help me - and when anyone came to me with this pretension, but fell considerably below the mark of a hero, I wished him to the devil and would have liked to kick him out of my door. Here in my house of meditation by the sea, I have learned to consider that the young priest possessed many talents, great learning, a keen knowledge of human nature, a clear, practical mind, an ambition careful enough not to seek base means for attaining the firmly desired goal, and a religious conviction which, whether inborn, acquired, or adopted, needed no further confirmation, and gave him sufficient tranquillity of mind to set himself with all his might to acquire the things which, among those his religion allowed, seemed to him the most desirable.

But oh! the deadly and sterile assurance of these people. Their confession of faith was not a living, blooming thing that under continuous distress and delight, daily revealed itself as richer and more beautiful; not a constantly changing, flowing stream, with its substance watering and making fruitful the entire world; it was a heavy, unchanging, tightly shut, square strongbox that stood in a comer of their lives, safe and well stocked, from which, at stated times only, and in proportion to their moral needs, they went to cut off the coupons of tranquillity of mind and spiritual consolation.

He was so astonishingly calm, so tremendously sure of himself, so well versed in his patriarchs, so practised in all logical disputes, so thoroughly at home in all the eaves and the alleys, the case-mates and the bastions of the citadel of his faith, that it seemed as though he might dare take it up with all the doubters on earth. And yet how poor he seemed to me, how naked and miserable, locked up in his formulated system, like a bug in the hollow of a dead piece of wood, helplessly adrift upon the wild waters of reality. He was not a narrow-minded fanatic either, and knew the issues of science as well or better than I - but he had his words, his formulas, his logical snares and ropes, in which he caught all these troublesome and unmanageable truths and hitched them to his car of faith: the true word, the correct argument, the convincing phraseology that is the fine and artfully painted panorama which the devil employs to separate us from the free true world.

I was exacting in those days and was not contented with the people, who were no better than they could be. I did not understand that they felt it as a duty to submit to the ideas of the group, just as I felt it my duty to break loose from it. I did not recognize the relative value of their virtues, because they seemed to me like cyphers, in front of which the unit of highest virtue, the naught-fearing love of reality, was missing. And I was still too timid and too modest to give every man his due cold-bloodedly, to break the bond of absolute sincerity with him, and to mount the steep path of pride which each truly pious man, - as you and I, dear reader, - alas! is obliged to take against his will and pleasure, under penalty of losing time, life and strength, and the subtle discernment of God's loving signal light, in idle strife and struggle.

I shall not name the man here at present: he is already a cardinal, and when you read this he may be pope. Through negative influence he has exerted a tremendous effect upon my life. My mother admired and honored him highly, and it was as though with her own hand she thereby took the shining halo from her head and smashed it upon the pavement. I could not be mistaken in this priest: the very highest humanity, the fine tentacles constantly reaching out toward the divine, the continuous growing and seeking, the true life were wanting in him. When I wanted to ascend this path, he became blind and lame and refused to follow, escaping and evading me by all kinds of winding rhetorical paths, with a perfectly innocent expression of ignorance upon his pale, calm and self-satisfied countenance. It was as though his eyes congealed - of my burning desires they knew nothing. He could say every thing that he believed, felt and desired, and the unutterable that made him feel and desire thus and so was to him a word, not a vehemently and helplessly loved and longed-for reality, as it was to me. This I saw, I felt, I apprehended; there was no possibility of doubt. And thus I learned two most important truths: first that all talk about the chiefest part of our being is mere talk, that is to say, prattle and chatter, worth no more, no less, and just as misleading and inadequate for mutual communication and conviction, as all speech; secondly, that even the best men in their most profound and sacred feelings let themselves be ruled by other men, or groups of men, not necessarily better than they, and that they do not realize this constraint, but go on thinking that they themselves conceive and feel and accept with independent judgment what is thrust on them by other human beings or human groups.

For this priest considered himself more godly, wiser and better than my mother and I, and all his masterly eloquence only proved the contrary to me; and yet I saw that my mother was servile to him and adopted from him what he again had adopted from the large group of his equals and kindred spirits, and that all this took place without their realizing it, through personal influence, and never, as they contended, through the clear sense of the absolute, with the free judgment directed only by God's subtle guidance. What became now of all the beautiful light of Grace and Revelation? persuasion! nothing else! impress of personality on personality! as the teacher impels the child, the market crier his peasants, the general his loyal soldiers, the judge the timid witness, and as the ruling idea - public opinion - impels every individual, wholly beyond all reason or judgment, or absolute sense, no matter how strongly, we all may imagine the contrary.

These are subtle, cruel truths that deeply and grievously penetrate a youthful spirit if it be open to them. You, dear reader, as an all-renouncing lover of truth, know them as well as I. You know how terribly corrosive, like a sharp acid, is their discovery, leaving scarcely any of our ideals uncontaminated and sound. And consider besides that my spirit was broken by the terrible memory of the struggle which for years I had carried on with my father, and of his awful death caused by my clinging to ideals that now indeed all seemed nerveless illusions.

In my artlessness I had thought that the church in which my mother found peace and consolation would elect none but chosen heroes among men as her servants and priests. The very best would scarcely be good enough for such a dignity.

Instead of this I saw how the first youngster that came along, with a little hard pegging and servility could work his way up to the priesthood; how the average stood no higher than the common masses; and how, among my people, they were more looked down upon and derided than venerated. And even the very best among them, the highest dignitaries, were not the heroes, the poets and the sages, who by virtue of their great human gifts were fitted to be the elect and leaders; but merely the clever and ambitious, who possessed a little more of that particular proficiency which helps one on in politics, too - but has nothing to do with the divine.

Frederik van Eeden

If ever I stood close to ruin, it was then. I had lost all hold. My beloved was far away in the arms of one whom I deemed unworthy; my saint had lost her crown; my father's voice now seemed to ask me with mocking emphasis whether it had not been better either to continue living with him or to go with him into death.

Do you know who saved me, dear reader? Not the beautiful Lucia, whom I pitied with tender compassion because she was, after all, nothing but a slight feather upon my mother's breath, - but none less than Satan himself. Satan saved me, Satan, dear reader; hold this well in mind! Here is the profound explanation of his nature: he saved me because he manifested himself so clearly and unmistakably that I simply had to continue believing in him. And whoever believes in evil as evil cannot be lost. Just as I, even as later the young scapegrace Nietzsche, wanted to make a bolt over good and evil, I faced Satan, and the evil one was so kind that he did me a better turn than any kind human being ever did me.

As if to manifest himself very plainly, Satan, following the custom of all mighty principles, became incarnate. I came into contact with a young seminary student, who bore the name of an archangel and with it a face that resembled that of the prince of fallen angels more closely than any known to me. He even, as if to emphasize this, twisted his black locks above his low forehead in such a way that two horns appeared to be hidden under them. His eyelids hung rather low over his brown eyes, that peeped out furtively, and narrowing, twinkled kindly, while the straight thin-lipped mouth, above the long chin, uttered the most cruel sarcasms in a high, almost feminine voice.

And yet it was just this man who attracted me more than anyone I had met in clerical circles. In the first place, by reason of his wit; for he was an Irishman and full of those sharp and delicious jokes to which I was very susceptible; but also, because he was the only one who seemed to understand something of my great, dumb, impotent wrath at the universal unwillingness of mankind - which at the time I had not yet learned to look upon as impotence - to recognize the contradiction between their teachings and their life. Once when he had attended a conversation between my young teacher and myself, in which, as was my wont, I had made fruitless efforts to make him sensible of what was lacking in the entire priestly institution and to free myself from the meshes of his arguments, he said in leaving:

"You come at an opportune moment, dear Count Muralto! The rôle of ingénue has long been vacant in our company. But you need not assume it any more toward the directors. They are already aware of it now, and there is such a thing as laying it on too thick."

This remark aroused in me great astonishment and interest. I immediately began to question Michael. Above all, I wished to know how he found it possible, with such thoughts in his head, to wish to become a priest.

"That's not so difficult," said Michael, "if only you learn to keep order in your thoughts. It all depends on order and exactness, on a careful double bookkeeping. Every good business man has a private bank-account which has nothing to do with the business. In the same way we must learn to keep our private thoughts out of the business. That is all."

"I am afraid that I shall never learn to look upon the most sacred office as a merchant's trade."

"Well played, dear ingénue!" said Michael; "but on the verge of foolishness. To look down upon merchants and business is no longer naïve, but foolish. Without merchants the Holy

Father himself would starve in prison. The whole world is a trading concern and there's no harm in that. Our business we rightly call the sacred business because, at all events, it is still the most trustworthy firm in existence. I consider it a great honor that I may be its youngest servant and am thankful that at the same time it can, if I keep my wits about me, also become a pleasure. The demand that I keep the private account of my ideas carefully separate from the ledger of the firm, so as not to cause confusion, I consider very just and moderate. It is so in all large and practical affairs. There's nothing like order, said the farmer as he screwed the lid on the coffin of his grandmother, who lay in a trance and wanted to get out again. Can you make a uniform that will fit every soldier? Can you fashion a net in which each little fish will find a mesh exactly fitting its own dimensions? No doctrine is true for everyone, and no law is just for all. Each must have a care that he get through the meshes."

"I must admit, brother Michael, that I think your cynicism more tolerable and more upright than the obstinate hypocrisy of our prelates. And what you say about the law that cannot be just for all seems to me worthy of consideration."

"Cynicism! hypocrisy!" brother Michael cried out with a silencing gesture. "My dear young man, how wildly you throw your rotten apples. A dog is a good-natured and clever animal, but for that reason it is not doggish to discriminate correctly. And as long as you artless blockheads do not understand that proper and successful hypocrisy is the primal Christian virtue, the practising of which belongs to the highest religious duties already taught by the Trinity, so long nothing will come of the Kingdom of God."

After this conversation, about which I said nothing to my mother, I changed and my attitude became more reserved, cautious and suspicious. More and more I began with profound amazement to understand the curious and appalling condition of our social system. But meanwhile the turbulent passions in me were not calmed and my difficulties remained the same. As long as I lived in the hopeful suspense of the shipwrecked who believes that the haven of safety is in sight, the dogs were still. But when this again ended in disappointment, they grew restive, bold and troublesome. With every weakening of the spirit and joy in life our wild beasts get a looser rein, as a ship when its course is blocked pays less attention to the rudder.

The more I was disappointed in humanity, the more I began to give ear to the women who in Rome, more vociferous than in London, rioting and ranting often like unto a band of mænads, go out at night, upon the hunt for men. And it was not many weeks before just that peculiar temptation which does not put itself forth with wanton or charming thoughtlessness, but with good-natured and cold shamelessness debases itself, had discovered me in my defencelessness and made of me an easy prey.

The complex feeling of self-contempt, shame, assumed light-heartedness, fear of undesired encounters, and yet more despicable fear of thieves and cut-throats, that in the shadow of the dark doorways of Rome's disreputable houses, luxuriantly flourishes in the soil of a bad conscience, is not deserving of envy; especially when, as in my case, there is the aggravating circumstance that, in face of an entire haughty priesthood, one has dared to consider oneself a better man, and has shown this more or less.

Thus it was a monstrous shock for me and a most miserable cold douche of temerity over my proud aristocrat's heart when at such a moment, my temptress having struck a match on the wall, the brightly flickering flame suddenly lit up the

Frederik van Eeden

satanic visage of brother Michael, who, after first having leered at me cautiously and a bit perplexed, broke out into a truly devilish burst of laughter.

"Well met! Well met!" he cried out in his mother tongue, and then the witches' words from Macbeth: "When shall we three meet again?"

I confess, dear reader, that I stood there most miserably confused and ashamed, absolutely and utterly without self-control. But I stuttered out something resembling a reproach and a justification:

"I, at least, wear no clerical garb."

"Neither do I," said Michael; "I am incognito on private business."

"Oh!" said I scornfully; "concerning the double book-keeping!"

"Exactly, dear ingénue!" said Michael, with his most sweetish smile. "Concerning the double book-keeping, you have remembered it well. But go on, don't let me disturb you! Perhaps I'll be back later."

But in my fright I had already turned about, and ran swiftly up the street, followed by some not very flattering remarks from the woman who had been disappointed in her pursuit. Michael overtook me.

"Two negatives constitute one positive," said he. "Two sinners together arouse virtue. It seems to me we might as well have converted the fair sinner also."

Like an instinct for self-preservation in the most desperate danger, so man follows an instinct of self-justification in the most hopeless disgrace.

"Brutes we both of us are, Michael, but I at least acknowledge it. I loathe myself. You, tomorrow, must don your saintly garb and hide under it your rottenness and foulness. I do not envy you."

"It does not befit us, dear Muralto, to loathe one whom God has created after his own image. We have every one of us been saddled with a portion of filth and it does not seem enviable to me to work that off alone, as you. I can go to confession and belong to a large friendly circle, where they one and all are bitten by the same fleas and must chop with the same hatchet. We understand one another, and trust one another and forgive one another and help one another. There are weak brothers and strong brothers, we all of us know that, and we do not despise one another for that reason. This seems to me a much more desirable way of carrying your burden than as you do, who shoulder it alone. We at least do not dissemble toward one another, but you play the part of ingénue, not only toward the entire commonalty, but even toward us who know quite well what to think of your pretension to moral superiority."

I felt that I should succumb to this struggle. I gave it up. With a cool bow I parted from him and from that moment avoided all association with younger or older members of the clergy. Though I was willing to assume that I had not met the best soldiers of the camp, still the honor of fighting in their ranks did not entice me. I preferred, after all, to fight it out alone.

From this moment on my seclusion begins: I felt that Michael was right - my pretensions were ridiculous, I had nothing by which I could claim superiority, I was a hypocrite, I played an underhand game as well as they whom I seemed to look down upon.

And yet - and yet - I felt that I was not understood, that my erring was different from theirs, and that my piety had a quality lacking in theirs. And this undestroyable consciousness of a superiority, which I could not make prevail, of an inner life which I could not find in anyone and could reveal to none, drove me back into total, absolute solitude and inner separation from the human world in which I had to move.

This is an old story that constantly repeats itself. You know it all too well, do you not, reader? And we are not the only ones to undergo this process. In thousands and thousands of every generation the new life attempts to break the old group-ideas. In most of them it is overcome and subjected to the old. In a very few it breaks loose, prevails for a moment, and then is annihilated in the tragic destruction of body and soul by a death of torture, suicide, or insanity, as an inspiring example for a few, as a disheartening warning to many. In still others, as in you and me, dear reader, it finds a way of maintaining itself in the hostile world, protected by a tough hide of pretext and disguise, as the tiny seed swallowed by the birds withstands assimilation and, thrown out, finds a way of growth.

Thus for twenty years I have wandered about like a stranger in the world, apparently wholly subjected and belonging to it, but inwardly totally estranged, leading an independent life of my own: all this time inwardly struggling without rest, without peace in a battle apparently hopeless; until, strengthened and taught by a brief period of bright, true living, of blithe, vigorous action and nameless, deep sorrow, I have now entered with wholly different feelings, with trust and resignation, this last voluntary hermitage, to build with glad delight and joyous insight upon the mansion of the future.

I told my mother that nothing would probably come of my priesthood. She listened to it with the passive calmness which had grown customary to her through continuous practice in forced resignation, but which did not hide from the subtle observer the undercurrents of very ordinary human passions and desires. I had gradually come to observe these so plainly that the lack of self-perception in her grew constantly more difficult for me to bear without irritation.

This time I saw that she readily abandoned the proud hope of seeing her son a priest, for the possibility of now achieving the realization of her favorite marriage scheme. But she intended to show only sorrow and compassion, and shaking her head, she said:

"So your pride is not overcome, the viper's head not crushed, poor Vico?"

"I am obedient to that which is most divine in me, mother."

"Your human sense, you mean? Or your human pride?"

"Mother, what other means have we for distinguishing the truth save the sense that tells us: 'this is true!' exactly as our eye tells us: 'this is light!' and our skin: 'this is warm!' Would you have me say: 'this is darkness,' where I see light, or 'this is right,' where I see wrong, only because you call it right?"

"I cannot argue with you, Vico. Do what seems right to you. I have learned to be resigned."

"But you desire my happiness, don't you, mother?"

"Ah, dear son, I wish that people would stop seeking for their happiness. It is all deception and vanity, a bright soap bubble. I have never known happiness, but have learned to sacrifice all pleasure and all joy for love of the Saviour."

"Listen a second, mother!" said I, now no longer wholly suppressing my anger; "if you tell me that there are phantom joys and false happiness and that we must be careful not to fling ourselves away on these, I'll admit you are perfectly right. But if you want to make me believe that the desire for joy and happiness, which was given to all of us, is a devilish invention that we must not obey - then I call your world a chaos and your life an offence. The very deepest, all-controlling basis of our passions is that for happiness and joy, for the true, lasting, peace-giving happiness, that we sometimes mistakenly seek in idle pleasures. If God has created us with the intention that we should not follow the most profound, all-controlling passion he has planted in us, then God is a foot who has given life to cripples. Profoundly as I have searched myself, I always find the impulse toward light, toward beauty, toward happiness - to wish to turn me from it is to wish to destroy me. Never will I be able to follow another guiding star, for I have none, nor do I see one in any other person. And to none, to none on earth or in the heavens, shall I subject myself so slavishly as to deny for him my true, profoundest nature."

My mother carried her handkerchief to her eyes and shook her head with a sad shrug of the shoulders, but she did not reply.

Then as a lure I dropped a word, to see whether I understood her rightly - better than she understood herself.

"Isn't Lucia coming? We were to drive to the Pincio?"

The handkerchief dropped and her eyes sparkled a moment.

"Lucia? Of course she is coming. I did not know that you intended to go with us."

Then I knew that I had guessed right, and it was this that estranged me from my mother, while I gave in nevertheless to her unconscious desire.

XII

Call Holland a dreamy country because its beauty is as that of a dream. Sometimes it is black, wildly inhospitable and dispiriting - and suddenly, in calm, mild weather, the entire country with its trees, canals, cities and inhabitants sparkles in an indescribable tender radiance, enhancing everything with a deep mysterious meaning impossible to explain or describe more fully, and resembling the peculiar beauty of dreams. One must have seen my little city from the sea on a still, clear September eve, when the sun goes to bide behind the bell-tower, flooding the cloudless, luminous blue-green heavens with orange and gold, when pastures and the shadows of trees merged in a fairy tinted blue haze unite in wondrous harmony - when the milkers come home with heavy tread, balancing at their sides the pails of cobalt blue - when all that sounds is harmonious from the striking of the clock on the tower to the rattling of a homeward driving cart, and all that breathes from the coarse Hollanders to the dull cows seems wrapped in this selfsame peaceful, poetic evening bliss - one must have seen it thus to understand how much all this resembles the wondrous illusion of our dreams, when in some inexplicable manner the simplest object gleams with a glow of heavenly splendor and unspeakable beauty and for days can fill our memory with the bliss of it.

But the inhabitants of this dreamy little country do not like to be called dreamy. As I understand the word, it is a compliment better deserved by my own countrymen; but the Hollanders themselves feel flattered, though quite erroneously, when I casually remark at the club that the Italians are a much dreamier people than they. To the Hollander a dreamer is a blockhead and a dullard, and our broker, a little fellow with gray beard and little leering cunningly-stupid eyes, who thinks himself very smart because he knows bow to eke out a profit everywhere and thus to swell his bank account, always states with much satisfaction that he never knew what it was to dream. When he sleeps he sleeps absolutely and is conscious of nothing, thus - of less even than when he is awake. And the doctor - a fat jovial young fellow of strong mulatto type and popular for his good-natured cordiality and stale college jokes - says that all dreams are pathological and the best medicine for them is a good cigar and a stiff rum punch before retiring.

A Dutch peasant in his blue blouse, on a meadow flooded by the golden evening sun, amongst the black and white cattle, with a background of white and pale green dunes in fine undulating outline, is a marvel of dream beauty. But he himself knows nothing of this, as little or even less than the cow beside him. And the broker and the doctor only recognize it when a dreamer such as Rembrandt or Ruysdaal has revealed it, and the papers record how many thousands of golden gilders their reverie has yielded. But in my country the humblest peasant lad, clambering barefooted and singing down the Piedmontese foothills behind his black goats in the golden evening light, is enough of a dreamer to have a clear conception of the grand concert of beauty whereof he is a single tone. In the cities it is of course equally bad everywhere, and dreamers are as rare among the sleek, smart officers and loungers of the Toledo in Naples as among the portly, blond-bearded sons of the merchants and shopkeepers in the Kalverstraat at Amsterdam.

Frederik van Eeden

Now it also seems to me that he who dreams is more awake than he who sleeps, and that he who spends a third part of his life in utter unconsciousness better deserves to be called a sleepyhead and dullard, than he for whom the dark nights are also vivid and rich with pulsing life. To me it has always seemed a shame to lie like a stone for so many hours, and to arise from sleep no wiser than when we sank into it. And after having experienced several times in my early youth that sleep possesses riches of sensations and a wealth of rapture that surpass the intensest joys of brilliant day, shedding behind them a radiance that penetrates the brightest daylight as sunshine penetrates an electrically lighted hall, - I began to pay more attention to my dreams and, especially in dreary joyless days, to look forward to the nights in which I had unmistakably felt the shining presence of such great treasure.

As to the doctors' opinion regarding the morbidness of dreams, I refer again to my observations on the philistinism prevalent among physicians, and I know from very positive experience that there are healthy as well as morbid sensations in sleep, precisely as in the day-life. I may speak with some authority because in my day-life I never experienced any serious morbid disorder and no doctor could ever cast a doubt on the excellence of my health. Yet for me a dreamless night is a bad night, and I call the man who passes his days in the following of perverted and inharmonious impulses, in deviations from the good instincts for refreshment and nourishment, for propagation and accumulation, for peace and happiness, and his nights in dull unconsciousness and thoughtlessness, dead as a cork, or at most, a little mad temporarily from foolish and confused dreams, - such a man I, with good reason, call sickly and abnormal.

For our highest instinct, that like a stately royal stag, proudly holding aloft his widely branching antlers, should take the lead of all the wanton and timid flock of our impulses and passions uniting and guarding them, is the impulse toward beauty, toward sublimity, and toward purest blessedness. Even the mighty passion for knowledge, which impels us so untiringly to seek for the secret of life, is subordinate to this, though it is the second in rank - the most beautiful hind of the flock.

And if in our sleep and dreams we perceive, more distinctly than in the day life, signs of the highest beauty and the purest bliss, - should we not then give them our closest attention?

And this I would now point out to you, dear reader, as the first new idea, strange - till now - to the present world, the first thought-child pulsing with life and future promise, born of the profound union of my experience and contemplation:

The solution of the secret of our lives lies in our dreams.

You think - do you not? - that this solution is not attainable to man. Nor indeed is it - at least not to mortal man. And yet all mankind, through the medium of its naturalists, is patiently and hopefully seeking it. But, though they have already unearthed much that is useful, measuring and recording and comparing with ever finer and sharper instruments, they are still digging in a direction that inevitably leads into a blind alley.

For the manifestations of day-life, the only ones that attract the attention of the searchers, do not reach beyond the grave and end with the withering of the body. But the manifestations of sleep, yet unexplored and unmeasured, begin where the eyes are shut, the ears do not hear, the skin does not feel, and extend into the regions concerning which we want enlightenment as much as - yes, even more than - concerning the sphere of day.

Frederik van Eeden

As long as I can remember, I have always been a great and vivid dreamer; therefore I know I must count myself among the breakers of suggestion, among the pathfinders, just as you too, dear reader and sympathizer, are one of them. And therefore, also, when the ideas of the group and traditional creed became too narrow for me and neither the words of my great hero brothers, nor intercourse with my contemporaries, nor the latest discoveries of science could satisfy me, I could forthwith see an outlet and discover light on a path which no one had yet pointed out to me and none, before me, had trod. Thus my alienation from the world has not made me unruly. Thus alone is it possible for me to find peace and contentment in this life amid narrow, sordid souls and barbarians. For aside from my monotonous daily life, with brief moments of rapture aroused by the beauty of these low lands and the sea, by work and study, I have the rich nights full of marvelous mystic realities which I gratefully and attentively observe and record by day. Thus, despite the loss of all that was dear to me, I am happy in the consciousness of being a useful laborer in the fields of the future, ploughing.

"For the promise of a later birth

The wilderness of this Elysian earth."

Before, therefore, speaking to you of my marriage to Lucia del Bono and the long, outwardly prosperous period following, I must acquaint you with my nocturnal observations.

The dreams of terror and bliss, that to you too surely are not unknown, I dreamed with vivid intensity. And it had immediately struck me that their vehement sensations - the inexplicable, deadly, hopeless terror and disgust or the wondrous, perfect bliss were quite disproportionate to, and could not be explained by, the things we saw and experienced in the dream. I remember a dream of a bare, gray room, without windows or furniture, and moving about in a corner some indistinct object, whose terrifying weird impression could make me shudder even by day; another one of a small, narrow, square courtyard enclosed by high walls overgrown with ivy, which was also gruesome and appalling beyond description, - and then again blissful dreams of meetings with a strange youth or maiden in some unknown garden, or in a rocky valley with gigantic golden-leaved chestnut trees, whose memory filled me with sweet delight for days and weeks - yes! that even now in my old age can make me happy when I vividly recall them.

No one hearing such a dream recounted would be able to comprehend its impressions of terror or delight. Only this was plain to we - that the blissful dreams dealt with love. In my earliest youth it was a boy whom I would meet in my dreams and who by a single word, without much sense, would make me marvellously happy and the scenery around him glorious; later it was a girl. The boy and the girl returned several times, though not very often, and did not resemble any friend or sweetheart of my day-life.

At first the weird terror seemed much more mysterious, for it was connected in some unaccountable way with the simplest and most innocent objects and scenes I dreamed of.

We, indeed, talk of nightmare and usually seek its cause in a poor digestion and the doctors talk a great deal about improper circulation and suggest all kinds of remedies. But throughout a long life I have been a close observer and have come to the conclusion that indigestion and improper circulation are no more the cause of this nightly terror than of rain and wind, though a frail condition will make the one as well as the other harder to endure. Wait, my reader, until you are as old and experienced a dreamer as I am, and you shall see for yourself these terror-inspirers and bloodcurdlers, these buffoons and jesters at work in the shapes in which Breughel and Teniers portrayed them in so life-like a manner. You shall learn to know their tricks and malicious inventions, and the queer furnishings of their dwelling sphere. You shall learn to track them, as it were, - as the dog tracks the game - by their peculiar scent of gruesomeness. You shall see them unfolding their loathsome and dark spectacles before you - their battlefields reeking with blood, their swamps filled with corpses - besmirching your path with mud, and playing fantastic tricks on you without its causing you the slightest degree of alarm or fear, or depressing you as it did before you knew the cause of all these things - because now you apprehend them in their wretched malignity and dare to face them and, if need be, duly to chastise them.

These are the creatures that Shelley calls

"The ghastly people of the realm of dreams,"

and of whose miserable existence and restless activity neither he, nor Goethe, nor any other of the world's sages and seers ever doubted.

Indeed, would not this doubt signify that we are ourselves responsible for the multitude of horrible, utterly vulgar, heinous and vile or obscene illusions that menace us at night and yet all bear an unmistakable imprint of thought and imagination, compiled with reason and deliberation, and thus betray a thinking mind though a low-thinking one? Do you not know the dream in which you know yourself to be guilty of murder, of bloody murder through covetousness, of theft, or of plotting to kill and inciting the innocent to it -with all the horrid retinue of fear of discovery and lies upon lies to escape it? And do you hold your own soul responsible for this? Or do you believe that chance can beget such artfully contrived complexities?

It was this sort of deception that incited me to indignant defiance. The war I had to carry on by day against my troublesome passions, also put me on my guard at night, and I would not absolve myself with the excuse that sleep renders irresponsible. For I knew that it was I, myself, I, Lodovico Muralto, an honest, well-meaning fellow, who in the dream-life of night had done and felt all kinds of malicious wicked and low-minded things, and I would not have it.

Not only the baseness, but also the absurdities of dreams, exasperated me. Night after night I was imposed upon and led about by the nose in the most ridiculous fashion. It often seemed as though my most earnest resolutions and most sacred feelings were the very ones to draw their shafts of ridicule. And morning after morning it was not only with surprise, but also with growing shame and wrath that I discovered on awakening, how absurdly I had again been fooled. This could not issue from myself, it must have been thrust on me; it was suggestion, infusion, that menaced and confounded my mind and judgment, and I was determined not to endure it. I would not stand it and earnestly sought a means of defending my healthy soul and free judgment. Thus I may say that my vehement lifelong struggle for self-purification and advance toward salvation was doubled, being carried on by night as well as by day, and indeed to great advantage. For it is the same soul, and they are the same forces which by night as well as by day act and react upon one another, and life with the physical senses of day has been made not a little clearer to me by the nightly senseless life.

I accustomed myself to memorize carefully in the morning what had occurred to me throughout the night, and in the evening before going to sleep to form fixed resolutions, auto-suggestions which should continue working also in my dream life.

And I realized that the first essentials were: observation, attention, self-consciousness also in dreams. Who would not be cheated must be on his guard. Thus while dreaming, I wanted above all to realize that I was dreaming and not to lose the tie of memory connecting me with the day-life. Every night I stood before the dark cavern of sleep, like Theseus with Ariadne's thread in his hand, and I knew, as you perhaps do too, reader, through chance experience - that such retention of memory is possible. Has it not happened to you often while dreaming that startled by some dangerous beast, or confronted by a steep precipice, you have calmed yourself with the vague consciousness: after all it's nothing but a dream? This consciousness I wished to cultivate and to strengthen until it should become fixed and lasting. And after a while, one night while dreaming of a blossoming orchard in Italy, I succeeded in observing with thorough consciousness. I saw the branches as they crossed one another, and the festoons of vines stretching from tree to tree, whilst I soared through, a few yards from the ground, with a pale blue sky above me. And while observing yet more closely I pondered how it was possible to reproduce so exactly and minutely in a vision obviously emanating from myself and which I had myself created, the apparent motions of these myriad crossing twigs and the confusion of the young foliage. And in my dream, and realizing that I was dreaming, I came to the conclusion that this vision must be a reality, an objective reality as the philosophers of reason would say, because to me - the observer - it manifested a distinctly personal existence. As I soared by, the twigs described their apparent motions exactly as I had observed by day, and how should I, who could not even draw a tree, be able to create these extraordinarily compiled moving images? And at the same time, now thoroughly wide awake in the midst of what I recognized as a deep sound sleep, I pondered upon the visionary impressions of day-life which have been explained by the effect upon the wonderfully constructed eye, of infinitely fine, infinitely swift vibrations of light, which are sent out from objects whose construction includes a no less complicated combination of billions and trillions of molecules - and how these identical impressions with exactly the same results were now attained, as a clearly felt and calmly observed reality, while my eyes were shut and the world of day-life remote - thus that there must be something which could reproduce all these infinite combinations of light vibrations and molecular motions with an absolutely equivalent effect.

And before having yourself tasted such delight, reader, you cannot imagine my elation when, on awakening, I found that my attempt had met with success, that I had gone on observing - attentively observing, and thinking - thinking deeply and clearly, with full recollection and calm self-consciousness in that mysterious, senseless sphere of wonder and deception.

The philistine philosophers will talk of "delusion" and contend that only the perceptions of day are real and those of sleep a mere delusion. But I have said it before: there is no delusion, or - everything is delusion. What realities does the day possess beyond perception? And because the perceptions of sleep are more fleeting, more unconnected, more mysterious, does it follow that they do not exist or that they deserve no attention? Through the very strangeness of their nature, which has no need of our senses, their study promises richer revelations than are found in day-life, but what they primarily demand is steadiness and clearness of the mind that would contemplate them, with the same purpose and precision with which the realities of day-life are searched.

My delight at this first success filled me all the day, and the

　　　　　Frederik van Eeden

comfort and joy found in this unexplored domain of study has not forsaken me to the present day and has helped me to bear a hard life with fortitude.

I now determined, by constant practice, to go further, to observe longer and with still greater accuracy and also, above all, to try to what extent I could act voluntarily in this senseless sphere. In my first elation I hoped that I might sometime reach the point where I could pass from waking to sleeping without loss of consciousness, and night after night contemplate the dream-sphere with all the calmness of day - thus doubling my entire life. Moreover, I hoped to fight the evil and demonic, to seek the pure and heavenly and perhaps also to dig up from the unknown world of perception, other precious facts.

Of course my exaggerated expectations met with disappointment. Only very slowly can we gain ground in a field so wholly unknown. I must content myself with leaving behind a series of honest and careful observations which will be repeated and put to test by others. To you, my reader, if the time be spared me, I will bequeath them in writing for your perusal, well ordered as a guide for further research. I know that you can follow the path pointed out by me and penetrate further than I.

For the present I will only briefly mention that although my expectations were not fulfilled in the measure hoped for, yet not any one of them was wholly disappointed.

To retain the clearness of mind night after night throughout the entire duration of sleep - that I never achieved. The moments of observation were and ever continued to be of brief duration, and they came at long intervals. Sometimes there is nothing to observe for weeks; then again two or three good nights follow in succession. The conditions for satisfactory observation are: excellent health, perfect equilibrium of mind and body, and the deep refreshing sleep toward morning, when the body and the senses are in a state of absolute passiveness and calm.

Nell' ora che comincia, i tristi lai

la rondinella presso la mattina,

- - - - - -

e che la mente nostra pellegrina

più dalla, carne e men da' pensier presa,

alle sue vision quasi è divina.

A few times only did I succeed in falling asleep with unbroken consciousness. This occurred when I was very tired and fell quickly into a deep sleep. Then all at once I would realize with a wonderful sensation of joy and relief that the desired sleep had come, and I thought, enjoyed, observed, determined and acted with calm deliberation in the glad conviction that my body, whose weariness I no longer felt, had found its needed refreshment without necessitating a suspension of the vital activities of my senseless and invisible being. But these extremely favorable conditions are rare; usually I feel myself gliding rapidly through the sphere of perception, anxious lest it should pass before I have made the most of it.

A long series of observations has made clear to me this above all: that there are various spheres which, on gaining consciousness, one immediately recognizes by their peculiar atmosphere, impossible more closely to describe. One knows what depths, what fields of observation one traverses.

There is a sphere wherein we see again the world of day-life - the earth we have seen with its landscapes and habitations - all strangely altered. It is not the same, but we know: this is meant.

Thus over and over again many a night I saw my paternal home in the city with its old-time luxury - but in its dream image. Moreover Lake Como and the forest of Gombo, near Pisa, and also England and the North Sea - but it is always the dream sea, and the dream forest, and the dream London, differing totally from the realities of day. But they themselves remain the same and without exception I immediately recognize them.

Thus there is a sphere of ecstasy and great joy. In this our consciousness of self is strongest, and it is impossible to give an idea of the wonderful clearness with which one views and admires everything, and the undoubted sense of a reality, though wholly unlike the reality of our waking hours. One sees vast, splendid, more or less clearly lighted landscapes, fashioned indeed according to earthy pattern, with mountains, trees, seas and rivers, but more beautiful and filling us with overwhelming admiration. And one sees them perfectly distinctly, with sharp intensity and full consciousness.

In this sphere one also possesses a peculiar body with very intense corporal feeling and definite qualities. One feels one's own eyes opened wide and sees with them, one feels one's mouth and speaks and sings at the top of one's voice - wondering meanwhile that the sleeping body should lie there still as death - one sees one's own hands and feet and the clothes one wears, resembling the clothes worn by day. It is all a little different, it is seen fleetingly as through running water, and it changes also through the influence of pronounced will. But one recognizes the dream-body exactly as one recognizes the waking body, when one has again returned to it. And one retains the sense recollection of both, each independent of the other. One remembers on awaking that the dream body has been actively stirring, but the waking body knows that it has been lying calm and still, though not wholly dead, for an unaccustomed noise would have wakened it. And the dream-body possesses all the sense perceptions and all the energies of the waking body and even more, for it can not only see, feel, hear, taste and smell, but also think very clearly and discern more delicate subtleties of mood. Yes! this last it does with such unwonted subtlety and acuteness that one cannot compare it to any sense perception of day and might with good reason speak of a new sense. And it can soar and fly. It feels light and free - though the waking body is wrapped in the deep sleep of weariness, the dream-body in this sphere is always supple, light and delightful beyond description. This ability to fly is always the infallible proclaimer of the advent of the joy-sphere. But this soaring power is not unlimited. The dream-body can safely descend into the deepest chasm, but it cannot rise to every height. Ascending requires exertion and often meets with failure despite the greatest efforts.

The careful observation of the reversion of the one body into the other on awakening is most remarkable.

One can always wake voluntarily from this joy-sphere. And to me it is an ever recurring and never waning wonder when the two bodies, each with its distinct bodily recollection, merge into one another. The dream-body, let us imagine, assumes an attitude, with arms stretched out and raised high above the head, and it shouts and sings, but at the same time it knows the sleeping body, still as death, is lying on its right side, with arms folded over the breast; this seems impossible, however, so distinct is the consciousness of speech, of the muscles, of the open eyes ? and yet there follows a single indescribable moment of transition and we regain the physical consciousness of the sleeping body with the memory of having lain silent, immovable, unseeing, in quite another attitude.

Who once has observed this, as I have hundreds of times observed it, no longer meets with flat denial the supposition that the decline and decay of this visible body does not exclude the possibility of reintegration and of renewed consciousness, will and perception. No more will he dare to confirm my father's opinion that we possess no sign or proof of the existence of any part of our being, whether we call it "soul" or "spectre" or by another name, that can separate itself from the visible body.

It was this sphere of joy which I always hoped to regain and the attainment of which made me happy all day. In this sphere I can make music and sing wonderfully - a talent wherein by day I do not, alas, excel. In this sphere I can also exert influence on myself and on the life of day. A strong suggestion uttered by my dream-body acts upon my waking body and drives away weariness, dejection and some of the slight disorders that sometimes trouble me.

But what is of greater importance - in the joy-sphere I can pray without shame or embarrassment. Then I pour out my whole heart - I who was never a good speaker - in lucid, fervent, flowing language, thanking, asking, praising.

Auto-suggestion? Yes, surely! Yet of very peculiar kind. For there is response. Response that has never wholly deceived me. When, in this wonderful sphere, I pray in transcendent rapture - subtle, silent, deeply significant signs take place in the wonderful landscape before my eyes. A soft veil of clouds obscures the light, as a warning of danger or calamity, - a great glowing brilliance rises behind me or at my side as an encouraging greeting, - a light layer of clouds gradually evaporates and a deep, dark, boundless, ravishing azure comes to view, filling me with unknown comfort. Blue, an incomparably beautiful blue, is the most characteristic color for this sphere. When I see blue I know that all is well, that I am going right and safely, that divine favor and support surround me. Blue is the cosmic color, the color of sky and ocean, of the vaster universal life, just as green is the telluric color, the color of the more limited earthly existence.

Very gradually, very slowly, by repeated observation one acquires a thorough knowledge of all these spheres and impressions. I have tried to describe this more minutely in other writings. The full meaning can naturally not be computed solely from my observations. Years of repeated investigation by following generations are still required. But an unknown perspective of seeing and knowing opens itself, where before we could only believe and trust.

If only for the purpose of rightly following the brief history of my career in life, it will be necessary to know something of this nocturnal life of observation, for it has greatly influenced my lot. I record it, undisturbed by the fear that these pages may fall into the hands of the herd of philistines. For they will look upon it as an idle phantasy, as curious invention, in the style of some of the wonder tales by Rudyard Kipling or H. G. Wells, conceived for their amusement. You, dear reader, and ready sympathizer, will easily recognize the note of truth. I am anything but phantastic, and am a faithful and devoted follower of the sober naked truth; but I do not deny her because she reveals herself by night instead of by day, and to me a revelation remains a revelation, whether it does or does not come to me through the senses.

That the dream-spheres adhere to a definite arrangement and situation as well as the area perceived by day, I consider

Frederik van Eeden

likely, because they appear in a fixed order of succession. Once only I was in a most profound sphere from which I could not voluntarily awaken and in which I had some very joyous encounters, - creatures resembling men but without mortal cares and a winged child which, in my dream, I already compared to Goethe's Euphorion, the child of Faust and Helena. This sphere lay still deeper - though one must understand the word deep wholly as a metaphor - than the beautiful joy-sphere with its vast landscapes.

The joy-sphere, however, is inevitably followed toward waking by the sphere of the demons with their pranks and spook. This sphere is easily recognizable. One sees the visionary objects sharply and clearly, but they have an indescribable yet very distinct spectral character. A single object, a brush, a horseshoe or anything of the kind may suddenly come before my eyes and by the horror and ghastliness issuing from it, I immediately recognize it as an invention of the demons.

A very common pleasantry of this demon pack is to let you awaken apparently. You imagine it is morning, open your eyes, look around and recognize your bedroom. When you want to rise, however, you see all at once that there is something strange, something weird and spectral about the room - a chair moves by itself, an empty garment stalks about, the windows, the light - everything is different, unaccustomed, and all at once you realize that you are not yet awake, that you are still dreaming and have landed in a world of spectres. The first few times this occurred to me, I was frightened and nervously made strong efforts to wake. But after a few experiences of this false awakening it no longer caused me the slightest alarm. The curious spectre sphere with its sharp outlines and intense light interested me, and I woke from it voluntarily as easily and as calmly as from other dream-domains.

This land of demons most dreamers frequent without knowing it, and even to the present day, when my consciousness and memory are not very clear, I easily let myself be deceived by it. Then come the mocking dreams, the vile, offensive, bloody, immoral and obscene dreams.

But when I come from the joy-sphere and thus have clear consciousness and presence of mind, I see the strange images themselves in action, while traversing this spectral world. I cannot describe them better than Teniers and Breughel have portrayed them. This, however, the artists could not convey to us: that they were constantly changing in shape and color. And they do this not only of their own accord but also at my command, and sometimes I amuse myself by letting them grow larger or smaller, black or blue, and by making them assume curious shapes. Amid throngs numbering hundreds of them I have moved about, and though my power over them varies, yet I never feel again the old nameless dread and when they become too obtrusive I can keep them at a distance by vigorous words of authority and also by a lash of the whip. This perhaps sounds strange to you, dear reader, but you must in truth understand that even in the senseless sphere, thought alone is not efficacious without a certain plastic expression in shape of a visible, audible or palpable form. If this spectral company becomes too much for me I must loudly command them, even shout at them, "begone," and if that does no good I must wish for a whip - which forthwith appears - and give them a sound thrashing. And I assure you, and you will yourself experience it if you test my statements by personal observation, that one never awakens more refreshed, never does there follow a happier, serener and freer morning than after such a successful struggle with the demons. Yet, it was this sort of fighting that, more than all my efforts by day, has helped me to overcome my low and vile temptations. Thus, much from the old transmitted tales regarding evil visitations and struggles with demons has

Frederik van Eeden

appeared true to me in the light of new experience.

Here I must warn you against a very strange and important peculiarity of our dream-body and our dream-nature. In many respects it is superior to our waking body - in sensitiveness of mood and feeling, in keenness of vision, in the sense of peace, comfort and happiness, and also in subtlety of thought. But in one respect it is weaker, namely - in the control of passion. Once kindled to passion -in grief, in joy, in rapture, in every soul-stirring emotion - it very speedily grows beyond control. It then looses itself in countless extravagances, which the contemplating judgment does not countenance, even deplores, but is powerless to check or curb. From this I draw the conclusion that we must learn to regulate and control our passions by day, for though the senseless life is enriched by everything the day-life conveys to it, it can only avail itself of well-mastered and disciplined passions.

Therefore abiding in the demon-sphere is never without danger. If, with a little too much self-confidence, I let myself be induced to assume a less haughty and reserved manner, if I associated a little more familiarly with the bold tribe, I soon repented, for I was carried along by their wantonness and folly, I could no longer subdue the laughter and extra-vagances, nor could I, to my own disgrace and sorrow, restrain myself in my wrath toward them.

And this most especially applies to licentiousness, of which they are particularly ready to take advantage. They are past masters in lascivious pranks and practised on my weakness with much success. I soon noticed that they are sexless and can alternately appear as man or woman. As long as I clearly realize this I have power over them. But when the clearness of my consciousness and memory is dimmed they get the better of me.

Thus you must understand me rightly, dear reader, as regards the salutary effect resulting from this demon fight. Struggling with demons is not struggling with passions. Demons are enemies and stand outside our own individual domain. But passions are our friends, the useful domestic animals belonging to our own household, to the economy of our own personal nature. The passions and emotions should be tamed, never combatted. And this taming is accomplished by day, for at night they are more difficult to master, and the body invisible to the senses, that which can remain after the fading and wasting away of our material body, has no longer the power to tame. It only harvests what is sown by day.

Yet this nocturnal life of struggle with the demon brood is extremely stimulating to the soul, above all through the knowledge, the clearer comprehension, the deeper insight with regard to our own obscure being and its no less obscure besiegers.

In the better, the higher or deeper dream-spheres impure lust and base lasciviousness do not occur. Love transports of unknown splendor do, however. But it is an almost unfailing characteristic of everything pertaining to the joy-sphere, that it passes over sexual matters with a curious disregard, and never carries with it any suggestion of that lust for which we feel shame and humiliation. Yet there are in it unions and raptures very similar to the love-life of day, though more beautiful and tranquil. But the peculiar quality that is vile and leaves behind aversion and disgust, is eliminated with subtle separation.

XIII

The things I related to you in the preceding chapter are necessary for the comprehension of my subsequent life. But they are the issues of an entire lifetime, and in the years previous to my marriage, when I lived with my mother and her protégée, I was only at the beginning and knew yet very little of all this. I did not speak of it either, and in all my later life I mentioned it to only one person.

As my plan of entering the priesthood had come to naught, we were all three glad to leave the sultry city of Rome. We went to Como, occupying our villa at the lake. It was an old house with wainscotings of yellow stucco and a sad air of ruined stateliness, of a splendor that even in its prime had pretended to more than it really was. It was quite different than my memory had pictured it. Much humbler, smaller - a weak and feeble reflection of the solid marble splendor of antique and renaissance which it affected to imitate. But this very decay now spread over it an involuntary charm. For the garden with its cypresses, mimosas, magnolias and roses had grown all the more beautiful in its neglected wilderness, and we inhabited only a few rooms of the great still house, making ourselves at home in the nooks and corners as though we were caretakers instead of owners. And directly in front of the garden was the lake, with its smooth extent of deep blue, with satin or moiré sheen according as it was touched by the gentle breeze, - and behind were the mountains with thousands of primulas, the purple erica, and the pink and white Christmas rose. The brooklet was still there - and the old pillared portico, where the stone showed from under the crumbling stucco and the roses had pushed their way through the stone paving and entwined the columns.

Into this abode I withdrew, gathering books about me, and by study and a quiet, temperate life endeavored to attain by myself the consecration which I could not find in Rome. Lucia with her maid continued to live with us, and I saw her and my mother at the meals, but aside from that not often.

They were rigorous, tranquil, secluded years, which may probably be reckoned among the good years of my life. I quietly went my own way and studied, following only the guidings of my inner thirst for knowledge.

But the women waited, waited, and I did not see it, or did not heed it. Bernard Shaw, the Benjamin and the enfant terrible among my brethren, tries his best to show the world that it is the woman who wins the man and not the reverse - and surely there is more truth in this than the common herd suspects. But if one were to believe him, one should imagine that the woman thereby considers only selfish ends and primarily cares for, desires and accepts the man, because she finds him useful to the interest of her deep-seated instincts, of the desired good and beautiful child. But after all this is not true, and the woman in her quiet, unnoticed, luring and combining activities does not want to take only, but to give as well, above all to give, and usually she values the husband higher than the father.

Lucia was a very gentle woman, yet of firm character. She had the large firm build and the regular, massive features of

Frederik van Eeden

Titian's women, but her eyes were softer, and showed less of that daringly exuberant spirit.

She was also characteristically Latin and un-Germanic in her feelings and sentiments. Without criticism she subjected herself to the spiritual teachings of the group to which she belonged. The conventional was an unalterable mental reality to her, tradition possessed for her all the power of the living and the sublime. Thus the conception of "honor" with all its personal and social facets was to her as fixed, clear, clean-cut and immutable as a diamond. That it might be variable, that some ages had called honorable what was now considered dishonorable, and vice versa, on that she never reflected and she did not seek for the lasting kernel of the changing idea. Through this she possessed a serenity and peace of mind which, in my perplexities, often seemed very enviable to me. She had no tendencies which she despised, but also no ideals which, as I, she must constantly curtail at life's behest. That a young bachelor like myself sometimes allowed himself dissipations, was a fact which she passed over with a light French step. And she bore allusions to it so undisturbed that it often impressed me painfully. She did not seem to feel the Englishwoman's need of upholding the illusion of prematrimonial purity in both husband and wife, and though I recognized that she had a perfect right to this way of thinking, yet it annoyed me and I preferred Emmy's ingenuous or assumed blindness.

But I also realized that Lucia's indulgence would be turned into an equally rigid condemnation as soon as conventional bounds were overstepped. What a young man did before his marriage had in Latin countries never yet jeopardized his honor. But her honor as a wife, the honor of the home, the honor of a family name - these were for her circumscribed realities, which might be menaced by certain actions, and which if need be she would sacrifice her life to defend.

She had been reared in luxury, and on reaching her majority had a large fortune at her disposal. But she never seemed to give it a thought, and lived in my mother's house with the utmost simplicity. That my mother cared just as little about it I dare not say, and for me this was another reason for maintaining my stubborn resistance. It impressed me most disagreeably to hear my mother forever talking of the miserableness and worthlessness of the earthly life, and of the blessedness hereafter as the only thing deserving of our attention, and at the same time observe how with unconscious motherly matchmaking and secret strategy she sought to arrange a rich marriage for her son. I therefore resisted her silent machinations as much as was possible without endangering the household peace.

It profited me nothing, however. I was bound to lose this game because I did not have my mind on it. The two women were determined to win it, not with conscious deliberate intent, but as women want a thing with all the obstinate strength of their mind, without ever saying a word about it or admitting it to themselves. And I was absorbed in chemistry and physics, in physiology and biology, my whole mind was engrossed in the great endeavor to decipher something of the mysterious writ of the phenomena of life and Nature, and in some degree to penetrate the dark recesses of my own nature.

Thus the conflict was unequal - and though it lasted for years I finally found myself conquered as by surprise. I felt that it was no longer possible for me to draw back, and moreover that I was alone responsible. There is no finer diplomacy than the unconscious diplomacy of women. I had been conquered and withal wholly maintained in the illusion that I myself was the acting, the attacking and the conquering party. But all this, mark it well, with the most devoted and unselfish love.

Actually in love, as with Emmy Tenders, I never was with Lucia del Bono: and this, despite my amorous nature, her great charm and our many years' companionship. I admired her for her beauty and for what everyone must call her stainless character. But she lacked for me just that certain mysterious, impenetrable something that in Emmy excited me to so mad a passion. I loved Lucia for the same reason that everyone must love her, because she really was a very lovable creature. But this rational sentiment, that to many would seem a more solid basis for a happy union than most paroxysms of love, never rose to the height of a passion mightier than all reason. And I believed, as do many sensible and staid people, and as my mother also believed, that I could make this well-considered affection suffice for making her happy, and for giving direction and balance to my own life. I lived in the very common conceit that I had my own nature entirely in my power and thus, from out the head-quarters of my self-consciousness, could freely dispose of it, always following the counsels of a reasonable deliberation.

That I should make Lucia happy by marrying her seemed beyond doubt. That I should ever feel for another woman what I had felt for Emmy, I could not believe. Then how could I do better than to devote my life to an excellent woman, to whom I thus accorded what she seemed to desire and who as my wife would surely never disappoint me? True, to save her from humiliation, I should have to feign a love which I never expected to feel. But I no longer faced mankind with the naive brotherly uprightness, and I saw no wrong in acting such a part with such good intention. I also considered myself perfectly capable of it, and again swore to myself an oath - no less sincerely meant and also no less fragile - that I would be a faithful and exemplary husband to her, and would at all times make my own happiness subservient to hers.

Now every human person is, according to the primitive meaning of this word, also a mask, and there is no person living, be he ever so simply sincere, so wholly uncomplicated, but has wrought for himself such a mask, has assumed such a rôle, according to his ideals of human worth, of fitness and breeding. And if he means it honestly, he tries to live himself into the part so that he can believe himself to be what he pretends. Thus, following his own or others' form ideals, he moulds and fashions himself into a personality which will be the more respected the more pronounced, decided, and unchangeable it manifests itself. But would he assume a mask, enact a part far removed from his own form ideals and unattainable to the plasticity of his true nature, he fails miserably, is called a scoundrel and a knave and is indeed a wretch.

Thus the part I played toward Lucia was not one entirely foreign to my nature. I simply tried my best to efface the boundaries between, and merge the emotional degrees of affection and love. This was not difficult and I honestly hoped that my true nature would some time really fill the assumed form: that thus I would become for Lucia the true lover and devoted husband she expected to find in me. I also related to her the history of my heart and my past, in so far as was essential to a just estimation; and she accepted it all reverently, as a pleasing and honoring mark of confidence, and saw no difficulty whatsoever. She followed the suggestion of her own desire, that everything would be as she wished it, with the same complacence with which she had trusted in my mother's wisdom, and she continued to hearken to the voice of the herd.

The wild, sultry sirocco had suddenly melted the snowy caps of the mountains to about half their former extent, the mimosas bloomed profusely, their luxuriant yellow masses standing out vividly against the deep blue ether, and up on the mountains everywhere beamed the hepatica with its myriad sweet flower-stare of faint and tender blue - when Lucia and I were to wed in the white marble cathedral of Como. I had acceded to her wish that all the ceremonies should be duly observed. More and more I had learned to divide my life, as the only means of keeping the peace with mankind and with myself. I realized that what in brother Michael had seemed to me despicable hypocrisy was nothing more than the brutal acceptance and shocking confirmation of a sad necessity, to which every deeply thinking person must submit. Was not Socrates far too wise a man to believe that if there really existed a god of medicine, Asklepias by name, he would please this personage by beheading and burning a cock? Yet he ordered this to be done in acknowledgment of the speedy effect of the poison that killed him; this at a moment when a sensible man does not usually jest or act. This poor cock of Socrates has often come to my mind; also on the day when I left my books and microscopes, my sprouting seeds and growing salamander larvae to array myself for the wedding ceremony. Even the very wisest man is obliged to offer to the gods of his time.

It was a lovely day and a brilliant scene. Lucia's distinguished family had arrived in full force and glittering pageant. Not only the violet but the crimson clergy were represented. The street populace of Como were lined up from the landing place of our boats to the cathedral as at the arrival of royalty. The street urchins ran before us, and there was even cheering as though this event signified an additional joy on earth. The church was fragrant with masses of roses and radiant with - hundreds of candles, and returning our gondolas formed a long multi-colored line on the lake, with draperies trailing through the water, and songs and music, as though we were still in the good days of the Borgias.

Lucia was serene and beaming with quiet happiness, like a blue hepatica blossom, a little bashful, but responding archly and merrily, and her fine clear eyes dimmed by only the slightest suspicion of a tear. She saw nothing ahead of us but bliss, a welcome happiness, a regular God-pleasing life. For me it was not hard to sustain my part in this beautiful scene. It was not so much a rôle or a comedy that I enacted, as perhaps a lovely dream.

When the sun sank I sat on the terrace meditating and contemplating the colors of the darkly shimmering well-nigh blackish green foliage of the magnolias, the snow of the mountains opposite, glittering golden in the evening light, above it the luminous, pale greenish blue sky, and below the purplish violet mountain slopes and the soft steel blue lake. The colors merged and became one with the fragrance of the lemon blossoms surrounding me, marking this as one of the unforgettable representative moments, to which we look back repeatedly on our journey of life as the skipper looks back to a buoy or lighthouse passed.

I thought of my dream-world and compared the sharp brilliant impressions of the night with those of the day, asking myself when I was most truly and really myself, and which of the two worlds was the more real - and why?

XIV

Time is a sphere in the dream-world in which you, dear reader, have surely been as well as I, but probably without distinguishing it as such. Without doubt it has happened to you that you dreamt very vividly of persons who have died. Then you may have observed two peculiarities, first, that you usually do not remember in your dream that these persons are dead, and moreover that if you see others with them, or near them, or shortly after having met them these others are also dead persons, whose passing away you had forgotten in your dream. Long before the day of which I told you in the last chapter, I had already observed the regularity in these visions, and had formed a presumption from it, concerning the relation of their causes.

A presumption I say - not without value for all that. All that we call proofs are presumptions of different degrees of certainty. Nietzsche scornfully says that God is but a presumption. It is so. But it is not nice of him to fool people for that reason, and to thrust the superman, whom no one has ever seen and who is even slighter than a presumption, into their hands as a waggishly contrived idol.

Believe nothing beyond experience, dear reader. But God and Christ are more experience than the superman, even though they be presumptions. Your father and your mother, too, are but presumptions, deduced from experiences, aroused by what their skin and their eyes seem to imply and to conceal for you.

Thus I presumed that the dead also have their sphere, and that when the dream-body of living, sleeping man enters there, he cannot grasp the difference between this sphere and his own and therefore always retains the illusion that the dead are still alive.

Now I had very often before this dreamed of my father. First that I was still sailing with him on our last expedition. But this belonged to the terror-dream of which I spoke before, which at the beginning regularly repeated itself.

This dream I consider nothing but the painful echo in the deeper chasms of my soul, of the violent shock that my waking body had sustained. Beyond this I attach to it no deeper significance.

But then came a dream of wholly different character, in a perceptibly different sphere, in which I walked with my father while he put his arm around my shoulders and cried. It seemed to me as though he was trying his best to show me the marks of tenderness which he knew I was fond of and of which he was usually so sparing.

I did not remember that he was dead and I walked by his side somewhat embarrassed, as the child that unexpectedly gets more than it has asked for. So as also to do something on my part to please him, I caught a fine butterfly with curious blue arabesques on his wings, and I pronounced a Latin word to let him see that I knew the species. The word I no longer remember and moreover it was only dream Latin, that is to say: nonsense. But my good intention was apparently evident to him, and pointing to the wondrous design on the wings he said something about "plasmodic" or some such word, just as nonsensical as my name for the species. But in the dream there is a wholly different relation between word and spirit, and one can construe sensible meanings out of nonsense and also interchange thoughts without words, - and I knew very well at the time and also on awaking that my father wanted to make me think about the way in which this butterfly decoration was formed.

Then I woke and it took me a long time to realize fully that my father was dead. And this realization suddenly struck me like a cold whirlwind, making me shiver from head to foot.

The first hours after waking I was sure that it was he who had communed with me, that he felt remorse for his rage at me in the last moments of his life, and therefore cried and was unusually tender toward me. I also thought his pointing to the ornamented wings of the butterfly important and full of meaning, albeit not yet clear to me.

But the impressions of the day are so different from those of the night, the two are so hostile, that they alternately seek to supplant one another as absolutely as possible, as though by turns one had been in the company of a religious devotee and an atheist, of a poet and a dull philistine, of a spendthrift and a miser. No man so firm in character but undergoes this influence. And it still regularly befalls even me, after so many years, that at the end of day I face the night with its wonders with critical unbelieving expectancy. Even when falling asleep I cannot realize the coming transition, and only the next morning I again know how everything was, and am surprised that I could ever doubt and forget it, just as we see again the face of one we love and are surprised that the image in our memory could have faded so completely.

The mightiest and most prodigious fallacy of men in this age, that cripples their aspirations, and like a deadly frost bends low and kills the tender blossoms of their young growing wisdom, erecting cruel steep walls between heart and heart, between group and group - is the fallacy that in this struggle between belief and unbelief a verdict can be reached through something that they call Reason and that bears as its weapon the True Word. But reason rules only in the realm of imagination, in the realm of word, of language, of scheme and symbol. In the realm of actual experience Reason is not what we call Reason, and only the young person and the childish nation, as that of ancient Athens, confuse reason and see in the "Logos" the actual, and in the logical the truth, expecting that patient reasoning must indeed lead to the truth. But did not father Plato himself get nearest the truth where his logos is most illogical?

Frederik van Eeden

XV

It was really she! It was in a long lane bordered on both sides
by dark spruce and beeches decked out in the golden brown
tints of autumn. The sunbeams, distinctly bluish in the fine
mist, slantingly penetrated the dark spruce, and fell in golden
radiance upon the pale green moss, and the blue ether and
the brown and green foliage shone in a brilliance of hue
suggesting the brown and blue lustre of the opal. I had
already seen her approaching from a distance, her white bare
feet noiselessly pressing the soft moss. I gazed intently at her
face; at the young fresh complexion; the softly waved
lustrous blonde hair with the little, fine loose hairs standing
out around her head, shimmering in the sunlight like a halo;
at the amber tints in the shadows of her finely modelled ear.

It was she, and she laid her finger on her lips as though I
should listen. But I heard nothing. I saw distinctly how the
round spots of sunlight glided over her face and her hair and
the shadows of the foliage fell upon her breast and shoulders
draped in white.

While I gazed at her, wondering what she would say, my
thoughts carried on their subtle play. The subtle play from
which they so seldom rest, night or day. I thought: "How will
the life after death be? Shall we perceive, see, hear, smell,
taste, touch then too? Surely the perception can never be as

positive as now - here. As clearly as I now see these trees and her dear face - now, now while I am alive and awake - so clearly I cannot perceive after death, without a body and sense."

While I was thinking this, she had come close up to me and I spoke calmly:

"Is it you, Emmy?"

Then I looked at her, somewhat doubtfully, as though there were something unusual about her, and she whisperingly replied:

"Not yet entirely."

These strange words did not surprise me. At the moment I understood very well what she meant to say with them, and I asked:

"Will you stay?"

Then I wanted to fold her in my arms. But I saw her shake her head and, with the slender fingers on her mouth, again motion as though I should listen. Then I heard sounds as of a wildly galloping beast, a trampling of hoofs that resounded hollowly on the wooded path. And all at once I remembered a heavy responsibility that rested upon me, and I knew that this trampling gallop was connected with it. It was to fetch me or to drive away Emmy, to put an end to this great serene happiness. And I felt a horrible, choking fear rising in me, while the sounds came nearer and nearer.

But Emmy smiled - a tender gracious smile and said:

"I shall come again."

Then, at the very end of the straight lane, where the alternating brownish red beeches and blackish green spruce appeared very small, and the light green mossy path gleamed up and narrowing met the sky, I saw the galloping beast approaching. It was black, a horse or a bull - I could not distinguish which - but it came nearer and nearer and my fear rose to terror. Then all at once, sideways through the row of trees, the pale face of my father appeared, and he walked toward Emmy as though to shield her, saying:

"It is too late!"

After this that strange transition took place, which is like a chaotic mingling of two spheres of life, a rolling together of space and light, one moment oppressing, then again relieving, as the sensation of the diver who, turning around under water, loses the consciousness of up and down until he regains his balance, air and daylight, the transition from dreaming to waking.

I had dreamt and only now actually woke. And meanwhile, only a moment ago, I had thought that there could never be such clear and distinct perceptions in the life without the body and senses, as those which now after all turned out to belong to the dream - to the life without body and senses. I was astonished and perplexed as on so many a morning on waking.

But then came a yet more dazzling, more overwhelming memory - Emmy! I had seen her as positively as I had ever seen her, her glance still lived in my eyes, her voice in my ears. It was Emmy - and we had wanted to clasp each other in our arms, we had tasted each other's love.

I opened my eyes and looked about the world in which I had awakened. I saw the cold, soulless luxury of a hotel apartment, mirrored wardrobes, thick red carpets. Out doors, bells were pealing, carts were rattling, and whips were cracking. Another bed stood next to mine and in it I saw dark, glossy hair - spread out dishevelled on the white cushion in the disarray of morning. It was my wife - Lucia.

A violent agitation seized me. My thoughts and feelings were stirred to commotion like a bee-hive which someone has knocked against. Vainly I sought to restore harmony and peace in myself by calm reflection.

My strongest feeling was one of guilt, terrible, inexpiable guilt. Much graver guilt than had ever oppressed me after my youthful errings. Guilt toward this gentle, dark-haired woman, who lay sleeping by my side, and whom I had permitted to become my wife. For after all it was deceit - Emmy still existed. I had seen her and spoken to her, and we loved each other, as I should never be able to love this other.

Emmy still existed - but where and how?

Then another memory came back to me which made me shiver with nervous fright. I had not only seen Emmy, but also my father with her. And I knew what this meant. Might her appearing to me so distinctly this night be an instance of the oft-propounded correspondence of death and the manifestation of the spirit?

In my anxiety I got up quietly, dressed and went out.

The air was keen and sparklingly fresh, the smoke from the houses rose up in straight columns. We were at Lucerne and the winter, which had already forsaken Italy, was here bidding a last farewell. A thin layer of snow covered the roofs and the mountains, and the transparent bright emerald green of the lake, the light brown of the antique wood work

Frederik van Eeden

on the bridges, towers and houses, and the soft tender white of the snow formed a cool and noble harmony.

I roved about in the woods and mountains and only returned toward afternoon - my spiritual balance restored, but more than ever estranged from the human world.

I sent a telegram to Emmy's family in London: "Wire address Mrs. Emmy Truant." And toward night came the reply: "Mrs. Truant died fever Simla January."

Not this night, but three months ago she had died. I attached no significance, as so many do, to the fact that the point of time did not correspond exactly. I knew that it had been she, and the certainty of her death made me calm. It was as though she was now really mine, and would ever remain mine.

I showed Lucia the message, thereby explaining my sad and introspective mood. She willingly forgave me and did not ask me more than I wished to tell, just as she had always met me with the utmost discretion in my, to her inexplainable, humors.

But if perchance she had hoped that my heart would now feel itself free, that my entire love would now be bestowed on her, she was miserably deceived. The effect was exactly the reverse. I only now fully realized what I had done, and only now felt it as a great wrong. I felt that I had a wife, but it was not the one who slept by my side and who bore my name. A fervent passionate desire went out toward the being whose fair image I had seen so clearly, whom I had wished to embrace with unutterable tenderness, and whose voice and whose presence had procured for me bliss such as the day had never brought me, and the clear, cold daylight could not dispel. I longed for the night all day long, - and with bitter certainty I felt that I should never be able to offer more to the poor woman, whom I had taken into my arms as my wife, than a friendly mask, an assumed appearance of loyalty and tenderness.

And the feeling of guilt, which in another might perhaps have been lulled by the news of her death, began to burn on my conscience with greater intensity than ever. I abused myself as a coward, a weakling, an adulterer, for something that no man on earth would ever have imputed to me as guilt.

But even then, while I writhed with pain, I knew that my free judgment never would have condemned as guilty one who had acted as I, thus - that remorse and the distressing consciousness of sin are not the logical and just consequence of a deed realized as bad and pernicious, but that it is the sad effect of a law, salutary for humanity as a whole, but often baneful and unjust for the individual, to which we must submit with love and patience for the sake of the sacred character of this law and out of respect to the sublime will of its Maker.

Frederik van Eeden

XVI

In order actively to carry out a thing in the dream world, I must resolve upon it betimes and definitely determine upon the plan. During the actual dream the time is usually too short, the incidents pass too fleetingly. Sometimes I soar on in swift flight so that everything rushes by me without my being able to delay the pace. It is usually after one of these happy dreams with full consciousness, that I plan out, that very morning before getting up, what I shall do the next time in my dream. And then, every evening before falling asleep, it is once more distinctly formulated and stamped upon the memory, so that like a ready tool it will be at hand during the moments of observation - just as astronomical instruments during an eclipse of the sun.

Thus I had determined on calling some one in my dream. And the first one I selected for this purpose was my father.

I had seen him many times in my dreams, but never with full consciousness, never with the memory that he was dead, never in the sphere of light and happiness.

I made up my mind to call him night after night, as soon as I should awaken in the sphere of observation. For it is an awakening just as much as our awakening in the morning, but the body sleeps on.

And I succeeded. One night I was dreaming in the usual way in the demon-sphere and they played one, of their familiar dismal pranks. We were acting a farce, some friends of my youth and I, and the stage was a cemetery and all the actors had grinning skulls. Then, firmly regarding one of these acting apparitions, I said: "There is no death," as though to resist this obtruding horror. The head grinned mockingly and, with a sarcastic expression, pointed to all the skulls and bones round about. But I repeated, now with fixed determination and in a loud voice: "There is no death!" and behold! the eyes of the being before me faded, the whole apparition vanished - and I felt it was by my will. Then I gained full consciousness, the complete remembrance of my day-life and waking sensibilities, and blithely and thoroughly conscious I rose into the sphere of knowledge and joy. Then hastily and animatedly I spoke to myself, and I felt my mouth, my breath, my whole body, the animæ corpus; and yet I knew that my day body lay sleeping and silent and did not stir. Hastily I spoke: "I am there! I am there! What is it that I wanted? I wanted to see my father. Oh yes! my father! I wanted to see my father!"

Then I saw a sunny, green landscape spread out before me, a little house, low and small. "He is inside," said I. "Here I shall find him." I ran through many rooms and did not see him, but I continued my search from room to room. And when I saw the last room empty too, I made an additional room. And behold! I saw him sitting there.

This time he looked exactly like my father as I had known him, only much younger than when he left me. He wore a dark blue suit, top boots and a felt hat. The expression on his face was mild, and his eyes shone clear and bright.

"Father!" said I; "Father!" and with a beseeching gesture I walked toward him. I heard him say: "Good day, Vico mio!"

Frederik van Eeden

And it was his voice, even more than it was his face.

Then I gave him my hand and he took it. He tried to press my hand and it seemed to cost him physical exertion.

I said, "Have you forgiven me?"

It was a warm, glorious sensation; I saw that he tried his best and he looked at me mildly.

He murmured something, but I could not understand it or I have forgotten it. Thereupon, with the utmost effort to express myself clearly and with sincerest fervor, I asked: "Can you give me advice? I seek for the best. Tell me what I must do, counsel me!"

But he said nothing.

Then an old question arose in me, unexpectedly and without my having resolved anything about it:

"Father," I said, "what is Christ?"

Then I heard him say:

"Ask the butterfly."

And I understood that he meant the butterfly in the last dream with the blue decorated wings. I asked:

"Can you tell me nothing?"

Then he shook his head very gently and everything in my dream vanished; I saw only his head shaking "no" - and with that I awoke. The day was dawning, and I lay thinking over everything and impressing it on my memory.

I felt absolutely certain that I had spoken with him.

I went to sleep again and dreamed, as frequently happens after a dream of this kind, that I related my dream, but without knowing that I was sleeping.

That morning I was extraordinarily refreshed and happy. And the whole day the sound of his voice was in my ears, with the words: "Good day, Vico mio!" And repeatedly I tried to recall the exact tones.

I had this dream some time before the first appearance of Emmy, and had asked for advice, because at the time I was still in conflict with myself whether I should take Lucia for my wife.

XVII

"How is it that they wired you so late that your little friend had died, so many months after?" Lucia asked me, some days after we had left Lucerne.

"Because I, myself, had only then wired to inquire about her."

Lucia looked at we silently and thoughtfully for a while, and then said with a kindly unsuspecting earnestness, full of delicate chastity:

"Oh, then I understand. Then she appeared to you in a vision, didn't she?"

I nodded and Lucia questioned me no further.

She had remained a strict Catholic and had retained much of the lavish popular superstition of my country. She attached importance to amulets, to trinkets blessed by the Pope, to the offering of candies to saints.

Regarding dreams she held a creed, elaborated in every detail, the accuracy of which she continued to maintain, although I never heard from her a single striking proof. To dream of flowers, of water, of money, of blood - it all meant something, but it was always equally vaguely asserted, equally inaccurately observed, and with equally little foundation accounted proved. For me it was absolutely worthless and I carefully guarded against contradicting her in these things and making her a partner of my own experiences.

But it was strange and remarkable that a certain dream to which she herself attached no significance and whereof her dream-lore made no mention, always repeated itself in connection with a certain experience of mine in my night and day life.

Whenever another woman stepped across my path in life, threatening to endanger the soundness of my union with Lucia, she would dream of a large, wild horse that frightened her or bore down upon her. Sometimes it was white, sometimes brown, sometimes black, - there also would be two or three of them; they menaced and frightened her, but did her no harm. She always faithfully and unsuspectingly reported to me when she had again dreamt of horses, without having the least idea that for me this was a stern and covert warning.

For it never failed, whenever I had fallen into serious temptation - which, after the peaceful and secluded years at Como, was quite inevitable on our numerous journeys - she would very soon come to me with her innocent story that she had again been worried by the troublesome horses.

And as I know that not only she, but my mother too sometimes, as well as other women I have known, have been warned in this strange way, I would advise you, dear reader, to pay attention to this. It may have been a strange chance and coincidence; it may also be peculiarly proper to me and the persons associated with me, - but it may also have a more universal meaning, and no wonder, if we take into consideration the presumable slight coöperation of the men, that the women have not yet ascertained this meaning. But we should make reservations before sowing suspicion between the innocent!

After my first vision of Emmy I lived in a peculiar state of outward calm and inward happiness. To Lucia I was kind, tender and solicitous, but I did not feel myself her husband, nor could I approach her as such without a sense of guilt. At Como the temptations besetting my life as a youth had vanished. The close application to study, the simple, rural life, the absence of temptation, the pure, serene atmosphere of the little domestic circle - all this had given me support and kept me out of difficulties.

And when I travelled with Lucia the strange fact revealed itself that, mindful of Emmy's love and her appearance to me, I charged myself with sin and baseness for what everyone considered just and lawful. The temptation against which I fought and to which, bitterly ashamed, I nevertheless repeatedly yielded, now no longer went out from hapless prostitutes, but from the beautiful and amiable woman whom I had made my wife. It would all have sounded very queer to other people, but once for all it was so, my spirit responded to life in its own original way and would not be forced. It was of no avail that I told myself how differently the world judged, and I was just as unhappy when I had yielded to Lucia's charms as when I had succumbed to the intrigues of a strange woman. But nevertheless one as well as the other occurred, for the incongruous relations in my heart and life were not ordered and the wild lusts remained untamed. While all who knew me accounted me lucky on account of my marriage, I led for many long years a hard and tortured life. My love and devotion to my wife and children were forced and strained, and I grieved bitterly that so much beauty and loveliness did not attract my natural interest. My task was a giant task that often seemed too mighty for me, and what I attained was nothing unusual, nothing but what everyone expected as self-understood. I was called a good husband and father, but no one knew the enormous effort it cost me, and how far I still fell short, and no one would have believed me or showed me sympathetic understanding.

When I had succeeded in summoning my father in the night and thus knew that I possessed this power, the nights in which I penetrated to the clear dream-sphere became all the more important to me.

And when I had seen Emmy in the common dream-sphere, in the sphere of the dead, but without being myself clearly conscious, my first thought that morning was to call her as soon as the sphere of clear perception should open before me. And with great suspense I awaited such a night, and morning after morning was disappointed and vexed that this clarity had not come. For as I said before, sometimes this perception eludes me for months and the dreams are on the ordinary confused, insignificant order. Then all at once some inexplicable cause summons forth the good, happy and clear moments of perception three or four nights in succession.

But at last, after all, came the blessed night in which my project was completely realized.

It was after a most tiring and not very pleasant day. A long mountain excursion in the rain. I dreamed that I walked in the street among a crowd of people. Beside me walked a little friend of my youth. Suddenly it shot through my mind like a ray of light that I would call some one, I would summon Emmy. Hastily I said to my comrade: "I beg your pardon, but I must look for some one, Emmy Tenders!" I did indeed think meanwhile that I was giving publicity to something very intimate, but the matter was too important, I had to say the name. Then I ran through the crowd searching and calling: "Emmy! Emmy!" Meanwhile, I thought that I should be heard calling in my sleep, that Lucia would hear me. I passed by trees and verdure, observing everything sharply and distinctly. Busily absorbed in my quest I murmured to myself: "Yes! I see it distinctly - autumn sun on elm leaves - small green apples. I can remember their position, but I must have Emmy, - Emmy!"

Then I saw a closed door, and I pointed to it with my finger, saying: She is there! if I open this door I shall see her!

I opened the door and saw - a slaughter house. Pieces of meat, a floor streaming with blood, men slaughtering, a disgusting stench - horrible! a demon trick to hinder me.

Profound disappointment. Well-nigh despair. I sobbed convulsively, calling "Emmy!" Meanwhile, again the thought: "I shall find the marks of my tears on waking."

I saw a piece of paper and wrote upon it with my finger dipped in blood: "I was here in my dream"; with a vague hope that this might serve as proof, one of the half-considered ideas that one sometimes has in these dreams.

Then, deeply grieved, I felt myself waking up. But I fell asleep again directly. And then I thought: "I shall go to her country," and I ran hurriedly as though I knew the way. I considered meanwhile: "How shall I get there? She is in India. I don't know the way and yet I am going there."

Then I felt myself soar and I saw a sea foaming beneath me as in the wake of a big ship, and I saw the gulls flying around above it, preying upon the refuse.

After that a luxuriantly wooded mountain and on its slope a

house. I hurriedly flew down and went into the house. I heard knocking and thought: "There she is."

I saw a door on which it said: "Waiting room," and it opened slowly. A figure emerged from it.

"Can it be she? She does not resemble her. And it so often happens that people are quite different in dreams. How can that give me assurance?" I came up closely. She had wound her thick blonde hair in braids around her head and upon it rested a wreath of myrtle and orange blossoms. I saw distinctly the small, shiny dark green leaves and the little reddish twigs - and I smelled the sweet fragrance of the orange blossoms. I looked at her and they were her eyes - very serious as though absorbed in her own deep thoughts.

Then I folded her in my arms and I knew positively that it was she and I called out passionately: "Are you there? How sweet of you that you came after all!" It was very happy - happier than any moment of my waking life has ever been.

I woke up, no longer sad, but very serious, and also, for the first time after such a dream, a trifle tired.

I did not find any marks of tears and I asked Lucia whether she had heard me cry or speak or making a noise in my sleep.

"No," she said. "You were lying still and tranquilly sleeping, I believe. I was awake early. I again had such a disquieting dream about that white horse. It was a splendid creature with a heavy full mane, a long white tail and red glittering eyes. I stood close beside him and he would not let me pass. I was frightened to death, but when I kept quiet he did not harm me."

Frederik van Eeden

XVIII

Very few people, you, dear reader, excepted, will find anything important or curious in these records. The lay philistine will consider them an idle play of the imagination for his amusement, and speedily forget them. The philistine scholar will smilingly utter a few words of authority, whereby he will consider the matter explained and settled. There is such a one, his book is lying before me, who pretends to have solved the entire mystery of dreams. Mind it well - the entire mystery. And then he pronounces a few hollow phrases, which as an "Open, sesame" should give admission to all the unspeakable wonders of this untrodden reality, saying: "the dream is a wish fulfilled." Then upon this the man is contented and glad, considering that he has said something.

I cannot furnish you with positive proof, dear reader, that it was surely my beloved who appeared to me at night as my betrothed. Some of the facts could probably be accounted as proof that my nocturnal observations are not merely creations of my own imagination, but that they concern a world with which others also are in communion, and which has a peculiar nature. There was indeed a correspondence between the words heard and the things seen by me at night and that which, unknown to me, had occurred in the waking life. But I had no need of these proofs. The primal feeling of certainty is a feeling that one gains by experience. The communication of this feeling along the lines of reason is an illusion that never subsists, nor has subsisted. We communicate primal certainties to one another along intuitive and suggestive lines, not by proofs. Though my proofs were clear as crystal and firm as rock, the obstinate would easily reason them away; while only those who by repeated and repeated observation have gained complete assurance can also value the significance of the observations. For what I observed is like the tiny spark from the rubbed piece of amber, like the contraction of the muscles of the dead frog that Galvani observed - a small phenomenon that the unbelieving ridicules, but in which the wise sees the germ of new, never-guessed-at conceptions and deeds.

From that night when Emmy appeared to me, at my summons, as my bride, I led for many years a double life, in which the incidents of the day did not seem more important to me than the observations of the night. A successful reunion with Emmy in the joy sphere of the dream was to me the best and most joyous event, that I desired more and remembered with more grateful satisfaction, than the most fortunate incident of my daily life. The few solitary moments in the night, recurring only a limited number of times during the long year, and perhaps lasting but a few minutes, in force of impression and deep after-effects outweighed the many days crowded with events, so that now it seems to me as though the years had flown by and I can measure and define them better by the visions of the nights than by the events of the day.

Yet my life was not empty, not barren in deeds and experience; but it was the ordinary life that thousands lead and that has already left so many wise and sensitive men unsatisfied, because they could not penetrate the deeper meaning, and saw death and destruction so unavoidably

Frederik van Eeden

threatening them at the end of their career.

In accordance with my father's wishes, which my mother sanctioned, I became a diplomat and lived and worked in different countries, first as attaché and later as secretary of the legation. Outwardly my life was as prosperous as could be and all who knew me envied me, without therefore showing me ill will or seeking to harm me. I had a sweet, pretty wife who bore me four fair, healthy children, I had money enough for a life of luxury and plenty, and did my work with apparent devotion and success. Transferal was the cause of frequent travel, and I saw a large part of the civilized human world. We lived in sunny Madrid, fragrant with acacias and carnations, with its subtle dangerous atmosphere, its elegantly indolent culture, its desolate surroundings; - in restless Marseilles, full of crime and rabble, where we never felt safe; - in orderly, methodical, soberly bourgeois Berlin, where they strive so sagaciously and diligently for culture; - in blithe and beautiful Paris, where they still live on happily in the illusion that they are the leaders of civilization; - in the not less self-satisfied London, immutably grim in its sombreness, hardened in its dangerous luxury and misery, full of intellectual life, but without much sign of improvement, like a strong, pros-perous, hardened villain; - in wanton St. Petersburg, with its extremely polished, yet withal ever equally barbarous luxury; - in vain, amusing Vienna, where all thought of the possibility of still higher culture has long ago been given up as insulting; - in the curiously grave and affected Washington, with its trim green lawns and white buildings of state in confectioner's style, with its blasé air of aristocratic calm and state in the midst of the bustling, bourgeois, informal but intensely living American world; - finally in the little, neat, doll-like Hague, that is so difficult to consider as real, where the good Hollanders play at Metropolis and where even the diplomatic world acquires the well-nigh comic aspect of a very chic and well-cast amateur stage.

I could not have borne this existence calmly, without the stay of my nocturnal experiences, without the constant preoccupation with the miracle that again and again befell me, without the remembrance of how I had last seen and heard Emmy, without the looking forward to her return, and the considering of what I would do and say and what I should observe in her the next time.

I did not therefore neglect my daily work; on the contrary, I performed it with vigor and perseverance solely on that account. But how others could cheerfully persevere in it I could not understand - unless they were insignificant persons, wholly governed by the power of formal religion and conventional patriotism. And I must admit, too, that the most advanced and independent of my colleagues did not continue their task without bitter self-derision and a sort of melancholy epicureanism. Diplomacy may be carried on with fine forms and on a grand scale, yet it remains nothing but an exceedingly narrow-minded bickering for the greatest profit, for the largest morsel. Something remarkable lies in the fact that the diplomat does not fight directly for his own profit, but identifies himself with the Government he represents. But what man fights for a really personal profit and not for a fancied one? Thus the zeal, the enthusiasm, the satisfaction of the diplomat is usually the same as that of the player moving wooden figures about on a board, and finding his pleasure in the making and the disentangling of confusion. But an earnest man asks after all: what is the good of it all? Wherefore do I work and let so many others work for me? My body which I keep in condition with so much care shall wither, the royal house or the Government for which I fight and exert myself some day shall fall after all; and though I fought not for myself, nor even for my Government and people, but for a still higher ideal -

humanity - will it not also die some time when the earth shall dry up and become uninhabitable?

These questions must be answered, for it is not true that it is man's nature to go on working with courage and zeal without their being answered. No; if he now still goes on working without an answer, it is because he does not reflect. But it is truly man's nature to reflect and thus he is still making his living by denying his nature. This is a contradiction doomed to disappear. And I witnessed with pity the endeavors of the so-called religious people, like my good wife Lucia, to escape the chill wind of the new knowledge by the fostering of a worn, patched and half-decayed Church system. Her cheerful acquiescence and placid contentment in the enervated, marrowless shadow of what was once, for a more childish generation, a solid joy, seemed pathetic to me. Faithfully she sought her daily share of consecration, edification and purification, that every human spirit needs as much as the body needs a bath. But it was a dead, nerveless consecration through sounds and impressions from which the living thought, the soul, had long vanished. How could the poetry of the Hebrews and the thoughts of the Middle Ages still touch her? Only the hollow tones of the declaiming priests and the outward magnificence of the churchly edifice brought something like a fleeting shadow of the true sense of the divine. And in the poetry or music which she could really and wholly feel, in the art of her age, in the thought and science of her age - the living, direct expression of God - in these she did not seek, because round about her no one realized that only in these consecration is found, and must be sought for.

But for me, that which had been indicated by the meditative of all the ages, in vague, and for the most part impotent, expression, began to acquire a new, wonderful character of reality. I had learned to speak, to hear, to see, to taste, to smell, to touch, to create things and beings, and to enter into relations with what seemed to me independent beings, without having the body - that which is positively doomed to destruction - take part. What generation after generation had repeated one after the other as empty sound, idle chimera, or suggestion, the existence of a world beyond the senses, had for me become actual experience. I knew now that I had another body, beside the ordinary one, an animæ corpus, with a proper world of perception; and this knowledge rested upon equally good foundations as every one's knowledge concerning the existence of his ordinary body. Time and again I faced the undeniable wonder of another space, perceived by the selfsame I, from the same centre of observation, as the space by day.

What some sages had presumed and concluded by specu- lation - that what we call room and place is nothing but one of the infinitely numerous ways of perception of our being that neither taken up room nor occupies space, the ego that is neither here nor there - had become for me an ordinary fact, the knowledge of which influenced all my thought. That I, without stirring from my place, could arrive in a totally different world, in many worlds, all with a proper space, all with the same evidence of real existence, all full of life, full of sensations, fall of beauties and transports - this became for me a matter of simple experience. And no one only knowing it from hearsay can realize how different and how much more profound is the effect of actual experience.

In this conjunction the eternal error of the human phantasy in wishing to fly directly toward the perfect and complete revealed itself. All the defective work of the human imagi- nation errs in wanting to make its creations too beautiful, in affording a soulless perfection, such as is manifested in human art by its decay after every period of bloom.

Frederik van Eeden

The insensible world is not full of pure loftiness and unmixed nobility. I do not constantly wander there in Elysian fields, absorbed in flowing conversations regarding important questions with spectres of noble stature and dignified bearing. As all reality, the reality of the beyond is unexpectedly fantastic, full of surprises and full of disillusions; but on the whole more stimulating and more beautiful than anything the imagination has pictured regarding it. And this is of supreme importance in the practice of our daily life - that the insensible world is in part our own creation, subject to our will, built up from the conclusions gathered in our day-life, with the faculties and powers which by practice and use we have in this same life made our own. To say for this reason that nothing new awaits us would be equal to the assertion that Beethoven had given nothing new to the world, because, after all, he only employed combinations of familiar sounds and tones. I again repeat - nothing in our actual day-life can equal the ecstasy of even a single awakening in the new sphere.

And who would now confront me with the assertion that then probably the dear being that appeared at my summons as my bride and made me supremely happy in her arms, was also my own creation - to him I can only reply as he himself would reply to the agnostic philosopher, if the latter asked him for proofs that the entire world of the senses, with his wife and children and the whole family included, were anything else than a product of his imagination.

Does it make much difference whether we give to one and the same thing, vehemently and intensely felt, the name of fancy or the name of reality? - and does anyone know a reliable mark of distinction between the two? Everything is the product of imagination, the sun and the stars are also works of God's imagination. But there is weak and strong, enervated and potently creative imagination; and very subtle is the boundary line between the idle thought image and the created one, endowed with personal being and reality.

How absurd, in the light of my experience, now seemed to me the common idea of the so-called believers - as though the earthly life with all its joys and its misery would break off all at once with death and suddenly, without transition, change into a bliss the purer, the more miserable had been the earthly existence.

All that we can expect is directly connected with what we attained here. Here on earth, imperceptibly and continuously, we weave our future, not by a right to reward from on high, as compensation for sorrow and disaster, accounted and awarded irrespective of any action on our part, but by personal activity, personal ability, personal achievement of the joy and ecstasy we deem the most desirable.

Therefore the closer knowledge and study of the immaterial reality does not lead away from the earthly life and coöperation with all striving humanity, as the fanatics and ascetics in the misconception of their idle and defective phantasy have believed and taught.

No, the blessedness that we all desire and can attain at will, must already be sought for here in our mortal life, in this earthly sphere. For only from the transient can the less transitory be compiled.

I now knew that my immaterial being with the repose or decease of the waking body, also lost the heaviness and the aches, the melancholy and dejection proceeding from the mortal, defective nature of this body: but I also knew that its joys and transports are dependent upon the happiness obtained by the day body through an active, wise life brought into harmony with the development of all mankind.

The more beautiful my days, the more crowded with effective labor my life, the gladder and serener my soul - the loftier also are the exaltations and transports of my nights, the more glorious the scenes I behold, the more beneficent the moods and the influences I undergo.

True, often a dream of most sublime splendor comes to brighten a time of the very deepest dejection; but only when this earthly affliction in the necessary consequence of the struggle for a higher and more common happiness, when I am after all inwardly hopeful and know that I am on the right road.

But, poverty, want, misery, affliction and loneliness are not good guides toward a better life, and smothered desires not good travelling companions.

The will for happiness may indeed burn so brightly in some of us that its flame shoots up all the higher through all the accumulated sorrow; but the spark of joy must remain visibly glowing, and to keep the sacred lamp of gladness burning is the primal duty of every human being.

It is true that man has often shown that he could not stand luxury and, like a child, broke out into folly when abundance came after a long period of want. But wealth is the only nurturing ground for the bloom of beauty, whereto in our striving for a higher life, we feel ourselves called.

Only in the land of abundance can we play the game of beauty which is our sole destination and which unites our nature to God's nature. And if we cannot stand abundance we must learn to accustom ourselves to it.

He who created us leads us by the line of joy, another link between Him and us does not exist. Though the way lead through dismal gloom, the luring voice of happiness continues to go before us. That is our will and God's will, disagreement is but misunderstanding.

Forgive me, dear reader, if I join the conclusions to the facts. I know that among them there are many confirmations of ancient, long-known truths. But you shall see that the very simplest and most well-known facts must be repeated to men over and over again, because they lack the courage and originality to keep their hold on them.

XIX

If so far you have believed and understood me, dear reader, it cannot fail but you will demand more of me than I can give. You will not demand further proofs, but revelations: communications from beings of another sphere, distinct, well-formulated communications concerning the beyond, concerning the meaning of our life, concerning the soul, concerning Christ, concerning God. Everyone desires these, not considering that for a distinct communication two factors are always required - namely, a good communicator and a good understander; just as air and fuel are required to start a flame.

I myself, as everyone would have, also sought for revelation, and many a time instead of calling Emmy I committed the folly of calling for Christ, or even worse, for God.

In the clear moments of observation of the night one can only effectually carry through one thing, there is no time for more; and it would happen that throughout the entire vision I would pray passionately, not thinking of Emmy, thanking God for his favors and beseeching him for enlightenment, and in the same way Christ. I could never do it by day with so much earnestness, conviction and eloquence. In the daytime I am not eloquent, but bashful and embarrassed, even when alone. I cannot pray by day for fear of feeling ridiculous, for gêne. But at night this gêne is gone and I abandon myself to prayer with a true passion, sometimes - even as all passions in the immaterial life - going beyond my control. At times my devout passion during prayer, even at the very moment, seems exaggerated and affected to me, but I am unable to restrain it.

But now the remarkable fact about it is that I never, absolutely never, have perceived anything in my visions that at my passionate and ardent invocation appeared as a divine image, as an angel or as Christ. Human beings, dead or living, came almost always when at all strongly urged; Emmy I saw many times in various shapes and circumstances. But at my invocations and prayers to these higher beings, whose existence man has always had to conclude from the signs of the world perceptible to the senses or from inner consciousness, I have never seen anything but what we call natural beauties - sunlight; blue heavens; flaming evening skies; radiant horizons, brightening or clouding with promising or warning significance.

And this where the history of human civilization is replete with stories of visions of angels, of Mary, and of Christ. We may explain this as we like, yet it proves that the simple wish, the invocation, the self-suggestion is not enough to create a visionary image. The demons of the Middle Ages I have seen, but not their angels, their Marys, their Jesus, their God the Father, while yet I often longed for it as a child and prayed for it as a man, until I was old and wise enough to understand that I had to be glad of their non-appearance, because the apparition of an old, bearded king as God, of a white-robed, long-haired man as Jesus, of a winged man as an angel, would simply have been nothing but fancied images, spectral deception or impotent human phantasy.

Does not our simplest reason tell us that all life that is more than human life, all higher beings, whether superman, or

Christ, or God, can have no form perceptible to man with his five senses? Do not all endeavors of art and imagination to create something above man, remain limited to a perfected humanity? Has not the sole conception of a superhuman being always been the impossible one of a man with wings? Yet we know that there is a higher being, higher life with more exalted beauties; but clear reflection must also teach us that its form remains imperceptible and unimaginable as long as our perceptive faculty and our knowledge have not, in a manner at present quite inconceivable, increased in a higher sphere, and that therefore all their awarded shapes, though formed by Dantesque phantasy, must be erroneous.

Sometimes, indeed, I saw worlds and sad beings that, much as they resembled the familiar and human, seemed to me to belong to a wholly different sphere. One night I dreamed of the sea, but it changed to something else, - a park, a landscape peopled with many creatures. I remember that the ground was moving like ocean waves, but magnificently blue and speckled with intensely yellow spots. There were also bushes and a multitude of happy, festive, richly dressed human beings. They were not demons, that I felt, but a species of men - happy, luxuriously living men.

Then I remembered that I was on another planet, and though my consciousness was not yet quite clear, still I began to pay close attention. Thus I remember that I gazed at the sky and seeing the blue color immediately drew the conclusion: "so there is oxygen in this atmosphere too," because it is oxygen that gives the blue color to our atmosphere. I went on and on and the landscape changed repeatedly. The inhabitants were extremely sympathetic and kindly disposed toward me. Of language or words I have no remembrance, but there was a cordial understanding. Then I saw trees and hills or something resembling them, and I fell into raptures. "0 my earth!" I cried, "it resembles my earth!" and I wept with emotion, because it reminded me of my beloved earth. Then I noticed that everything differed somewhat from earthly things and yet resembled them. "Just as America resembles Europe and yet differs from it," I thought in my dream.

Upon this I came into a barren and uninhabited part and I saw a perspective of mountains, a mountain chain rising out of the sea, luminous and steep, but so affecting and terrible to behold that it oppressed me. The perspective stretched out farther and farther - a dizzy extent, and all the way my eyes travelled along the ridge of faint-rose-colored rocks. Below me, at the left, was a mighty abyss, also, a distant mountain prospect. I saw everything with peculiar sharpness and distinctness. My mind was clear at the time and I was fully conscious - the terrific depth made me dizzy.

Thereupon I saw two strange beings in the wilderness. Human beings also - not demons. One was slate-colored like clay, the other brownish red like baked earth. They were hard at work - and the thought crossed my mind whether these were perchance the proletarians, who in this land supported the luxurious people I had just now seen. They were busy with a fire and I asked them something, about food or wood I believe. Laughingly they explained: "That is scarce here." Then I pointed back toward the land where I had left the people living in affluence:

"Yet it is not scarce there." Thereupon they laughed, feigning indifference, and intimated, how I no longer remember, that they were not envious of this, that these things were not essential, that it should be so. I awoke pondering the meaning of this dream, which I did not comprehend, and even now would not dare to explain entirely.

All that the perception during sleep teaches us, demands exactly as much scientific thought and comparison, critical analysis and selection, and building up into fixed, universal and lasting truth, as do all our waking perceptions. There can be no other true revelation than that of creative art and of science, established by all and for all. What would a personal revelation signify, that depended on the receptivity of a single individual, and could be affirmed in a few words and, by suggestion, forced upon the unreceptive? Would it not be as though the Divinity entrusted to the apostle the work of convincing thousands, where he himself had found only one - the apostle - susceptible to persuasion? Can such a revelation, spread by inculcation and pressure, by authority and servility, be anything else than passing fancy, and fleeting deception?

Therefore the study of the immaterial did not draw me away from the world of day, but caused me to work in it with all the more zeal and satisfaction, because I learned to look upon this world as our real field of labor, where the riches that shall count on a higher plane of vision are prepared.

Dreams only give us slight hints; the work must be done in this life.

But my dreams also showed me that solitude and seclusion could never lead to the highest joy and purest bliss. Unspeakably happy as were the moments of meeting with my dream bride, they were surpassed by those in which a universal joy, a great and transcendent enthusiasm simultaneously filling many beings - human happy beings - carried along myself and my beloved in a wave of radiant festive bliss.

I have had them often, such dreams, and they were the most beautiful of all. I know not whether they were the proclaimers of future or the dawning of already existing reality - but I would see spectacles of countless enthusiastic multitudes, processions of festive people streaming together and marching in solemn rhythm, with jubilation and sound of clarion. And we two, my beloved and I, were a part thereof, we belonged to it; and a feeling of festiveness and of unlimited confidence toward all possessed us, lifting us up into a bright and joyous mood, and yet not detracting from our mutual affection, but transfiguring and strengthening it.

Thereby - as through repeated experience I learned to understand them - truths were pointed out to me in a peculiar symbolical way. Thus I once saw in my dream many people building a large house and laying out a path, and they did it with marvellous alacrity. And there was no one to command them, to give directions, or point out anything.

The incredible swiftness with which the work advanced was due to the fact that each one of the builders, down to the very least, knew and comprehended the entire work and therefore did not need the slightest direction.

I understood these hints better and better, and more and more clearly comprehended what hindered man on his upward path - the dawning rays of pure universal blessedness shone for me ever more brightly from out the chaos of our confused personal and social life. But all the more tormentingly I felt my impotence to bring about an effectual reform.

XX

Ah, what could I do, imprisoned as I was in the cage of my honorable position, my definitely-prescribed sphere of action, my distinguished connections, my luxurious domestic establishment, my reputation and my money? The better I saw what society lacked for leading man toward the highest development, the more I felt myself paralyzed when I wished to contribute something toward his deliverance.

I felt as does the sailor on board a ship in distress who sees the safe waters and rescue close at hand - he alone, of all the others - but he has no authority, he knows that they would not believe him, discipline prevents him from speaking. Then it is harder for him to do his duty than for the others who plod on blindly, obedient to their superiors, without seeing deliverance.

I saw how men suffered misery through gigantic misunderstandings, which like great clouds of mist enveloped and confused the nations. I saw them blundering with their tongue and their words as children who have their first paint box and get as much color smeared over their dresses, hands and faces as on the paper. And on this mess-work they build their treaties, with this mess-work they enact laws, and thus messing, blundering and squandering they prepare their food, their clothing and their habitation.

From words wrongly understood and wrongly employed arose the bloody frenzy of revolutions, the grim party-rage, the useless slaughtering and disputing and the fatal dissipation of thinking and working powers. In their blind faith in reason and the True Word men destroyed their own and each other's joy and happiness, not realizing that they all wanted one and the same thing, for which they employed many different terms.

I saw how they all acted from the mighty impulse of the herd-instinct, the group-sense, the sacred gift of Christ, warrant of their power and safety - but at the same time how they all thought they acted from personal, independent judgment and reasonable conviction, to their own miserable confusion and wretchedness.

I saw the grouping into rich and poor, because the wholesome craving for luxury and abundance is corrupted and weakened through neglect of the tie of love, so that the individual thinks that he alone can be luxurious and happy in a world of wretches, and thus no one attains blessedness. And this once more: - because there are no two people who with the same word know that they mean the same thing.

And I saw the demagogues taking advantage of our good instincts, of the craving for luxury, of the group-sense, to start up fatal currents through the influence of hollow catchwords and ridiculous over-estimation of self. As though the poor who had known nothing but poverty and envy would be better proof against luxury than the rich; as though self-insight and self-restriction were possible without culture; as though the perfect maturity of every individual, which demands the very highest organization and efficiency, and which in name is called the Christian ideal, could be attained all at once, without practice, without development, without patient discipline.

Frederik van Eeden

All this I saw, and what could I do? My sphere of activity bound me to fixed duties and to my superiors. I worked in a definite group-confederacy, the political world of diplomats, and to go beyond this meant immediate expulsion and ostracism.

Well, yes, in the clubs and "circles" people speak more freely. There one sometimes hears the entire diplomatic service ridiculed with cynical sarcasm by those of inferior rank, and the superiors listen smilingly, as though regretting that their higher dignity forbade them this freedom of speech. In these circles many a sharp word would sometimes escape me too, in regard to the structure of national prosperity, still everywhere based upon the want of the weaker, and also regarding the mighty ones on earth with whom I associated, and who were yet so often embarrassed and foolish when obliged to say something concerning the highest human gifts - wisdom, art and beauty. And from some vague confusion of thought, characteristic of the chaos of their ideas, I was known there as "the red duke," or sometimes too as "the Christian diplomat."

But nothing could weaken my conviction that the chaos is busy arranging itself, at first blindly, with a cruel indifference to suffering, driven by an inscrutable impulse - but by degrees with clearer consciousness, more insight, more skill, in proportion as higher wisdom gradually pairs itself with wider active power.

It was plain to me that if there ever was a time in human history in which men were awaiting a hero, a Messiah, a redeemer, it is ours. No opinion is more foolish than the one that in our age there would be no room for a prophet. But he must not be a moralist preaching repentance, not a speculative builder of systems, not a man of lamentations and warnings, but a poet in very deed.

Riper than was the French revolution for the advent of an organizing and suggestively powerful general and ruler like Napoleon, is our time for the advent of the wise and high-minded administrator, who will make use of the group-confederacy, the herd-spirit, so much stronger and more consolidated to-day than ever before.

I also knew what the qualities and talents of this hero should be. The time of the great generals is past; the brute power of force is no longer needed for establishing, only for preserving. The commercial alliance covers the entire world course, and tolerates war only as a secondary aid. The honor of the soldier becomes that of the police, the peace preserver.

But the qualities of the general, the ability for organizing, for ruling and for the bearing of responsibility, these remain equally necessary.

The Messiah of our time must be the hero-organizer who brings order into the confused operations and the half-conscious action of our society. And as in the time of the generals, it was only the poet-generals, the great dreamers of a world-realm, such as Alexander, Cæsar and Napoleon, who shone out through all the ages as heroes and geniuses, so in our time, it will be the poet organizer, the dreamer of a world fellowship, who will attain still greater heroism, and much more lasting honor.

The time of eloquence is also past. The elusive phrases of oratorical logic only blind young nations, and even America is outgrowing the authority of the orator who is solely an orator.

But the time of the drama and of music is not past, and he who knows how to handle these mighty suggestive expedients can turn the course of humanity. The herd will follow him though he lead them into the wilderness or the desert. Wagner and Ibsen have proved it.

But some day, and probably soon, it will come to pass that the hero of the new times, the poet organizer, will join hands with the one suggestively mighty through music and drama, or perchance that these rare powers shall be united in one man.

And only then shall the herd be led into green pastures and shall be satisfied and shall see the day of maturity dawning.

I say it, I, old hermit among the philistines, and my peace rests upon this knowledge. I had not the gift for ruling, for organizing, for leading. I was not eloquent. I had not the power of music or drama. I could not attempt to be this hero, this "Sotèr" of mankind, for I knew what was required of him. But I knew and still know that he shall be born with the infallible certainty with which statistics foretell the number of geniuses and defectives, the number of those above and below the normal. His birth is approaching, and speedily moreover, as surely as the birth of a majority of sons after a man-slaughtering war. For the race has need of him, Christ requires him.

And if I myself cannot be he, still I can be his John the Baptist, testifying of him, happy and enthusiastic in my solitude, in this desert of caddishness and provincialism.

XXI

I had been married seventeen years and my youngest child was eight years old when I returned to this same Holland, where so many strands of my rope of destiny are fastened. Little had changed in my life. Order and peace reigned in my family, prosperity in the sphere of my activities. Lucia seemed wholly satisfied and ruled her household with quiet devotion. My children were fair and well brought up. I felt my growing attachment to them and to their mother, as every creature is attached to the creatures and the things that have long been its daily companions - an affection from symbiosis, I might call it. Yet with my inmost being I remained a stranger to them, and my affection for them retained its forced quality. An ever-growing discontent was gathering in me. The older I grew, the nearer I saw the time approaching when age would make me powerless, the more intense became the strain. I felt as though I should die without really having lived. I did not fear death, but to be doomed to die without having revealed my true life, this was a prospect quite unbearable to me.

I lived on, strengthened only by my dream nights, but it seemed as though they were driving and spurring me on to something more - to an act, to an outbreak. They became rarer and I encountered greater difficulties in attaining the light and in seeing Emmy in my dreams. Often it was but a

Frederik van Eeden

desperate struggle to force my way through chambers, garrets, and corridors. I could no longer see the unobstructed blue sky, I could no longer attain the ecstasy of joy so greatly desired, I could no longer pray in earnest, the voice of my dream-body grew husky and weak, sometimes when I called Emmy, it sounded as though I spoke in the tones of a dying man.

Moreover my temptations became stronger. As soon as the flame of life burns more dimly, the demons regain their influence and their wanton tricks are more successful. Lucia's maternal instincts were satisfied, and her allurement, which had always seemed the same as seduction to me, lost its power and was most easily evaded. But the old tormenting life in the big cities began anew, not easier but harder to bear with the advancing years, for the shame and the self-contempt are greater; and the contrast between what one appears to be before the world, and what one knows oneself to be, becomes more painful the older one grows.

And the while I knew that I harbored thoughts and intentions and even planned deeds for which everyone, and above all, Lucia and my children, considered me too good, I at the same time felt something like contempt for their complacence, their content; I felt angry at this careless, happy household, in this great, imperfect world, full of misery, ugliness, error and confusion, this open wound from which it behooves each of us to suffer until it is healed.

The great love that burned in me, the great love for Christ, led me to what most people would call godless ingratitude. I cursed my prosperity and only with difficulty bore my apparent wedded happiness. I felt as does the soldier, who is left behind at the warm, comfortable hearth while the army to the strains of music marches out to take the field.

The first thing I did in Holland was to buy a little sail yacht. It was anchored at Amsterdam, as from there I could sail on the Zuiderzee. One day I had made an engagement with a colleague from the Austrian legation, a clever, strong, young Hungarian to sail to E—, the little town, then still unknown to me, where I now write these pages.

In those days I was passing through the gloomiest period of my life, I was nauseated with all the sweetness around me, the oppressive semblance of happiness suffocated and palled on me. I saw absolutely no deliverance, not even an accident that might threaten to change the course of my life - new abilities I should surely never acquire, nothing seemed in view that could bring about a change in my unreal existence. I was indeed willing humbly to submit if I must - but there was something that incited and disturbed me, as though submission was the very greatest sin.

Wanton suicide before I was brought to the last extremity filled me with aversion and disgust. But the perils of my sailing expeditions had again acquired for me their former attraction, as in the days when I sailed the North Sea with my father. To die the death of Shelley, my greatest-bard, is an honor I had desired from boyhood, and I thought: If after all it must be, then why not now, before I sink still deeper?

The day before our expedition I was deeply depressed. The wind was blowing strongly, but it was a summer day and my companion thought as little as I did of postponing our undertaking.

When I fell asleep that night, I knew that I was falling asleep and I retained perfect consciousness. In wondrous transition I suddenly rose from the deepest dejection to the light, free, joyous, soaring life of the dream. "Thank heaven!" I thought; "let the body sleep now, I rest, and really I am not at all tired now. I can sing and move about, fly and soar with thorough perceptive enjoyment." Soon after I was out of doors in a vast wooded landscape under a sunny blue sky. For a long time the dream world had not been so beautiful. I was enchanted and grateful and soared upward. I met a bird, and talking aloud to myself all the time, I said that I not only wanted perceptive enjoyment but a being to understand me - spiritual and mental communion.

I saw a white bull - the animal which in ordinary dreams most alarmed me - the most feared dream-animal; but I felt no fear and soared high above him over a sea; there was no danger.

Then I called my beloved, just as always. But before I myself knew it I had called not "Emmy," but "Elsie," and this same mistake I repeated, without noticing my error. From out a dim valley I saw a maiden approaching, younger and smaller than Emmy, with smooth blonde hair. But I went to meet her nevertheless as though it were Emmy, and I walked and talked with her. I talked Dutch, which I had pretty well mastered by that time.

Then the maiden pointed to a dark, threatening thunder cloud which was slowly drawing up over the blue sky. This was a symbol of disaster. But I was proud and happy and not afraid and wanted to fold her in my arms. But she was gone; the perfect clarity of my thoughts declined, but not my sense of happiness. The dream then attained a symbolical signi-ficance, as often happens. I saw a long line of human beings in bondage, like a procession of slaves, and among them many priests. And I said things that I knew would cost others their life, heresies about the evil brought about by false religion, and I saw the poor creatures growing pale with fright and the priests pale with anger, but I soared out above them, and their hatred was powerless. Then I saw a large building, a most peculiarly beautiful and impressive temple, with mighty pillars of gray stone and carpeted with green moss. There none might enter without permission of the priests. But I soared far out above them, entering it from above by the windows. And everyone saw me and was astonished, and there was a sort of silent recognition that I was the only one that could do this, and the priests tried to deny the fact and even to seize me. But I laughed at them, and when they wanted to touch me I paralyzed them with a gesture.

And there was no palsied pride or hatred herein, but a calm self-consciousness of freedom, personal authority and triumph - a good and beautiful emotion.

When I awoke I was surprised that I had talked Dutch with Emmy. And I doubted whether it had indeed been she, although the face was like hers and I had indeed seen her in such youthful form before.

The following day we sailed with a stiff sou'-wester toward my little city, which I was then to see for the first time. From time to time there were rain showers, mist, with a rough and rising sea. My companion and I had donned our yellow oilskins and we had our hands full to keep the frail little craft in the right course. The sea was deserted, the fisherman had taken refuge in the harbors. When we saw the harbor of E—before us and the little city veiled in gray mist, the waves were dashing over the rear of the boat and the little yacht was sinking her nose deep into the billows. We had to keep up bailing her busily, and with mute suspense we gazed toward the pier for which we were directly heading, expecting every minute to see the boat fill with water or the rigging break. We could distinguish the people on the stone pier which ran out into the sea. A crowd had gathered and stood watching us with mute interest, anxious to see whether we should make the landing safely. I was unusually calm and happy. I would have drowned with perfect composure, but I knew that this time it was not yet to be.

The black eyes of the Hungarian sparkled with pleasure and pride when at last, by dint of skilful man?uvring, with furled sail we ran safely through the narrow entrance of the port. He shouted in his excited way, and the sober Hollanders, sent up a little answering cheer.

Then as we glided along past the line of people who stood thronging the stone quay, amid the stupid indifferent or coolly critical boys' faces and the faces of the fishermen, rough and weather-beaten as though carved out of wood, I caught sight of a pair of eyes full of intense interest and attention, that seemed to light up gladly as with relief, in a little face still pale from suspense or anxiety. Amid the men stood a young woman, bareheaded, the wet, blonde hair blowing about her cheeks. She had thrown a dark gray shawl around her as though she had run from the house just as she was to watch for us. She looked straight at me with an expression of concern and gladness.

I nodded to her, as every Italian, seeing a sweet woman manifesting concern in his danger which has aroused the general attention, would do. I nodded gaily and waved to her as though to thank her for her sympathy. She just gave a little smile and nodded back, not blushing, nor embarrassed or prudish - but grave and confiding as though she had expected it.

At the exchange of this greeting and these glances I had a curious sensation. It was as if I had forgotten myself for a moment and did not recognize myself, and as if everything I saw did not fit in the life of the day. I thought of my dream and without yet consciously drawing any inferences or comparisons, I for a moment was entirely gone from the ordinary waking world and in the land of dreams again.

"Hallo! Muralto - the boat hook!" my Hungarian called out.

With a shock I came back to earth, and it seemed as if I had been off a great way and as if everything I saw had been familiar to me, as though I saw it again after a long absence.

Before I came back to my senses sufficiently to hand over the boat hook, my eyes once more sought those of the young woman. But she had vanished from the quay. I only just caught sight of the slender figure in the gray shawl as she crossed the little square of the port. She hurried along with a glad, light step as though she had come solely for us and now went home, calm and well satisfied.

"What's the matter? What ails you, Muralto? Do you see anything particular - or anyone?"

"Did you see the young woman standing on the quay?" I asked.

"No!" said the Hungarian, "I didn't remark her. I knew of course that there were pretty girls here, but not that you knew them."

"I know no one here. I'm here for the first time," said I curtly, abstractedly.

We went to the hotel and dried and warmed ourselves and ordered the dinner. I looked at everything that, despite the rain, was to be seen of the little town, later so dear to me, - the pretty gables, the narrow little streets, glistening with water, the sombre elms creaking and groaning in the storm, the yellow raging sea. I also saw the house, in which I now live, and thought it a pretty, dignified little structure with its free-stone gable, and its tall windows.

After that we regaled ourselves with food and drink, and my companion said that after all I must surely have seen some good acquaintance of mine, some little friend or other - for I was so quiet, so abstracted and yet so merry.

That night I slept without dreams of any significance. But sleep itself had a character of gently elevating joy, and the morning found me without a semblance of the melancholy that so long had possessed me.

The weather had cleared, the wind gone down, the sky was blue. We decided to sail back early.

As we were leaving the hotel and stopping a moment in the vestibule, with the blue and white tiled marble flooring and the brown wooden ceiling, the young woman, who yesterday had stood upon the quay, came from the out-building and, running past us, went into the upper chamber. Again she looked me straight in the eyes and nodded cordially. I was even more confounded than the day before. But nevertheless I had time to remark that she was very graceful and that she had fine and noble features and long, aristocratic hands. Her eyes were bright and had the clear lustre that I had seen in only one pair of eyes, and an expression as though, together with me, they knew innumerable, unutterable secrets.

My Hungarian comrade now again saw my agitation and, moreover, the cause of it.

"Oh! was it she that you saw yesterday?" he cried out in French when the girl had passed. "Then I comprehend your dumbfoundedness."

"Do you know her?" I asked.

"Certainly, she is one of the sights of the town. All the strangers know her."

"Is this her home?"

"Of course! and not to the loss of the hotel-keeper. She's his daughter or his adopted daughter. But not interesting to me, because notoriously unapproachable."

"What's her name?"

"Elsie - Elsie van Vianen, or Elsje as they say here."

On our prosperous homeward voyage over the sunny sea I was even more quiet and even merrier than the night before.

Frederik van Eeden

XXII

As soon as I could make myself free for a day I went out sailing again. I now knew the way and the water and took no one with me this time. At daybreak I left The Hague and was beyond the locks before eight o'clock. I had not mentioned my encounter to Lucia, but nevertheless I felt none of that secret sense of guilt of a married man, who feels himself charmed by a strange woman.

To-day it was a warm summer's day with a light eastern breeze blowing. The great yellow sheet of water looked as peaceful and friendly as it had appeared wild and wicked the time before. The little waves sparkled in the sun and with sweetly soothing murmurings splashed against the little boat. The shores with their steeples and windmills lay rosy and placid round about me in perfect dream splendor. I was six hours on my way instead of three, as before, and they were hours full of light and sunny bliss. My little city lay as sweetly pensive in the bright glow of sunlight as a drifting isle of the blessed. The round, leafy, blue-gray crowns of the trees with the little belfry peaking out above them, appeared as if tranquilly floating above the sparkling silvery sheet of water -

"Du bist Orplid, mein Land!

Das ferne leuchtet -"

I sang. I smiled at the contrast between the meaningless and trivial life of the people, who presumably lived there, and the wondrous magic glory it all assumed through the power of my imagination. I meditated on the land Orplid - the youthful phantasy of Möricke - to which with a few measured words he was able to lend a deep, mysterious, glowing splendor, which has filled thousands, like myself, with a yearningly passionate thrill of beauty, yes, with a real longing. Is not the dreamed Orplid that for so many shines afar, more real than all the lands that waking we behold?

When I landed there was hardly anyone on the quay; the fisherman sat caulking his boat, a few boys were fishing in the dark green waters of the harbor - everything exactly as I can still see it to-day - my future dwelling-house already looked at me with familiar friendliness from out its cool, dark window-eyes; the doves cooed in the softly rustling elms; it smelled of pitch and tar and of the inevitable Dutch peat-smoke, which rose from the stove pipes of the fishing smacks lying in the harbor, where the fishermen's wives were cooking the dinner.

I went straight ahead toward my goal as though I were already a loved and longingly expected lover, smiling and myself wondering at my assurance. I went past the little rope shops, where the door-bell sounded loudly through the empty street when a solitary visitor in Sunday attire stepped out of the shop, past the barber shop with the brightly polished brass basins, past the few stately mansions with ancient stone gables representing "Fortune" or "Love," where the daughters of the house, from dark side chambers peeped out, from behind the inevitable Clivia Hower-pot, at the rarely passing stranger, on to the hotel "de Toelast."

I have, indeed, as I have already with shame confessed to you, been out a couple of times on gallant adventure, but never with such point-blank, unabashed directness as on this summer's day in my beloved little Dutch city. I also felt none, absolutely none, of the shyness, the conscientious scruples, the nervousness that usually attend the gallant adventures of a married man. I felt like a schoolboy going to claim a prize after a successful examination. My heart only beat a trifle faster with glad expectation - perhaps too with a little fear at the thought of the type that would present itself before my eyes as the father.

I asked directly for the hotel keeper. At my first visit he had not made his appearance. From the out-house, after a long wait, a big lazy Dutch man came shuffling on in a very slovenly and ill-fitting gray suit, a black silk cap, a soiled shirt in place of the missing collar and tie, an open vest full of cigar ashes, a cigar in a paper holder in his mouth, and worn, flowered, green slippers on his feet. When after some little conflict with myself I finally looked into his face, I saw a flushed, full-moon countenance, clean-shaven except for a drooping moustache under a small crooked nose - and in this face one sleepy eye; the other had perhaps once been there, but now was lost.

"Are you Mynheer Van Vianen?" I asked in Dutch, which at the time I still spoke with a pronounced Italian accent.

"No!" said the offensive father, without taking the cigar from his mouth.

"But you are the hotel-keeper at any rate?" I asked in a disagreeable state of uncertainty.

"Yes," came the answer just as curtly, as though he wanted to say, "Are you through soon now? Then we'll go to sleep again."

"But are you not then the father of Juffrouw Van Vianen, who lives in this house?"

"No!" said the man. "She has no father. She's a foundling."

I could have embraced the unsightly boor. His indelicate communication seemed to me the happiest compliment and the gladdest tidings that I could have expected from him. He could not know that his brutal rudeness, which he in Dutch fashion seemed to take for lusty candor, something like "I won't be bothered talking around the subject" - that this rudeness was for me a blessing. The advantage of not being descended from him he would indeed hardly be able to appreciate. I breathed more freely; it was one of the loveliest moments of this lovely day. The word "foundling" was for me like an opening blind in a dark chamber of boorishness and provincialism, suddenly revealing a vista of distant, mistily romantic perspectives. To be sure I had comforted myself with the thought that the race can, at any time and anywhere, bring forth geniuses through atavism; thus also in the family of a Dutch provincial hotel-keeper, a womanly genius of noble grace, charm and distinction; but this was after all much sweeter solace. With a foundling one could presuppose noble ancestors of any nationality. I too now found it unnecessary to talk longer around the subject.

"Then would you kindly tell Juffrouw Van Vianen that there is someone who urgently desires to speak to her?"

The cigar now fell from the gaping mouth and the solitary eye also opened perceptibly wider like that of a hippopotamus emerging from the water. I was scrutinized a while.

"Urgently?" he growled, as though such a thing were most

improbable and also improper.

"Yes, urgently."

"Hm!" said the Dutchman. He stuck the paper mouth-piece with the cigar back into his mouth and shuffled back on his slippers to the out-house, the while a remarkable stirring seemed to be going on in the brains underneath the black cap.

A moment later Elsje came. This time she blushed deeply when she saw me, although there was now really less reason for it than last time. But I knew it was joy, for I also saw her eyes sparkling.

"Oh, is it you!" she said with restrained surprise. "Did you wish to speak with me?"

"If it is convenient to you, Juffrouw Van Vianen?"

"Just step into the upper room. Didn't your French friend come with you?"

"I crossed the sea alone. The other gentleman is a Hungarian, and not a particular friend of mine either."

"Oh, good!" said Elsje, leaving me in sweet doubts as to what she found good.

We went into the upper room. I can remember a red table cover, cane chairs, a crocheted cover over a tea-set, horrible steel engravings on the walls. Everything lovely and adorable - what would I not give to see it once more! But "de Toelast" has long since been rebuilt.

I felt somewhat embarrassed, yet not oppressed. I refreshed

myself by gazing quietly into her soft, bright eyes. I could see only the eyes clearly. Whether the face was pretty or homely I could not judge. It was too intimate, too beloved, too much a part of me.

"Did I guess rightly that you stood watching on the pier out in the rain only on our account last Sunday?"

She nodded gravely. "Yes! I was afraid that you would be drowned. It has indeed happened quite frequently that little yachts were sunk with that wind blowing. And there was no way of saving them."

"Yes, we came off well. But how did you know that we were coming?"

"Well, I saw the people looking out from the quay and I realized that there was a boat in peril."

"But would you have done it for any other boat too?"

Then she remained silent and looked at me long. I thought I saw a mist gathering in her eyes. Her answer sounded timid, as though she dared not say it or feared to be laughed at.

"I was uneasy all morning. The night before too. I have never felt so strangely anxious. Only when I saw your face did I become tranquil."

"Then did you know my face? Had you dreamt of me?"

She shook her head. "Not that I know of. But yet I cannot say that your face is strange to me. I have surely seen it before this." Then as though to herself she whispered: "Where I do not know."

"You knew the Hungarian, didn't you? He seemed to know you."

Elsie laughed, the short clear laugh that has later so often made me happy.

"Oh, he! - yes, he has been here before. He surely hadn't much good to say of me."

"Quite the contrary!" said I. "He paid you a great compliment. He said that you were unapproachable."

Elsje laughed still louder.

"How conceited these foreigners are. Especially these dark foreigners who speak French. If you just treat them with ordinary civility they think they can allow themselves anything. I cannot be careful enough with these persons."

That was meant for me, I thought. I made a little bow and said:

"I thank you for your warning. I shall try my best not to foster any illusions and to give you no cause for exercising caution."

She became so embarrassed that I regretted my words.

"Oh, you!" she said with charming emphasis and naive candor: "I really didn't mean you! - with you I don't have to be careful - I saw that directly."

"Who knows, Juffrouw Elsie! for I am one of those dark foreigners too, and my Dutch is not yet quite irreproachable."

"You are no stranger to me," she said again, softly

and earnestly.

I believe that we said nothing for a long time then, and gazed at each other without finding it in the least embarrassing or oppressing.

We both felt as though the responsibility of our situation did not rest with us, but with One who probably knew best in everything and in whose keeping we were safe.

At last she got up, saying: "You surely want your room put to rights again. It has not been used since you were here last and I saved your bed linen."

"Did you know then that I would come back?"

"I thought you would."

"Did you hope so?"

"Yes!" she said artlessly.

This was so totally different from what other women I had known would have replied, that it made me feel confused. I had no conception or experience of woman's love that can dispense with playful dissembling, and so thought that I was mistaken after all. I began to consider that I was already quite an old man and she apparently about twenty years younger. Perhaps I resembled some one she had formerly known; perhaps she took me for her unknown father or sought in me a substitute for her unengaging supporter. I prepared myself for all this, firmly determined not to disappoint her.

"Will you do me the favor of being my guide about the city this afternoon? It looks like such a pretty and attractive little town to me."

"I?" she asked with evident pleasure. "I'll be very glad to. But first you must eat something."

"Will your ... stepfather have no objections?

Elsje smiled surprised and a bit scornfully.

"Who? - Jan Baars? - Why no! that makes no difference to him. He has no authority over me either."

How thankful these proud words made me. Hastily leaving the room she said:

"I'll see that you get something to eat quickly. Then while you're eating I'll get dressed and at three o'clock I'll go out with you."

And I remained behind, blithe as an angel and full of expectancy as a child on his birthday.

When we went out she had dressed, and it was astonishing to see with what simple means she achieved an appearance of tasteful distinction. A round straw hat, a white standing collar, a well-tailored light gray suit, a lavender silk tie - and she was a lady among the boorish and bourgeois women of her town. For on the point of dress the artistic Hollanders, as soon as they discard their quaint old national costume, are probably the most tasteless people in the world, and of these the women of a North Dutch provincial town are probably even the very worst dressed.

As we walked along the hot quiet streets we saw the residents peeping at us through their wire window screens with amazed, well-nigh angry glances.

"Do you see how we are being stared at?" said Elsje. "That will give them something to talk about for a whole week again."

"And don't you mind that, Juffrouw Elsje?"

"Why, no!" said Elsje, with a pretty expression of power and personal dignity: "I have taught them that I do exactly what I myself think right. Now there isn't one left who dares accost me about it. It does them no good, anyway. And what they say to each other I do not hear, nor am I anxious to find out."

We went to the museum. It was silent, cool and deserted there. The door-keeper sat nodding in his corner. Amid the relics of that old, stout, merry people that, a few centuries ago, strove to surround their earthly life with beauty and comfort here, amid the prints and paintings of the graceful, gorgeous, flag-bedecked vessels; the portraits of magistrates, charmingly elegant and autocratic, the muskets and cuirasses and lances, the medals and placards, the rare bibelots and the fine porcelain from the East and West brought together in this little sailor's hamlet, we spent a few hours of profound intimate happiness.

Elsje knew very little, but she was quick to understand, and she listened to my explanations with such eager desire for learning, with such rapt attention, with such unlimited faith in my knowledge, that it made me feel confused and I begged her not to take me for an oracle - for though I had indeed read much and seen a good deal of the world, yet I was by no means a scholar such as is demanded in our days.

"Ah! I live in such a small narrow circle here. To me you are the great, vast world," said Elsje with a charming deference.

When the daylight faded and it grew cooler, we wandered

　　　　　　Frederik van Eeden

out through the old, dark gateway up across the thickly wooded dike into the open green fields, where we watched the sun setting in flame-colored majesty. We walked to what is now my nursery, and I drew her attention to the marvellous flight of the gulls soaring motionless against the wind, to the colors of the sea and of the heavens, to the brightly-sparkling Venus glittering greenish white against the rose-colored background of the sky, and I told her all I knew.

Then I came back to our conversation of the morning.

"Have you often such forebodings as when I was approaching in peril on the sea?"

"Yes, always when something important is going to happen to me, good or bad, I know it before. It never fails."

"This time it was good, though, I hope?

"Yes, good," she said, smiling sweetly, "but alarming nevertheless. You must not sail so recklessly again. Boats like your little yacht should be in the harbor with such a wind blowing. Even all the fishing smacks were in and they can stand quite a bit more rough weather."

"I was calm and assured. I knew that I would see you. I had dreamt of you, of your face and of your name."

"Really?" said Elsje, looking straight at me with her frank, innocent eyes.

Before this look my heart melted with tenderness. I felt a desire to kneel down before her and cover her hands with tears and kisses. But I controlled myself, for I reflected that I was an Italian and that it was a Dutch girl I had to deal with, and I did not want to risk my fragile happiness by foolish extravagances. And there was a subtle relish in this sobriety and this respectful self-control. But I wanted to be honest too - my happiness must rest on a firm foundation of uprightness - I wanted to make my position clear.

"Yes, really, Elsje; and yet I had never heard of you, and no one had spoken of you to me. And now, tell me, had you never heard of me either? Do you know anything about me? Do you know my name?"

"I saw your name in the hotel register. Otherwise I knew nothing of you until I saw you."

"Really not? Also not ?"

"What?"

"That I am married and have a good wife and four children?" I burst out, almost roughly in my brave effort to spare myself nothing and to risk the worst.

Elsje without starting gazed at me long, attentively and thoughtfully. What I distinctly discerned in her glance was a questioning doubt and a tender compassion.

"A good wife and four children," she repeated softly, pensively. "I thought that you were probably married. But you are not happy after all, I know it."

"No, I am not happy, Elsje, that is true. Or rather - was not until to-day."

She asked nothing more after that, as though she thought that I would probably myself tell her what I deemed necessary for her to know. But I knew enough, and I also saw that she

Frederik van Eeden

knew enough and we spoke no more about ourselves that day. We felt as one does in dreams - one understands and communicates without words.

I slept very little that night. With me also, well balanced in mind as I am, sleep grows more elusive with the advancing years. But it is not care, but happiness, that drives it away. I lay all night silent and happy in a bright cloud of joy, thinking of her who now lay peacefully breathing under the same roof. Then toward morning I had a short dream, which by its dark terror gave me a measure for the brightness of my joy. I dreamt that I was back in my office at The Hague and, coming home, I found a letter containing my transference to Japan. My sailing excursions, my little city, Elsje - it had all been a dream and I was again deep in my old, gloomy life, worldly and yet estranged from the world. My anguish was terrible, I cried and sobbed desperately and woke up in that way, my face and my pillow now really wet with tears. And then - the relief, the transition, the glorious realization of the reality of my newly-found happiness, my dawning memory of yesterday's beautiful day, of Elsje's winsome ways and the frank, fervent look in her eyes, her ready sympathy and tender compassion. Only then I really comprehended what had been given me. I was no longer a stranger in the world - life, the sacred human life had won me back. I would not die after all without having been entirely human.

At my solitary breakfast in the upper room, into which the sun was shining, Elsje, amid the pressure of her domestic duties, stopped a moment to greet me. I said that I had no time to sail back, but would go home by train, leaving the yacht anchored in the harbor, to call for it the following Sunday.

"That is well considered," said Elsje, with a roguish little laugh of comprehension.

And at my departure I saw my peaceful, friendly little city, with its venerable old church steeple, stretched out calm and sunny in matinal activity. In front of the ugly, bare little station I turned, and stretching out my hands I blessed the little city with all my heart, murmuring in my glowing, passionate mother tongue:

"Benedetto sia 'l giorno e 'l mese e 'l anno

E la stagione e 'l tempo e 'l ora e 'l punto

E 'l bel paese e 'l loco ov' io fu giunto

Da duo begli occhi, che legato m' hanno."

XXIII

"Dear Lucia, will you hear me a moment? I have something to tell you and would like to have it off my mind before we go to bed."

We had just come home from a court banquet and in our gala dress stood looking over the letters which had arrived that night. Lucia looked up interestedly.

"Come to my room with me then," she said, and then regarding me: "It is surely something good, isn't it? I haven't seen you in such good spirits for a long time."

I followed her silently. When we were seated quietly I realized what a vast abyss yawned between our two worlds and what a foolish undertaking was the endeavor to bridge it. I spoke slowly -

"Yes, it is something good, something very good. But I don't know whether I shall succeed in convincing you of that."

Lucia harkened attentively, and again and again I paused a moment, so as to proceed with careful precision in my endeavors to bring about an understanding.

"So you have noticed that I am in better spirits now, or rather that I am happier than I was. It is so and it proves to you that something good has happened. I was not happy because there was something lacking in my life, something that I can with difficulty explain to you. And now I have found it, and it opens up for me a glorious prospect of peace and rest, of the highest content that any human being can expect. A vast sea, a calm ocean of peace and joy.?"

Lucia waited and listened intently.

"Let me begin by saying that I am profoundly grateful to you for your faithful love, your care for me, for our children, our home. And also this - that my affection from the day of our marriage until to-day has never weakened, but constantly grown deeper. Will you believe me when I tell you this?"

Lucia nodded mutely. But I saw the shadow passing over her pretty, placid countenance and the frown contracting the white, still youthful brow.

"If you have ever loved me and believed in me, I now call upon this love and this faith. Does not love signify to desire the happiness of the loved one and faith to believe that he himself can best know and judge of this happiness??"

"Well?" said Lucia. "Where are you leading to?"

"Would it be possible for you to believe that it detracts nothing from a great affection, nothing, nothing, to have a still greater love complement it? Yes, that the power of a very great love even strengthens and unites in us all other affections. Can you feel something of the truth of:

'True love in this differs from gold and clay

That to divide is not to take away.'"

Frederik van Eeden

Lucia bowed her head and stared fixedly at her hands, which she clasped together convulsively. The frown was deeper and a bitter expression settled around her pretty mouth. Then she whispered hoarsely:

"Who is it?"

Now once and for all I saw the hopelessness of my endeavor. But I went on.

"First contemplate generalities, Lucia, and from those judge the particular. Do you know the truth which I indicated? Do you disagree with any one of the general facts that I cited?"

But she followed the train of her thoughts:

"Is it Countess Thorn?"

This was a well-known, mundane beauty who, it was said, had come to live at The Hague on my account.

"What motive have you, Lucia, for being anxious to know the person that gives me so much happiness? You care for me, don't you? What feelings should one cherish toward some one who makes a beloved person happy and does him good beyond measure?"

Lucia laughed, a short, scornful laugh of contempt. She glanced at me swiftly and furtively.

"Come, Vico, make an end now with these miserable sophisms. I always thought that you were better than other men. But I knew that this was hanging over my head just as it threatens every woman. That you disappoint me so now, you, that is terrible enough. But don't make it worse by foolish self-deception of this sort and by childish nonsense, as though I ought to be thankful to her who has destroyed my domestic happiness. That only makes you sink still deeper in my esteem."

Only then I really felt the absolute impossibility of what I had attempted. But I did not regret it and I resolved resolutely to persist. It was essential to the clearing of my life from falsehood at which I had so hopefully begun. I did not answer directly, and she went on.

"I appreciate it, Vico, that you immediately speak to me about it. That is what I expected of you as a gentleman. But then do speak openly and loyally too, without these wretched sophistries. Tell me what I have a right to know. Tell me who it is. Let me know what I have to hope and to fear. Tell me ? how bad it is. Say it as directly as possible, so that I may know whether it is but a passing infatuation or ... worse. That I may know what awaits us - we ... and our children."

At these last words her voice began to tremble and the tears came.

Falteringly, in my anxiety to be well understood, I continued:

"It is wholly unlike a passing infatuation. If you call the reverse of this 'bad,' then it is as bad as you can possibly imagine, or worse ?"

"0 Lord!" Lucia sobbed into her handkerchief. "Who is it then? Who? ? Do I know her?

"No! You don't know her at all."

"Not?" she pronounced this with great astonishment. "Does she live at The Hague? Have you known her long? Is she a person of rank?"

"She does not live at The Hague, Lucia, but in a little provincial town of Holland. I have known her only a very short time. Her rank is housekeeper in a hotel - thus no rank."

Lucia looked up, surprise and relief on her tearful countenance.

"0 Vico! is it that? But then ?" She paused, reflected, shook her head. And then again: "How is it possible? ? What unhappy creatures men are! Is she young and pretty?" . . .

Drily and coolly I answered:

"I could say neither one nor the other exactly. I don't believe that you would think her pretty, but I do think she is quite young."

"Haven't I been a good wife to you, then, Vico? Wherein did I fall short?"

"In nothing, dear Lucia; you have been a good and excellent wife to me. I appreciate it, and am grateful for it. I tried also to be a good husband to you."

"That you have been too, Vico. Until now I have had nothing to reproach you for. And we were just so happy. Vittoria was to make her début this winter. Guido is entirely well again. Oh! that this should never fail to happen! How alike all men are in that respect."

"Forgive me, Lucia, I realize that you have much to forgive. But I was not happy. I feigned happiness for your sake."

"And what was it you missed? Was I not enough for you? Must a man then have always fresh excitement? Am I growing too old?"

"No, dear Lucia, it is nothing of all that. It isn't that by any means. But I see no possibility of making you understand it. I was spiritually unhappy and often longed for death. I wanted something that you could not give me."

"Poor man, but why didn't you speak sooner? Why didn't you warn me?"

"Because it would have been useless."

"Why? Tell me what you missed. Let me try to give you what you long for. I will do what I can for you. What is it? What has this ? other that I should not be able to give? Can I not prevent you from sinking so deeply? Can I not save you from this sin? It is only two weeks you say that you have known her - can it be that in so short a time you should be so irretrievably lost? Let me help you."

Deeply pathetic was the expression of eager helplessness with which she gazed at me beseechingly. And deeper my hopelessness of making her understand what had happened.

"I not only have known her but a very short time, Lucia, but have even only spoken to her twice, and never touched her - except her hand. And yet ?"

"What!" said Lucia, with vehement and happy amazement. "Is it nothing more? A spirit friendship?"

"A spirit love, I would rather say."

"With a hotel maid? I believe you, Vico; you do not lie. I know you as a man of honor. Men have such phantasies. And ? and ?" with whispered emphasis and wide, searching eyes:

"will it remain so?"

"No, Lucia, I don't want to deceive you. It certainly will not remain so."

Then she rose and walked about the room in violent emotion.

"Oh, but my God, Vico, what possesses you? You are contemplating the greatest wrong, the deepest offence to me, the disgrace of your family, the eternal ruin of your soul - you can easily turn back, nothing yet is lost, and you don't want to! You don't want to! Is this woman a witch then? An enchantress? Oh, now I know that you have no religion! Now I see what it is to have no religion."

I did not answer, and in my mind I compared the two spirit-worlds that here confronted one another, weighing the one against the other. And there is none who reads this and has read the preceding chapter, not even you, dear reader of original mind, but shall waver on this subtle boundary line. And yet in his heart he shall have to choose and range himself on one side or the other. For we human beings may proudly raise ourselves above good and evil, saying that no sin may be accounted as guilt to our frail short-sighted nature - the choice, the terrible irrevocable choice, with every irrevocable second, is not spared us, and must be made.

My choice was made. I no longer wavered, but I pondered on the awful power that forces us to choose where we can yet distinguish so poorly, that relentlessly pushes us on into the dense fog with its dimly gleaming lights.

Lucia however interpreted my silence as irresolution, and with the exertion of all her powers she attempted a desperate attack upon my heart. She threw herself down on her knees before me, sobbing and crying and kissing my hands. She begged and implored me to have pity, if not with her then at least with the children and with myself.

Then I said:

"Dear Lucia, no more than you have the power to change day into night for me or night into day, no more can you make me call the light that I see darkness or deter me from following it. I can only leave you this choice: do you wish me to deceive you, or would you have me be upright? In the latter case you must control yourself, for the more I see you suffer, the stronger grows the temptation not to be upright toward you."

It was even more the tone in which I uttered them than perhaps my words that made her realize that she had nothing more to hope for.

She got up and dried her tears. Then recovering herself, she said:

"I see, Vico, that a Satanic charm has been cast upon you. Of course I desire your uprightness. I shall endeavor to bear everything and to make the best of it and I shall pray for you."

"Thank you, Lucia," said I, rising.

But she came and stood in front of me.

"Yes, but . . . what now?"

"What do you mean?" I asked, not entering sufficiently into her thought-life.

"You now put me into a position which I have known only from hearsay and never thought myself to experience. Thousands of women live in this position, that I know. But you will surely have so much consideration for me, that you will spare me as much as possible. That after all I may duly claim from you."

"Of course, Lucia, I shall spare you as much as possible."

"I do not ask it for myself, but for our children. You will respect my good name, won't you? You won't bring public disgrace upon us? You won't drag the honor of our family, the name of our children into the streets?"

The intuitive tactics of a woman are like those of a shrewd and careful general, who saves his best troops until the battle seems almost lost. I felt that now she had declared herself ready to yield in the main point, I could refuse her no concession.

"What do you demand of me, Lucia?"

"That all this remains a secret between us. That you avoid all public scandal. That before the world our household remains as it was."

I could not suppress a slightly disdainful smile.

"So you would withhold my uprightness, which for yourself you so greatly desire, from the world?"

"Oh, Vico, you will promise me that. You do care for us, don't you?"

"Of course I do."

"And you are sensible of your obligations toward your family. Even the most corrupt man is sensible of those."

"I too am sensible of them, Lucia."

"And you do recognize that you have wronged me."

"That I have, Lucia - not now, but before this."

"But then you surely want to make some amends, to somewhat mitigate the blow - when it's so easy to do it. See I shall leave you absolutely free. I shall not question you, not pry, not even make an allusion. But do you then spare our family too. That is all I ask. Spare our children this disgrace."

I was not prepared, and it is not easy when taking a critical step in life to go just far enough and with neither half-heartedness nor exaggeration. Therefore my answer was weak.

"Very well, dear friend," said I. "I shall as far as possible take account of your desires."

Then we wished each other a good night, well knowing that we had pronounced an idle wish.

XXIV

It was not a strict and definite promise I had given. But still it was a yielding from tender-heartedness that I deplore, though without self-reproach. He who chooses the high, unbeaten tracks should have overcome all tender-heartedness that leads to half measures. What is counted as virtue in the faithful member of the herd, is vice in the seceder. But I knew, how immediately beyond the safe confederacy of the group, skulked the wolf of fanaticism. I knew how difficult it is to keep one's balance upon the steep, lonely paths of originality, how easily the pathfinder, overwhelmed by the giddy sense of unbounded freedom, falls down into gulfs of fanaticism, hysteria, bigotry and madness.

Who shall always know how to find the exact medium between bold consistency and reckless extravagance?

The tendency toward self-sacrifice is an instinct, like all others, beautiful and useful when it remains in harmony with all our other instincts, and helps along in the common battle for Christ, who has given them to us. But this instinct can be perverted and run wild into asceticism and a passion for self-mortification, as hunger into gluttony and thirst into drunkenness.

I knew that heroic consistency must lead me to unite myself

openly with the being who had re-awakened in me the highest, holiest and most blessed emotions - and this meant declaring an open feud against society. For without doubt I should have the whole world against me, my own children included. I should lose my position, be expelled from my circle. I should have to brave poverty too. My mother was still living and I myself had nothing save the high salary which I would lose. And to live on Lucia or my mother remained absolutely beyond consideration.

I did not fear all this so much for itself, as for the danger of fanatic self-torture I saw in it. For above all, in the arbitrary breaking of the bonds between myself and my children there lay a refined torture, and I also knew that Lucia's suffering would not let me rest a day, no matter how firm my conviction might be that I had done right. I should feel remorse just as well then as I should if I did not do what I deemed right. Two consciences would always be at war in me, whether I turned to the right or to the left.

And then - what would my conflict with the world signify, powerless as I was? Should I convince anyone by my action that it is right to break a mock union, to clear an untrue life, to assert our true sentiments and feelings, to pursue the things eternal and the pure blessedness, and to remain true to Christ in the face of the world?

It would merely be said: "There's another fallen into the bog," and I should disappear like a stone in the mire.

I do not want to excuse; I only want to explain. To make it clear how it was possible that I, after this first vigorous wrench at my fetters, nevertheless for many years still led an irresolute double life, apparently the same happy pater-familias and prosperous man of the world, hiding my real, true life in the little seaport town and restricting it to the hours that I spent together with her, who had awakened it and who kept it alive.

When I went to get my boat and was starting the night before for E—, my son Guido, a sport-loving youngster of fourteen, asked whether he might accompany me. In my sense of guiltlessness I would perhaps have raised no objection, but his mother immediately interposed, with quick intuition guessing at the object of my journey and by a clever pretence thwarted his plan.

Elsje was awaiting me at the station and we had a long conversation, in which I for the first time experienced what a blessing it is to be able to give oneself freely, to show oneself as one likes best to be, to hold back nothing for fear of being misunderstood, even though one expresses oneself as always, with but the same limited means, toward a human being having the same limited comprehensive faculty as all men. For here was the infinite love with its magic interpretive power, that completes the defective, and from a few faltering phrases is able to erect a lofty structure of sympathy and understanding, because the beautiful plan in both speaker and listener has from the very beginning been designed by a higher wisdom, and no intellectual material is made use of and applied but must be in harmony with this fixed plan.

"I have spoken about us at home, Elsje."

"With whom?"

"With her whom the world calls my wife, the mother of my children."

"What is her name?"

"Lucia."

After I had spoken this, I have nevertheless quite frequently forgotten myself and spoken of "my wife." But Elsje never, not a single time.

"What did you say about me?"

"May I tell you quite frankly, Elsje? And will you tell me just as frankly whether what I said was right?"

"Yes," said Elsje, shyly and softly.

"I said that I had met a woman of whom, at first sight and after two brief encounters, I could say that she would give me the great love which was still wanting in my life. Was that rightly said, Elsje?"

"Yes," I heard a whisper beside me. Arm in arm we wandered through the dark lonely streets of the little town which was going to rest. The confidential pressure of her arm in mine was a never experienced joy.

"It was not quite understood, Elsje. It was taken for self-delusion and the entire case treated as a common gallant adventure. That's not surprising and it will appear that way to everyone. We must resign ourselves to that."

"Of course!" said Elsje.

"But I had a difficult half hour, for Lucia begged me not to see you again."

"Poor Lucia - does she care for you very much?"

"Certainly - and I told her that nothing was taken away from my affection for her. But she wouldn't hear of that -"

"Of course!" said Elsje again. "I shouldn't accept that either. Why should she?"

"Look, look," thought I smilingly; "even the rivals among women yet ever conspire together."

"I thought it might be a consolation. But I seem to be mistaken in that. I remained firm, though I told her that nothing would hold me back from Elsje."

"Oh, if I am only worthy of it! If only I am worthy of it!"

"That is fear of responsibility, Elsje. That we both have. But it is a weakness."

"And did Lucia yield?"

"She first asked whether it could remain a spirit friendship. I refused to promise that." Elsie remained silent.

"Do you think that was right, Elsie?"

She nodded.

"Then she yielded, but on one condition."

"What?"

"That before the world I would remain her husband. That everything would be secret."

"Oh!" cried Elsie vehemently with anger and surprise. "Then she never really cared for you either. Never!" And then indignantly: "You didn't promise that though, did you?"

There I stood, poor sinner, and hadn't a word to say. And I felt while seeking to defend myself that by nature a man always remains a sophist.

"Dear Elsie! remember that this consideration for a proud woman like Lucia is of much greater import than the sacrifice for us. Consider how much I have grieved her. Consider how few women would so nobly forgive this to their husbands. Consider that after all the past makes it my duty to care for her and my children. Disgrace is a very dreadful thing for them, something much more dreadful than you can probably comprehend."

"I consider just that a disgrace," said Elsie, illogically, but to the point, "to want to keep up a lie before the world."

"Consider then, Elsie, what it would mean for me. I should not see my children again. They would not want to recognize me. I should bring a terrible sorrow upon them, and I am very fond of them."

"Would none of them try to understand it, to forgive it?" asked Elsie.

"Not one of them, I fear. Even were it only on account of their mother, whom they adore. And remember that, beside my children, I should also lose my position. My wife ? I mean Lucia is wealthy, but I am not ?"

"Would your health suffer if you were poorer?" asked Elsie, with naive directness and perfect sobriety, though the question almost sounded ironical to me. In a very impolitic fashion I had again reserved my weakest argument for the last.

"Not that! Not that! ? but perhaps I am too much spoilt ? I

should have the whole world against me ? and I don't know if all that ?"

I felt that I was going wrong, thus I would end by myself casting a doubt upon the self-sacrificing power of my love. Elsie helped me out of it.

"May I now speak quite frankly with you too? Yes? Then listen! I am so dazed, so overwhelmed by the greatness of that which I receive from you, so suddenly and so bewilderingly, that you must not expect me at once to judge rightly. It seems ridiculous to me that I should not be satisfied with the least that you would offer me, now that I am getting so infinitely much more than I ever could have hoped for or expected. Though I never saw you again after this night, yet I should be eternally grateful to you. But forgive me if in your difficulty I judge too much according to my own feelings. Your grief for your children - that I can comprehend. But all the rest I don't understand; it is strange to me, contrary to my nature. Of the world and of the money I should not think - I don't know these things and have not experienced their power. I only know that I should like to be with you always and should like to confess it openly before all the world. And if I were in Lucia's place, and really cared for you, I wouldn't want for one moment to bind you, cost what it would to me. I shouldn't be able to bear it, that you lived beside me and were looked upon as my husband and secretly cared for another, I should think that much more terrible than all the sorrows of a divorce."

"Lucia would never agree to a divorce. That is a matter of religion with her. A Catholic marriage is indissoluble."

"And are you, yourself, also a Catholic, devoutly Catholic?"

"Lucia says that I have no religion whatever."

Elsje looked at me anxiously.

"Is that so? And I had just hoped to learn so much from you concerning that. It occupies me all day long. Even now I have a hundred questions ready, for you. I had put all my trust in you."

"In what faith were you brought up, Elsie?

"Brought up? I wasn't brought up. I must make another confession to you?"

I saw that she hesitated and was troubled. I began to fear some unpleasant secret or other.

"Speak without fear, Elsie. It is safe with me. Trust me."

"That I would like to, but see, I know you are a distinguished man of noble birth."

"That signifies nothing, Elsje - I am not so proud of that."

I was joking, but she understood me.

"No, you are not proud, but still you have assurance. That I have not. Do you know how I got my name?"

"Well?"

"They called me Van Vianen, became I was found near Vianen. I have no parents."

She said this deeply humiliated and ashamed. And in my heart I laughed, because now after all she too showed herself apprehensive of the voice of the herd, and because she felt as a disgrace, the very thing that, as an aureole of romance, had delighted me.

"Oh, is it only that!" I cried; "that I already knew. All week I have thought of the poor, dear little one as crying, it was laid down upon the grass by a desperate mother. Likely it was a royal child, Elsje!"

Elsie laughed, reassured and happy.

"They let me become a Mennonite. Not Jan Baars, but his sister who took me into her home as a child."

"Ah! Mennonite!" said I. I hadn't the slightest idea what theological, ethical and ritual peculiarities were attached to this creed. I only knew that it must be one of the innumerable variations or sects of Protestantism.

"To be sure it's a good custom of the Mennonites that they don't baptize you as a child, when you don't yet know whether you would rather be a Roman Catholic or an Israelite, but later, when you are confirmed and can yourself choose. But look! when I was eighteen I knew just as little what to choose. And now I don't know yet."

"And still you let yourself be baptized?"

"Why yes, there was surely no wrong in that. But if they would have you choose well they would first have to let you serve an apprenticeship with the Romans, then another with the Protestants, then another with the Jews and then with the Mohammedans?"

"Not to mention the Hindus, the Buddhists and the Shintoists," said I.

"So that you would need seven lives before you could let

yourself be baptized, isn't it so? And yet it is so necessary, so very, very necessary that you choose the right thing, isn't it? I never can understand how all people just live on carelessly, and all believing something different, and never consider that they might perhaps be wrong, and how terrible that would be. They simply assume, and only feign assurance, and you never hear them talk of it, so they probably do not break their hearts about it. And if you were to believe them, then everyone who thinks differently than they is a miserable wretch. But they all think differently, and so one or the other must be wrong, and yet they are all equally certain and assured. How is that possible now? Why it's absurd!"

I thought it was already a great deal for Elsie, in her solitude, to have arrived at the realization of this absurdity. Then I threw out my sounding-line -

"What do you think of Christ, Elsie?"

"I love best to read of Jesus; I think it wonderful to read - especially toward Christmas time - how he came on earth as a little child, and about the star and the shepherds. When I think of Jesus, I always think of him as a little child with Mary his Mother. I should like to have a picture or an image of them, but that's considered Catholic. Do you know more of Jesus and can you tell me all about him?"

"I asked about Christ, Elsie."

"Isn't that the same?"

"They are all only names from which we can choose. I prefer to say Christ, because I don't believe that there lived a man called Jesus who was Christ. But I do positively know that there is something that all men call Christ, and that lives and knows and loves us. And this Christ they already knew long before Jesus is said to have lived. I have seen images of the Mother with the child exactly like the one you would like to have, and it was thousands of years older than Jesus and made by the Egyptians, and instead of Mary and the Christ Child they spoke of Isis and the Horus Child, and the Chinese too made such images."

"And what do they mean by it?"

"Ordinary people mean a holy mother with a holy child, a saviour. But the few wiser ones probably mean the earth mother and the child humanity. I at least presume it, and when men now speak of Christ, then I believe, Elsje, that the most and the best, those who really mean something by the word, something real that they have felt - that they mean something that is equivalent to humanity."

"Humanity? that means nothing to me. Jesus for me is a living, beloved and loving being, who helps and supports me, an exalted, holy being. Humanity - that is nothing to me, an empty word."

"Right, Elsje, I readily believe it. But empty words can be filled with knowledge. There are learned professors to whom the word Jesus or Christ is entirely hollow or empty. But the word humanity implies for them a real and well-known thing, the entire human race which in its development and growth, in its expression and forms of life they have studied minutely. These professors again would be able to fill the word Christ with the exalted and tender feelings which it arouses in Elsje, if they had learned to feel like Elsje. And now it is my personal opinion with which, so far as I know, I stand quite alone in the world, that Elsje and the professors, were they to compare one another's observations, would come to realize that it is precisely the same real being that fills the word Christ and the word Humanity: the religious word Christ and the biological, scientific word Humanity."

"But humanity - that is not a being, not a personality ? that is a lot of people. People that I don't know. How can I care about them and how can they care about me?"

"A tree, Elsje, is a lot of roots, branches and leaves. Yet we call it a tree. A swarm of bees are a lot of bees, and yet one swarm. You cannot discern humanity because you cannot see all people at the same time, and not how they are connected. But I don't believe either that one leaf can see the whole tree or one bee the whole swarm.

"But humanity is yet a great deal more than all men together, just as the tree is more than all the leaves. And humanity is after all perceived by Elsje in her own heart - all humanity. That is thus much more even than the professors can discern of it, and why should it not be a personal, thinking, loving being? It is that, I think, that Elsje means when she speaks of her exalted Jesus, and it is that I prefer to call Christ, because I like that name best."

"I am such a stupid, ignorant creature, and you are so learned. Forgive me if I still find it somewhat too difficult."

"Of course, dear Elsje, you find it difficult, because you do not know what the professors have observed concerning man and the human race. But really, the professors would find what I said equally difficult and incomprehensible, because they don't know - at least most of them do not - what Elsje has observed concerning Christ. Only they would not be as modest as you are; they would not recognize that it is their ignorance. And I am no professor and no Elsje, but I stand sort of between the two and know something of the observations of both, and I know quite positively and see quite plainly that they both mean the same thing and that they require each other's knowledge."

"So you do know my Jesus, my Christ too, thank God!"

"Yes, though perhaps not as well as Elsje, yet better than the professors. And I believe that it was this Christ who brought me to Elsje so that I should learn to know him better, - and perhaps should better testify of him. And through him too I gained courage and steadfastness to remain true to Elsje, and not to give up, though the whole world stand against me."

Here the woman found good opportunity for bringing the man from his world of speculation back to practical life.

"But does not Jesus, or Christ, want you to do it openly, before all the world?"

"I don't know ? I don't know, Elsje. His promptings and suggestions as they proceed clearly from out the original fount are by no means always equally positive and distinct. But I assure you - I would swear it to you, had I not vowed once for all never to swear again - that I shall stop at nothing and spare nothing as soon as his light shall shine clearly and unmistakably for me."

"We Mennonites may never swear either," said Elsje, with pretty pride in her creed, confessed with so little conviction.

"That is good, that is indeed one of the best things the Bible Jesus is said to have taught. Therefore it is surely followed least of all. I not only swear no more - I even dare not promise you anything, for I know myself too little to foretell my future actions."

"You do not promise to be true to me?" asked Elsje with mild disappointment.

"I do better, I assure you of profound love. So profound that I do surely believe it will be true. But what would my faithfulness be to you if love grew weaker? It would become a lie, a feint, wouldn't it?"

"I shall be thankful for all that I get," said Elsje, "and never ask for more than you wish to give me."

I had to laugh when I thought what my acquaintances from the diplomatic world - friends I do not call them, I never had a friend among them - what they would say of a gallant adventure with so much theology at the third meeting.

But you, dear reader, will probably long have comprehended that I draw from the same reservoir, what others keep separated in water and air-tight compartments, and that theology, science, poetry and love to me are not only brothers and sisters, but often merely names and masks for one and the same inward reality. So that you will no doubt allow me to tell yet a few more things that in my amorous theologizing with Elsje, I learned and taught.

You will also probably understand without my remarking it that I did not speak in quite as fluent and succinct Dutch as I have here written down. But I could make myself understood just as well as if it had been thus spoken, because Love served as our interpreter.

XXV

I will not yet decide whether it was prudent discreation or rather, fearful and narrow-minded timidity, that deterred me from the great resolve of abandoning my family and my sphere of activity, to alone remain true to Elsje. It was for many years a hard and fearful struggle. It was indeed the hardest period of my life, albeit not the darkest. The gloom and dejection this most feared evil, marked by the relaxing of the highest vital spirits, dread warning of the powers that guide and rule us - this evil had vanished. I struggled and suffered, but was no longer miserable and wretched. Only I did not see my way clearly and vainly sought for help and guidance.

The wicked charms and temptations also were dispelled. I desired one woman - without faltering, without shame. I knew what my desire signified, and all my soul pronounced it right. To be sure the demons still carried on their nocturnal sport, but I minded them no more than barking terriers, and the wild passions were now tamed because the hand of the master had grown firm and he knew what he wanted.

My dreams attained their former sublime splendor, and for the first time in my life I had some one to whom I could confide them. I still saw Emmy in my dreams occasionally, but not so often, and it will surprise no one to hear that it did not excite Elsje's jealousy, and that she begged me to tell her of her. Elsje also asked me whether I would call herself once more. And I did it and saw her, and Elsje hoped devoutly that she would be in some way sensible of it.

But greatly as I should have desired it, and much more impressive and more convincing as it would have been for her and for you, dear reader, the truth is that she never noticed anything of it, or rather, to be exact, that she never remembered anything about it.

I for my part did not require such evidence. I have obtained stronger evidence through strangers, who let me know without my ever having told them anything about my dreams, that my summons had been heard - but all this belongs to the science of the supernatural, which awaits more general investigation and for which, dear reader, I refer you to some of my other writings.

I now lived separated from Lucia, although before the world our relations remained the same. And a most remarkable and peculiar fact is that Lucia assured me that her dreams were much more tranquil, since I no longer shared her room. The wild horses that lately had troubled her in her dreams more than ever, now stayed away. I consider this remarkable, because it seems to show how corporal proximity also affects supernatural influences.

One thing I had fully resolved on, and this was - that I would never abandon Elsje for good. And as often befalls the man in doubting attitude, I expected relief from destiny. Should fate threaten to tear her from me, then I would offer resistance and stay with her, no matter what the price. Should that which everyone in the diplomatic service may expect, befall me - sudden transference to another country - I would then deem the moment arrived to free myself entirely and for good. I know this attitude too was a weakness, but who does not see clearly must remain weak, and it is of no avail that he feign strength and act as though he were quite capable of distinguishing. And with our human tendency to argue that our own conduct is right, I consoled myself with the consideration that my children were still too young and still too much in need of my guidance.

Often too I prayed in my dreams, imploring counsel and enlightenment. But my experience is that sign or counsel is never accorded us before we ourselves have decided or acted, or before the approaching event has already been determined without our help and knowledge. We are never helped in a choice, though we are comforted and encouraged after we have chosen to the best of our knowledge. Many times this seemed cruel and unreasonable to me, but I am inclined to believe in the beneficent and salutary significance of it.

The secrecy toward the world, so much desired by Lucia, soon however assumed an altogether different, unfavorable and undesirable aspect. My frequent trips to E—, though explained by my passion for sailing, could not fail to arouse comment, especially as I usually went alone and also declined the company of my son Guido, no matter how often he asked. And E—is a favorite port for sailing yachts, ten or twelve of them sometimes landing there at the same time on fine summer days. Thus my acquaintances from The Hague, the men in the first place, very soon knew what attracted me to the little seaport. This by no means aroused any great agitation or indignation in Hague circles, as everyone acquainted with these and similar circles will readily understand.

I was looked upon as a very moral and honorable man, simply because I did not mix up in scandal and never spoke of things of that kind, whether they concerned myself or others. It now caused many a one satisfaction that the halo of chastity which, despite a total absence of display or moralizing toward others, yet by its mutely reproaching presence is ever in painful evidence, - that this unpleasantly spotless reputation was now fittingly and modestly obscured. I was almost congratulated upon it. No one thought of judging hardly of such a thing or of pitying Lucia on that account. She, herself, heard nothing of these rumors and lived in the illusion that everything retained its former aspect. I believe I was praised - behind my back, of course, not to my face - because I had had the decency to seek my diversion so far from the vicinity, and not, as more shameless ones, in The Hague or Amsterdam. As long as I did not arouse publicity or scandal, I could do what I wished; these were my private affairs. And Lucia and the gentlemen of my set seemed to agree in this - that it was worse to bring publicity upon a woman than to deceive her. The herd only resents any assault upon the unity of the group - for the rest it permits everything.

For me this was a twofold torture. Instead of one deceit I was now practising two. I was honoring a mock union and I was permitting a true union to be suspected and profaned. I felt myself locked in an intolerable fashion between two falsehoods. What as a tender secret I had wished to hide from the world to spare Lucia, the world had soon discovered. And yet it spared Lucia and myself, at the cost of this same tender secret, which it looked upon as an infamy: an infamy of the kind from which I had just felt with pride that I had freed myself. It was all equally unbearable to me, the friendly, sarcastic generosity of the world that spared me and acted as though forgiving me a sin, where I felt virtue beyond its comprehension; and the condemnation of Elsje, to which I was now most painfully sensitive, though it went out from this same unintelligent herd.

Frederik van Eeden

As often as I saw Elsje again, I read in her look of anxious suspense the question whether I had now at last taken the great resolve. But only her dear eyes asked, and her pale little face, her lips remained shut. She did not question me about my family either. She waited until I should speak. We spoke of our love and of everything that was nearest our hearts, of the difficulties of life, why we had to toil and struggle so and bear affliction, of the great world full of men and what would grow from it, of my dreams, of the best and most beautiful that we could experience and of the way we could conquer the difficulties and attain the purest blessedness. And we spoke a great deal of Christ, groping and seeking in the dawning truths, trying to help and to understand each other. And at every parting I felt again that something had remained unspoken, whereof she would yet have heard so gladly. And never did I leave her without a sense of the blessing that I had her, and without a heavy heart because I must let her wait and suffer.

For she suffered, she suffered as only pure, tender womanly natures made for love can suffer. And by degrees I could not hide from myself that she suffered more than she could bear. The power of endurance of a pure, delicate soul like hers is infinite as long as in the kernel of her being, in her love life, she is satisfied and contented. But the sorrow that touches the kernel consumes her both body and soul.

Remorse is a bad thing, a weakness, a morbid symptom. I permit no remorse in myself, for I know that it harms and weakens the best that is in us. But against the self-reproach which is the punishment for these years of wavering, I struggle in vain. It is always there, like a dark demon, silently awaiting its favorable opportunity in the third or fourth hour of the night, when sleep evades me - then it sits upon my breast and questions and awaits my answer: - why I let her mutely ask and ask so long and wait for an answer, till the bright eyes sank deeper into their darker growing hollows, and the red blood had gone from the fresh cheeks, and the delicate nose became so thin, and the soft lips so colorless?

And in my luxurious home everything continued as of old: the children healthy and happy: Lucia the housewife correct and diligent as ever, not unfriendly toward me, without sign of spiritual suffering, amiable and hearty.

Pardon an old man, dear reader, if he spares himself and does not expatiate on these anxious years. He is not a friend of tears and does not like to give in to melancholy.

One night the end of the struggle was at last proclaimed to me. I dreamt I was walking in the park at The Hague and saw an old man sitting with an opened letter in his hand. I comprehended that the letter was for me and saw my name and title on the envelope too. But the old man said, "This is not for you!" and I understood that he meant that I no longer had a title. Then I saw too that it was a large official document from Rome, and I knew that the long-expected transferal had come. Thereupon I dreamt that I was fleeing with Elsje and that I carried her across a great plain of ice. The ice cracked under my feet and every crack was a snapping spark of bluish fire like a flash of lightning. This betokened ill, but Elsje was not afraid.

The letter of which I had dreamed came a few weeks later. But it was the same. I recognized the envelope. I also knew positively what the contents would be, and I felt a glorious sense of relief, and a "Thank God" escaped my lips.

Lucia had also seen the letter and it now appeared that she had awaited it with equal longing. Her face was bright.

Frederik van Eeden

I had never wanted to ask the ambassador for transferal, detained by the thought that I should be deceiving him by doing so, but I had a suspicion that Lucia was secretly exerting herself in my behalf. She too expected relief from it, but in another sense.

"From Rome," she said. "That seems something good to me. Just look, quickly!"

"It seems something good to me too," I replied; my hand trembled and my heart beat.

"Where?" asked Lucia, the while I read.

"Stockholm," I replied, "with advancement."

"Thank Heaven!" said Lucia; "then the wretched story here is ended."

I looked at her a while severely and gravely, so that her bright look darkened and a shadow of anxiety fell upon her face.

"The story here is not ended, Lucia, but has reached a turning point. I am not going."

"That's impossible," she cried out; "you can't refuse."

"No! but I can hand in my resignation."

"Your resignation - and then??"

"Remain in Holland."

"In Holland? And without a salary? Live on my money? And continue this liaison? No, Vico, that you can't demand of me, that is too much."

"Lucia, there is something else I want to demand of you."

"And that is?

"That you release me. That you allow me to put an end to this falsehood. The world takes us for man and wife and we are not?"

"Release you? Don't I grant you as much freedom as I can? And are you not still the father of my children? The head of the house?"

"I have a wife, Lucia, who is really my wife and whom I want to make my wife before the world. I ask you whether you will give me the opportunity to do this by dissolving our marriage."

Then her Italian temperament revealed itself in all its intensity. She spoke with rage and animosity upon her face, and with vehement and dramatic gestures, as I had never seen her before.

"Give you opportunity? Opportunity to break what God cannot break? Are you crazy, Vico? How many women would do what I did - pardon and bear the deadly offence? Would you now cast me off still further and humble me yet more? Would you have me give up my rights for an ordinary bourgeois woman, whom another would long ago have poisoned? Should I yet abet her and you in the wrong you are doing me and the disgrace you are bringing upon me and upon my children? - Go, Vico, and don't provoke me, for I still love you and should be capable of murdering you. - I have borne this because I pitied you and hoped that you would soon have enough of it and come back to me. - But now that on top of it all you do this, now I shall yield nothing more, nothing. A marriage cannot be dissolved. - Off with you, man, - you are crazy or drunk. That can be your only excuse."

"I go, Lucia, - but understand me well, I am going for good. You will not see me again."

"Are you going to her? And what shall you live on?"

"I don't know. Surely not on your money."

"And the children?"

"I shall gladly see the children if they will see me. But they won't, you will surely see to that."

"I'll see to it. You shan't see them. Poor children!"

"Be good to them, Lucia, and advise them to get entangled in lies as little as possible. For some people it is distressing. Others are better able to cope with it. Good-bye! So we need not hope for a reconciliation or an agreement between us, need we?"

"Never! I swear it by God and by my innocent children."

"I do not swear, but you need not fear that I shall make any further attempts. I shall demand leave of absence this very day and hand in my resignation. We shall probably not see each other again. Forgive me if I have grieved you. I intended no ill."

A sarcastic laugh -

"Oh, come! intended no ill! Say that to Satan when you stand before the everlasting fire. If you want to go, then, go right off too. - And God have mercy on your soul."

Then I thought it time to end the torture. I packed up some clothes, regulated my affairs at the legation and was in E— that same afternoon. I had wired: "I am coming for good." And, sobbing and laughing, Elsje embraced me at the station before the eyes of the officials. It was the first time in public.

"There is as much reason for crying as for laughing, Elsje!" said I. "I haven't brought along much money."

"Oh, we need so little and I can manage so well. And you are so good and so clever, you will surely be able to earn money again."

"And we cannot be lawfully married either. Lucia will never give in to that."

"That's nothing," said Elsje, "if only the world may know of it. The ceremony we can well dispense with. Now you shall see how well I shall grow, and how strong."

XXVI

My mother was still alive and was living in Italy. I wrote her a letter, earnest and upright, to inform her of what had happened. This was one of the things I did to establish my position, to make it final, without myself believing in the success of my action. The answer was such that I had to hide it from Elsje, and shall also refrain from repeating it here. There is something awful in seeing persons whom one has known and loved as tender-hearted human beings grow hard in age. And for me there was something still more awful in the chief reproach contained in my mother's letter - that I, her only son, for whom she would have sacrificed her life, and who should have been the support of her declining years, now poisoned her life and made her old age lonely and miserable. Of Elsje she spoke with scornful, malicious contempt, as of an immoral, shameless monster, a she-devil who had beguiled me with sensual charms and had wantonly destroyed my domestic happiness. And this I had to hear from my mother, who so long had been my saint! I realized that we were lost for one another.

I had taken lodgings in "de Toelast," from there to regulate my position as far as was practicable, and to effect the rupture with my superiors and the entire sphere of my activities as correctly as possible.

I had been an active, helpful worker, and what made me popular everywhere - harmless, impersonal, without any unpleasantly obtrusive originality in actions or opinions. In the diplomatic world above all, a vigorous originality is quite intolerable unless it manifest itself in a ruling personality. And even then this personality must not raise his aspirations too far above the average of the masses. That is to say, the aspirations which he manifests in his actions - his private thoughts may, if he be but a strong ruler, wander where they would, upward or downward. Just because I was more original in my private thoughts than any of my compatriots, there was absolutely no possibility of turning these into aspirations of practical account, and thus in practice I remained an efficient aid esteemed by all and feared by none. My sudden breaking away was looked upon as a lapse, and I was in fact more pitied than scorned. I was said to have fallen prey to an ambitious, selfish woman, as indeed sometimes happened to the best of men.

I received many kindly admonishing and gravely moralizing letters from my chiefs and from former compatriots. I saw that they did not like to lose so efficient a power. They even organized noble endeavors for the saving of the poor drowning man. But I remained obdurate and would not let myself be saved and even concealed myself from all callers, faithfully assisted therein by Jan Baars, whose good Dutch qualities beneath his apparent unpleasantness I learned to respect. Jan Baars was the touchstone so to speak, the training that taught me to tolerate a Dutch environment. Without the schooling of Jan Baars I could not have endured my present life. He was a boor, a dolt, a dirty lout, a narrow-minded churl, but he did all sorts of kind and generous things. Once convinced of the fact that my intentions toward Elsje were honorable, he stood by us through thick and thin, and did not trouble himself about conventions, nor about gossip, nor about the minister, nor about the burgomaster, nor about the baker and his customers. And I have later noticed that a Dutch provincial world is not as dangerous by far as it is sometimes pictured in novels or comedies. In the beginning there is a buzz and hum as in a disturbed beehive. But if one goes ahead quietly and, just as the experienced beekeeper, lays hold with a firm hand, if one is not afraid and shows that one intends no wrong, the excitement and asperities subside wondrously quickly and the petty world tolerates what it contended it could never endure.

But not knowing this, I had feared a wretched life for Elsje and had made greater plans.

"Elsje!" said I, a day after my arrival, "I have wavered so long, not only because of all we must brave, but also because I did know how this rupture with my world should increase my usefulness in life. For I have perhaps achieved something, but under the direction of others, and my own will I have restrained and suppressed. For I did not have the qualities and the capacities for making my originality prevail. And I asked myself, if I now seek my personal happiness with Elsje shall I thereby be also doing some good to the world? I know, of course, that Christ calls us through the light of joy, and that we must follow the highest happiness, the brightest light; but I also knew that we can never find this for ourselves alone, for the highest happiness is universal happiness. If personal joy does not in some manner radiate over the world, it is not the highest, though it be ever so alluring to us. And I did not see how our happiness would be anything to the world. On the contrary, I saw only a dark, foul misapprehension that would arise from it. Do you understand me, Elsje?"

"I believe I do. But it seems to me it must after all always have a salutary effect, when people see that some one dares to do what he considers good and honest, no matter what it costs him."

"Yes, Elsje, but then people must also see and feel that it is for something better that he abandons the less good and beautiful. And that they don't see at all in our case. What impelled me they do not know, and so they cannot consider it good and beautiful either. They say: Poor Muralto, he has wrecked his life, he has become the victim of a woman, he could not restrain his passion, now he throws away his prospects, his happiness - some will add: his eternal blessedness - for a love caprice, an amourette. That is nothing new for the world. It happens frequently. And also that the unhappy sinner moreover deceives himself, pretending that he acts from noble motives and for a fine and righteous cause. That too is very common, for no one really sins in his own eyes, every one takes his follies for wisdom, and man understands no art better than that of deceiving himself."

"Poor, dear man!" said Elsje, now for the first time alarmed by the true realization of the world's attitude toward my act.

"And the world is usually quite right. It must cast out whoever menaces the unity of the group. For in this unity is its security, it is sacred, holy, 'taboo,' as the Polynesians say. And it cannot possibly investigate each particular case, whether the seceder is perhaps a faithful follower of Christ, a truly original spirit or simply an eccentric fool or weakling. That the seceder must himself prove In the face of the world's condemnation. Do you understand me rightly?"

"No!" said Elsje, "not quite, I believe. I don't know whether you think it good to secede or not."

"That I shall explain to you. Humanity consists of two principal kinds - of herd-men and seceders. Both, Christ has need of. The herd-men form the mighty unity through which he lives; it in his great organic body, whereof the individuals are the cells. The better they cohere, the stronger, mightier, more beautiful becomes his unity, his judgment, far exalted above our comprehension. Therefor the union of the groups in holy and good and every disturbance is met with vigorous resistance. But Christ is growing. Humanity has not yet attained its perfect growth and the union is still incomplete, defective. The tree is constantly developing new branches, bursting through the old bark, sending forth new shoots. That is the function of the single cells that burst the old union, forming the kernel of a new, better organization. Our body too has two principal kinds of cells, the corporal cells that constitute our organs, and the germinal cells from which new organisms are developed. The germinal cells in the body of Christ are the seceders, the original spirits who will no longer tolerate the union of the group and are directly called and guided by the Genius of Humanity, by Christ's own voice. But they must then also be men, with great strength and patience, designed for stern endurance and constant struggle. The world must hate them and persecute them and if possible annihilate them. For only those who can withstand this process of persecution and annihilation are the real, true seceders, elected by Christ and able to create a new and better union. Therefore it is good to be a herd-man and to respect the existing union - the existing order as it is called - if one has the strength for that and nothing more. But it is good to break this order if one feels oneself very distinctly impelled to it by the inward light of Christ, by true knowledge, by the firm consciousness of truth, and moreover knows, knows with absolute certainty, that one has the power and the abilities for enduring and struggling, for resisting the inevitable enmity of the world, for surviving her hatred and persecution, for proving indeed one's good right to secede and to be original. It is not just to denounce the world and to glorify the martyrs. Christ does not want martyrs. He wants conquering triumphant originals. The patience of the martyrs is a virtue, which he bestows on the originals, his privileged servants, but a virtue with which to conquer, not to yield. And a virtue which must not be sought for its own sake, but for the sake of the victory. The world punishes according to his deserts him, who breaking from the union has over-estimated his power to persevere and to triumph."

"Thus my dear husband will not be a martyr," said Elsje, as always practical, and keeping to the point.

"Not if he can help it. If I came before Christ with only a crown of thorns, might he not ask them: 'Where is your gospel? And what joy for my world have you bought with your anguish?' We are dealing with his goods, Elsje, with Christ's goods; our sorrow is his sorrow, our joy is his joy and we may not squander anything for nothing. Even the Jesus of the Bible-drama bought his gospel of joy too dearly. The just price for his crown of thorns has never yet been paid; the gospel is there, but the joy has yet to come. Though his kingdom is not of this world, the joy of that kingdom would also brighten this world, as soon as we could all believe in it. But no heavenly kingdom of joy shall be built of material as poor as mortal life to-day still is. I did not want to yield for nothing, nor do I want to sacrifice Elsje for nothing. Therefore I wavered so long, for I know how weak I am and how little I can achieve for Christ. Understand me well, Elsje, I do not want this just account for myself, but for Christ in whom I live. I am quite ready to pay with personal sorrow whatever is for the benefit of Christ. For his good is also my good. But naught for nothing."

"But you are so strong and you know so much, and there is so much you can do for the world," said Elsje, with her charming pride.

"I lack the very things that are most essential to make oneself prevail as an Original. I have not the qualities of an orator, nor of a poet, nor of an administrator, nor of an organizer, nor of a composer, nor of a dramatist. The only things I have are patience, insight and conviction."

"But then you can communicate this to others who help you."

"See, Elsje, before I tore myself away I doubted of this. But now I see better how Christ works in me. As soon as you take one step in his direction, though it be in the pitch dark, then he makes the two following steps clear for you. The great relief in my heart and my speaking much and freely with you, dear Elsje, has made so much clearer to me. I believe that I can do something in the world after all. And I feel that I must attempt it. And though it does not succeed, yet I am sure that I shall gain something by it that shall be worth fighting and bleeding for. Will you support me, will you join me, will you venture what I venture?"

Then Elsje threw both her arms around me joyfully crying:

"Oh, my Husband! what would I not venture where you are beside me. Whither leads our journey and when do we go? I am ready, though it were to-morrow."

"It is not to-morrow, but the day after. And our journey leads us across the great ocean, to the new country, where the new life is stirring, and foaming, and seething most intensely."

"To America?"

"Yes, Elsje; are you willing? We shall escape the evil tongues in Holland. Evade the painful proximity of my old sphere of life. We shall not bury ourselves in some remote corner of the earth, but shall stand in the very midst of the most fiercely burning life, in the most intensively growing human world. There I can best become aware of what is to be expected of mankind, best divine what Christ intends with us and what he expects of me. If I can achieve anything indeed - it is there. I know it, for I know the country and the people, though I am not yet quite sure how I shall go about it."

Elsje looked grave and thoughtful: not appalled or frightened by the prospect, but as though in a whirl of new overwhelming images. Then she asked shyly:

"And in this battle will there still be room and time for a small, peaceful home? And for a little, tender child?"

"Why not, Elsje? There too are peaceful dwellings and many tender little children also are born there. The fighting does not go on constantly."

"I shall see that I am ready," said Elsje. And she was, in good time.

XXVII

We stood upon the deck of the great trans-Atlantic steamer and our color-thirsty eyes drank in the rich scene of the cliffs and hills of Ireland, rising above a calm sea under a sky heavy with rain. Dark grayish-purple, light gray and white rain clouds to one side, above us a clear limpid blue, a short fragment of a rainbow rising out of the light emerald-green sea, and stretching straight across the faded brown and dull green land with the little white houses, on to the blackish-gray cloud which flowed out into mist and against which the bright colors shone dazzlingly. Thousands of white gulls round about the ship, like a whirling, living snow flurry, glittering in the bright sunlight and contrasting sharply with the dark background of clouds - screaming and screeching wildly and ceaselessly.

"The sign of the covenant," said I, pointing to the rainbow.

"Do you really believe, Vico, that God gives such signs to men?"

"What do you mean by 'God,' Elsje?"

Elsje looked at me with pensive wonder.

"Do you then only believe in Christ and not in God?"

"When I employ a word I want it to mean something. After many years of thought and observation I am beginning to mean something more or less distinct when I say Christ. Why? Because I have obtained so many signs of Christ, outward and inward, that I could form a fixed idea from them - not a picture, not an image, but an idea, what the professors call a hypothesis, and in which one may believe as every scholar may believe in his hypothesis, without absolute certainty, but with an ever-increasing degree of probability, so that one can make predictions and see them confirmed by experience. This is the faith that poets and scholars and originals and herd-men are all equally in need of."

"And does God not give such signs then?" asked Elsie.

"Patience, child! first come the signs and only then do the conclusions follow. I behold here a glorious, beneficent and comforting spectacle. That is a sign. But of what and of whom? Of a higher being than Christ? Surely. For earth and sun, that made this sign, are more than humanity. But our inward perceptibility experiences emotions which point to a supreme Being, the Almighty, who created the sun and the earth and all the stars, on whom all we know is dependent and to whom all is subject. No matter what we think we must always arrive at such a Being. It is impossible not to - whether we call it Nature or God or something else, or better still give it no name."

"Yes," said Elsie; "but for me again God, just like Christ, is a living, feeling, loving being. And Nature, sun, earth - all that is not living and feeling, is it -?"

"Dear Elsie, only in the beginning of this century, before the professors had yet thought out their impossible hypothesis of a dead matter and a soulless Nature, there was a poet who in a few words set forth the wisdom which the professors have forgotten and which they will have to remember again, before we have gone half a century further. This poet was named Shelley, and when he was not older than twenty, he wrote:

'Of all this varied and eternal world

Soul is the only element...

'The moveless pillar of a mountain's weight

Is active, living spirit. Every grain

Is sentient both in unity and part,

And the minutest atom comprehends

A world of loves and hatreds.'

"Remember these words well, Elsie, I will repeat them once more and translate them for you."

And I did so, for Elsie's knowledge of English consisted only in what she had learned from me. Then I continued: "These words issued from the strongest and most magnificent original spirit the world has brought forth since the poet of the Jesus-Drama, and every child ought to learn them, more necessarily than the multiplication table or the Lord's prayer. The world has called their maker an Atheist, just as did Spinoza. But all modern natural science can be brought back to God, that is to the truth, only by these words."

"Then is this glorious spectacle a living sign of the earth and the sun?" Elsje asked.

"Of course!" said I; "but it shall yet be long before we

comprehend such an outward sign. All we understand of it is: splendor, beauty, sublimity. These are also the characteristics of all that is divine. But their nearer relations to our inner emotions of love and joy - these we do not comprehend."

"And God?" asked my wife.

"All the outward signs I have seen point to the operation of limited, imperfect beings or deities - as humanity, the plants and animals, the celestial bodies. But these all seem to work in a power that is fixed and unchangeable. The signs thereof are what the scholars call 'Laws of Nature,' as the force of gravitation and all chemical and physical laws. These alone can be signs of life of the Almighty. And still we are not sure that they issue from the supreme Power.

"Our inner consciousness tells us that the supreme Life cannot be finite, temporal. But the sensible signs of the supreme Life according to our faulty perception are temporal and point to an end. The Universe that we perceive is not a perpetuum mobile. The laws of motion that we know all come to a standstill. As the scholars put it: there is increasing entropy and there are irreversible processes. This does not satisfy our inward consciousness of the supreme Life. It must be a local, temporally restricted condition. We know irrefutably that the highest Life is more, and we shall also discover the perceptible signs of it."

Beside us stood the second-class passengers of a large emigrant steamer, gazing across the bulwark toward the last land of Europe, and vainly trying to catch something of our conversation carried on in low tones and in a language strange to them. Small, dark, Slavonic women, with gaily-colored scarfs around their heads and children in their arms; Poles in shabby coats and astrakhan caps; tall blond Scandinavians, square-jawed, cool-blooded and patient;

short, sturdy Italians with felt hats and gay cravats; a handful of pale-brown Siamese jugglers or gymnasts with flat gold-embroidered caps on, and tired, listless faces, melancholy and pallid from cold and seasickness. And amid this dirty chattering human assemblage, devouring nuts and oranges, sometimes making music and gaming, all half dulled and frightened by the usual fierce and anxious battle of life they had gone through and with the vague expectation of future wealth and pleasure in their eyes - amid these I saw my sweet, delicate wife with her eyes, now dark-rimmed but shining with joyous fervor, and her pale, delicate features - and amid the singing, eating, chattering and gaming our subtle quiet conversation grew like a strange exotic plant amid rubbish.

But Elsje put to shame my false pride and gladly and helpfully busied herself with this little troop of humanity blown together from all the quarters of the globe, making herself understood and loved in all sorts of ways in the overflowing joy of her new life.

I myself was not very cheerful, but more often profoundly grave and sad, though with that rich and gentle melancholy that leads to sublime thought. Above all the memory of my children could make me deeply dejected and silent for hours. When I imagined that they would fall ill, or that they cried because of my absence, it was as though my inmost heart was torn, or strange hands were wringing the entrails of my soul. I had heard nothing of them before my departure with the exception of one brief, comforting word from my second daughter, the third in age of my children, a shrinking, gentle girl of sixteen. She wrote in Italian:

"My dear father, I don't know why you have gone away, and I dare not ask mother or the others about it, for they don't quite understand and take it amiss and won't speak of you.

But I will think that it had to be and say that I am not angry. You had better not answer, for that would annoy mother.

Your loving little daughter,

Emilia."

This letter also made my grief vent itself in tears; they were not tears of remorse, however, but of an unavoidable mournfulness. At such moments Elsje respected my feelings with a sacred veneration for which I was unutterably grateful to her. She felt that in this she could not heal or comfort.

The first stormy days in the European waters were the wont. Then I was painfully sensible of my poverty because it compelled me to let Elsje live in the midst of these often unclean and unmannerly people, in the close steamer atmosphere surrounded by sick people, in the sleeping quarters separated only by curtains, with the primitive washing accommodations and the lack of everything that I would so gladly have given her - beauty, cleanliness, comfort. But Elsje did not complain and adapted herself to the circumstances with bright inventiveness and good humor.

At last came the warm, dark, transparent, deep violet-blue waters of the Gulf Stream and the sun began to shine refreshingly and the light-hearted folk made music and danced on the deck. Then for us too it became more endurable and we sat for hours hand in hand gazing at the glorious play of colors on the waves, blue-black, seething light-blue, and foaming snowy-white. From time to time we spoke of the great things that always occupied our thoughts. For we felt that in these great things alone could lie our justification and our peace of mind.

"Dear man, you have taught me much that is comforting and

true," said Elsje; "but yet it sometimes seems as though you had made God very distant and inaccessible for me. This beautiful, wicked, awful sea - a thinking, feeling being is already terrifying in its profound incomprehensiveness. And then, moreover - the sun and the stars!"

"Still it is good, Elsje, not to wish to hide the truth, even though it is oppressing. Inwardly God remains just as near. There is no further or nearer there. And Christ I have really brought nearer to you, haven't I?"

"Yes, but also robbed him of his perfection."

"True, and therefore made him dearer, more intimate and real. When we are children we consider our father and mother perfect. Thereby we wrong them. Later we see that they do indeed stand above us, but that they have faults too. And then when we can love them, faults and all, then they are most truly our beloved and trusted confidants. It is a stupid, childish tendency always to expect and to demand perfection in all that is above us. The Bible-Jesus spoke truly when he said that there was but one perfect Goodness. I will add that there is but one I and one Memory. And only then will man be able to follow Christ to the pure blessedness, when he learns to feel that there may be incomprehensible sublimity, loftiness and superiority without perfection: that there may also be faults in the power that has created him and in which he lives: that there are yet an infinite number of higher beings, all above him, and powerful and wise and lofty far beyond his comprehension, and yet all of them humble and faulty and weak in the power of a Most-Sublime, who is equally near to all and penetrates all with equal profoundness."

XXVIII

I do not propose to give you dramatic surprises, dear reader, and you must not look for thrilling excitement in the story of my life. Elsje's parentage has always remained unknown to me and the pretty motive for a romance of the foundling is left unused. For that sort of thing you have your well-stocked public libraries and Mr. Conan Doyle and his colleagues.

So I will rather tell you directly that my trip to America resulted in what everyone, and I myself too at first, considered a complete failure.

But I wish to make you distinctly realize that man may fare as the soldier, who, ordered to maintain a position without knowing that the position is untenable, faithfully perseveres in his charge, though aware that the endeavor is a hopeless failure - later to learn that his perseverance and his failure were foreseen in the great plan of the general and have helped to bring about the victory and peace.

It is possible that, even though it seemed otherwise, my efforts were after all beneficial and fruitful, that I sowed seeds that are still in a state of germination and only long after I am gone will shoot up as plants. I do not know this and I need not trouble about it. I have carried out the order, as I understood it, to the best of my abilities. But I do know

Frederik van Eeden

what I have gained in new knowledge and understanding. And this has made me so rich that I regret none of my sacrifices and repent none of my actions. And this alone also lets me find peace and contentment in this quiet lonely life, because here I can write down what has enchanted and stirred me go strongly, and the assurance never forsakes me that my words shall find their way and, like a mighty ferment, work on in the heads of those who as you, dear reader, have experienced the painful blessing of originality, and know what it is to live in immediate contact with Christ, the Genitive Spirit of humanity.

Through all the dark confusion of my vain efforts and painful experiences, through the continued terrible anguish of mankind, ever increasing and void of beauty and sublimity, one light shone out with an ever steadier and brighter glow the wonder of the true marriage.

This is so difficult to describe, because every one professes to know it and to respect it, and insincere eloquence and insincere enthusiasm have poured themselves out over it in riotous streams. So that one scruples to employ any word wherewith to indicate the true wonder, because all words have been polluted and defiled through a horrible misuse.

The true wonder is so great that the man of original spirit who has found it would, if he had the power, not hesitate for a moment to destroy all domestic happiness and domestic peace among the great human herd, as long as these rest only on a conventional imitation, a miserable substitute, of the true glory. I have lived in what to all the world seemed a happy union. I have endured the terrible anguish of a violent rupture of firmly-knit bonds of attachment and affection - but how insignificant is all this, how sorry this apparent happiness, how slight the anguish compared to the mighty and transcendent things that were gained - the perfect tenderness, the real intimacy of true conjugal love, the complete melting into one of two cells in the great body of humanity.

I have good reason to believe that most marriages - oh! by far the most - are of inferior quality and falser than my own false union. And also that in this matter with most men - oh! by far the most - the elemental susceptibility to true conjugal happiness is still inborn, that even the weakest conventionalist and herd-man would in this respect turn back to this deep elemental instinct, if he were left free to do so - that with the majority Christ herein still works directly and immediately, because it is the most deep seated, most absorbing passion with which he has equipped us.

And even with a clear vision of the ocean of grief, confusion and disaster that would arise were the herd to apply itself to follow the lead of the Originals and in fanatic zeal break all untrue bonds - even with this appalling knowledge I would not hesitate to lead them on to such a crusade against the matrimonial lie, since I know the glory and the riches of the promised land to be regained. Many would perish on the road and pine away, many would be trampled on and perhaps curse my name and denounce what they had began; but the prize is worth the sacrifice.

Marriage is without doubt one of the most sacred human institutions, but only sacred through inward truth, and no civic formula or churchly ritual can make it sacred if the inward truth is wanting in it. And better a thousand dissolved and broken false marriages than one true marriage prevented or one untrue one with the semblance of sincerity and sacredness upheld.

But Christ is yet in distress and anguish. He is yet in the throes of birth, in the pains of growth. Our world is as my brother Hebbel said: a wound of God. But as I add: a healing wound; therefore not less painful. And what distinguishes the true marriage from the untrue is this very quality of pain. Never did I suffer through Lucia what I suffered through Elsje. In the apparent happiness there is contentment and complacency, in the real an everlasting gnawing and torturing longing, a desire for more, more - the desire to express oneself more fully, the desire to be more closely united, to be bound together more firmly, more indissolubly, more everlastingly. Elsje and I were constantly tormented by our powerlessness to express to one another the depth of our emotion, by our anxiety for each other's welfare and happiness, by our uncertainty in regard to what life and death would bring us, by our wish never to be parted and to experience constantly the blessing of each other's company.

Even when, in the serenest, most peaceful moments, I sat by her side gazing at her with devout attention so that Moricke's words arose in me:

"Wenn ich von deinem Anschaun tief gestillt

Mich ganz mit deinem heil'gen Werth begnüge?"

even then there was a mysterious, tender quality of pain in my love, independent of all the considerations and cares concerning present and future - like a gentle, never wholly dying echo of the great world sorrow. And through this I knew that our love-life was one with the great love-life of Christ. By the tang of pain in our cup of life I recognized the water from the world-stream.

I had worked out no definitely elaborated plan for my campaign in the new land, amongst the new people. I had a few thousand guilders that belonged to me and a few hundred from Elsje. We had selected the cheapest travelling accommodations and would live very simply. I hoped to have enough for us to live on until I should have found a means of subsistence and a field for my labors. I had plenty of acquaintances in the most distinguished circles, but I knew how little I could count on them. Yet I had to try to find among them the few that were susceptive to original thoughts and had the ability to turn them into deeds.

I argued thus: that all individuals live in an invincible group-union of morals, customs, traditions and institutions, which originated wholly beyond their reasonable will and which are mostly in conflict with their own deeper convictions. That they live thus is the result of their nature and character as group-creatures. They cannot do otherwise and may not do otherwise. No individual can live apart, he must have a group or grouplet, no matter how small, whose ideas, customs and morals he shares. It is absolutely vain and useless to wish to draw him from this union by logical, sensible arguments. Though logically he can find nothing to say against such arguments, though the system in which he lives conflicts wholly with his original disposition, he must continue in it, because otherwise he would run wild, and he will sooner twist and falsify his ideas and feelings completely than be disobedient to the voice of the herd in which be finds his conditions of life.

But these group-ideas and these group-formations are continually changing. Not through the influence of the mass, the herd, which may not judge independently, because otherwise no union would be possible. The strength of the group depends on the obedience of the members to the voice of the herd. Did the members think and act independently, they could not subsist as a group.

But the group-formation is changed through the influence of some few individuals, original enough to understand humanity's own voice, the voice of Christ, and powerful enough to make themselves followed by the herd. And the influence of these few shall be the stronger, the closer their original ideas stand to the ideas of the group. All the members of the group feel something of the Original element, of the Genius of humanity, they are all still bound to our Genitive Spirit, though not nearly as closely and as fervently as the few originals. If now the original individual is all too original, the herd does not follow, but hates and destroys him. That is the martyr the man who is "in advance of his age."

But if the originality of the single individual is felt by the herd, then it follows and respects and reveres him, and later it erects statues in his honor and eulogizes him. And all the more if the seceder possesses a personally suggestive power, and impresses people by the display of some one amazing talent - organizing, dramatic or musical. Meanwhile this leader and example has done nothing more than bring the outer organization more in unison with the inner life of humanity, Christ's own being.

This consideration led me to seek for a man sufficiently intelligent and independent to absorb my thoughts, and yet in his inclinations and feelings standing so much nearer than I to the herd, that he could exert an influence. Moreover, some one with the prestige lent by some extraordinary quality or other - as learnedness, or still better, organizing talent - and with the ability, the aplomb, the ruling power which the herd tolerates and demands. Thus a mediator between me, the all too original and practically unqualified, for whom an attempt to make himself prevail would signify a useless martyrdom, and the herd, that in its unoriginality is yet so greatly in need of the stirring ferment of my ideas.

Before we neared the American shores I had made my

choice from the persons that had come to my mind as qualified for my purpose. I shall call the man Judge Elkinson, concealing his real name, as he is still in the public eye. He had been governor of his state and at my arrival was a member of the Supreme Court, the highest tribunal in the United States, sovereign in its judgments and only admitting to membership the most trusted and esteemed men of this mighty realm.

- - -

It was a clear, cold, bright day when we steamed up the Hudson and saw the white building masses of the giant city rising from the centre of the wide, grayish-yellow stream. A strong icy wind was blowing from the blue sky, and the valiant little tug-boats rocking on the turbulent waters and amid shrill whistles running quickly in and out among the great ships, like sea-monsters hunting for prey, were covered with a solid coating of ice from the splashing water.

Upon the elongated island protruding into the wide mouth of the river stretched the mighty city, a densely packed conglomeration of houses piled up toward the sea, block upon block, so that the tall masses of masonry at the point of the island appeared to be heaped up one upon the other like pack-ice. There where the blocks were the highest and stood facing each other like giant building-blocks set on end, there was Wall Street, the centre of activity, where the stony growth seemed as though spurred on by the restless stir, the yet unregulated and uncomprehended instinct of accumulation.

As we drew nearer we saw the delicate, fresh colors, the soft reds and creamy whites of the buildings in the clear, smokeless atmosphere, the white exhausts of the beating systems, standing out like little white flags against the light blue sky, and the myriad dark, twinkling eyes of the houses, row upon row, severe, square, strong, firm and light with a myriad grave, fixed questioning glances reviewing the new arrivals from across the sea, who streamed from all the quarters of the globe to this land of future promise and expectation.

Then followed the confusing and confounding impressions of the landing, where the great nation, compelled by experience, seems to guard itself against the instreaming invasion of undesired elements, and investigates and selects with humiliating, apparently heartless strictness, as though we were animals to be examined.

Elsje's smile and cheerful endurance alleviated for me the bitterness of standing in the long line for examination, ordered about by the gruff officials - I, the proud aristocrat, who had never come here otherwise than surrounded by luxury, and treated with distinction as an honored guest.

When we were finally released and found ourselves in the noise and tumult of that tremendous life, where the selfish seeking of the few is by a secret and uncomprehended power forced together into a mysterious and curious order, - as out of the seemingly aimless and orderless agitation of ants or bees one sees a well-planned structure arise, - amid the rattling of the trucks, the shuffling of thousands of feet upon the worn and ill-kept pavement, the ceaseless thunder of the elevated trains running between the graceless buildings and signs, designed solely for doing business or attracting attention, in this so preeminently incomplete, imperfect, half-barbarous and half-polished world, I saw my dear, delicate wife, overwhelmed and confounded, cling to me as though she sought everything that still attracted her to the world with me, powerless to find it in this tumult of life.

I did not remain in the city a day, knowing everything that here preys upon the inexperienced arrival, but went directly to one of those vaguely scattered villages in the immediate vicinity of the town, where spots of nature, still wild or again run wild, can be found in the midst of the remote, neglected precincts of a quickly and carelessly growing human colony. There in the woody, rocky territory little, dingy, wooden houses are to be found, built of unsightly boards, outwardly no better than sheds or barns, as though put up temporarily by people who would probably move on further soon - houses that one may occupy for comparatively little money.

It did not look inviting for a woman accustomed to the choice solidity of a Dutch house, and the well-sustained intimacy of a Dutch landscape, where man and nature through long-continued symbiosis have grown together in a harmonious union.

Everywhere all through the woods were tumbledown houses, heaps of rubbish, crockery, old iron and dirt, trees chopped down and left to rot, burnt underbrush, annoying signs of the proximity of a heedless, careless, prodigal human world. And close by, between long rows of signboards, monstrously drawn and painted in glaring colors, rushed the trains, besmirching everything with their smoke.

But after all it was a home, and with all the energy that the long years of suffering had left in her, Elsje joyously began to turn the dear illusion of these years of pining and waiting into reality.

And when the humble dwelling had been made somewhat habitable, when there was a pantry stocked with provisions, an extremely fresh and spotlessly-kept bedroom, a table with a cover upon which the kerosene lamp threw its circle of light at night, so that I could sit and read the paper while

Elsje sewed and mended busily, her head full of tenderly solicitous domestic thoughts, and when to the great satisfaction of the housewife a young negro girl had been found who came daily to help a few hours, thereby giving to the household, according to Dutch ideas, a necessary air of completeness - then I saw upon Elsje's wan countenance and in her clear, dark-ringed eyes a light that shone out above all gloomy memories or sad forebodings.

Only then I saw her faithful, loving nature in its perfect radiant glory, but also, alas! with the distressing realization of its frailness.

XXIX

The so universally-recognized type of human excellence indicated by the term "gentleman," cannot go hand in hand with true originality that makes itself prevail. For one of the chief characteristics of the gentleman is the respect for group ideas, the obedience to the voice of the herd; while the characteristic quality of the Original is precisely his breaking away from the group union, his reversing of ideas, his making himself obeyed instead of obeying.

The seceder who is not able to change the ideas of the group and to make the herd follow, is annihilated and deserves annihilation. In the human economy he is only harmful and his existence is unwarranted.

The gentleman on the contrary has a pre-eminently useful and important function. He is that member of the group who without separating from the union retains most of the original element. He combines the highest possible originality with the strictest subordination to the group nature, which only very few exceptional natures can defy with impunity. He changes nothing, but he inclines toward the original, thus making the entire herd more adaptable to change, while be lacks the ever-dangerous tendency of the originals to break loose, and keeps alive in the herd the lofty, indispensable virtue of respecting and upholding the

Frederik van Eeden

sacredness of the union.

The more the group ideas diverge from the elemental ideas of human nature, the rarer the type of "gentleman" becomes in the group. And so my little brother Shaw's lament that the true English gentleman has become extinct is comprehensible, as in the entire tremendous herd of the nations of West-European or Anglo-Saxon civilization, ideas are current which every original immediately recognizes as conflicting with the nature of humanity, as hostile to Christ.

The term "un-Christian" is with just consistency applied to them. Un-Christian means the enriching oneself at the cost of others, the enriching oneself by means of craft, the enriching oneself without bound or measure. In many groups of ancient times these things were not lawful. But the great herd of the nations calling themselves Christian, include these so unmistakably un-Christian actions among the lawful, even honorable and generally admitted. And this moreover in the very worst form. It is one of the group-ideas of the great herd, that without oneself doing any work, one may enrich oneself unrestrictedly, by means of craft, at the expense of the very poorest. Only the unprecedented magnitude of the herd and its unparalleled firm coherence made so great a deviation from Primal Reason conceivable and possible.

The type of "gentleman" has changed, however, and grown rarer in this process. It is well-nigh impossible to preserve one's originality without separating from the union of the group, or without, as the socialists and anarchists, forming new groups that stand hostile to the great herd. The respecting of group-ideas and at the same time preserving one's original human feelings, demands a forcing and straining of truth that only few sagacious and honest people succeed in.

Judge Elkinson still represented the fast disappearing type of gentleman, and I knew that for him this was possible through an extraordinary suppleness of mind, fineness of tact and feeling, and a philosophic broadness of view.

Honest in the strict sense of the word, with naïve uprightness - that he could not be any more than any other faithful member of the herd, with some astuteness. But he was at least capable of giving everyone the impression that he always desired to be honest. He forgave himself the necessary distortion demanded by the group union, as the humane physician does not charge himself with the lies he tells for the good of his patients. He also comprehended the relativeness of words, the vagueness of conceptions, the faultiness of all communion, but was nevertheless not so broad-minded that he found extenuating circumstances everywhere and for everyone. His great power lay in his demand for fixedness of opinion. Growth and development were thereby excluded, but he sacrificed these, for the sake of the support so necessary to the herd, that positiveness and regularity afford.

One could depend on him absolutely; he was called "a man of character" and thereby exercised the most beneficial influence at the cost of personal development, actuated as it were by unconscious love, by a preservative instinct for the masses. His moral code was as broad as the group-ideas allowed, but beyond that point - immutable. He maintained it with the same sacred respect which as judge he demanded for the law, though his philosophic reason told him that neither could by any means exclude injustice. He called a rogue a rogue, though he realized that complete comprehension means complete forgiveness; he considered an anarchist an enemy to mankind, a harmful monster, even though he had to admit that the anarchistic criticism of society was well founded.

If the group-ideas and the group-union of those calling themselves socialists, had not been so wretchedly vague, confused and based on pseudo-science and hollow rhetoric, he would perhaps have joined that brotherhood. For he had the full measure of American courage and resolution. And he would have represented the "gentleman" in that confederacy just as well as in the old union. But, as every "gentleman," he had the intuitive dislike of bad company, the natural and wholesome aristocracy that makes one shun a group if it is represented by inferior people. And in the socialist herd he saw nothing much better than uncultured followers driven by fanatic leaders, a very sorry realization of the Originals who had brought about the movement. Moreover the union of this group was so weak, so entirely based upon the negative, so badly formulated, that it was impossible for him to transfer to it his natural respect for the union.

With this man, then, I considered that I might try my luck. He had grown very rich by clever, but according to group-ideas perfectly lawful money transactions, as commissioner of all sorts of large undertakings, and he had a fine mansion in Washington and in New York. Toward me he would, as a philosopher, sometimes jokingly excuse his wealth, referring in this connection to the example of Seneca the sage.

I called on him as soon as I knew he was in New York, and was received most cordially.

Elkinson had a large, bony head upon a lean, muscular body. He was not yet sixty, and his clean-shaven face was of a youthfully fresh and ruddy complexion. His hair was snow-white, but still thick and full, parted in the middle and trimly cut. His strongly-pronounced jawbones, large teeth and firm chin, lent him an expression of will-power and energy; the thin-lipped large mouth and the clear, gray, steady eyes commanded respect and marked the man who would not let himself be imposed upon or put out of countenance; his eyes twinkled at the slightest occasion with an expression of subtle roguishness, evidence of the general American inclination for jesting and joking.

"It is very kind of you, my dear Count Muralto, very kind indeed to look me up again. Have you been assigned to the post at Washington again? And how are the countess and the children?"

"Don't bother about using my title, Mr. Elkinson. It must be distressing to your democratic spirit."

The mocking eyes twinkled as though they enjoyed my sally.

"On the contrary! on the contrary! - that is atavism! It does us good. We are above such things, to be sure, but just as eager to do them as a worthy professor to sing the college songs at a reunion."

"Then I regret that I must deprive you of this pleasure. I am no longer a count and intend to become a citizen of your republic."

"What is that you tell me? Well, well, well! that is a remarkable decision."

"Your enthusiasm is not as hearty as one should expect of a true American. I believe you think that something is lost by this transaction after all."

"Perhaps I do! - Italian counts are rarer than American citizens. With these titles it's the same as with sailing vessels and feudal castles. They are unpractical and out of date. And yet it is a pity to see one after another disappearing."

"Would you put me into a museum and have the state support me?"

"No! No! - we are glad to make use of such excellent working powers. We need men like you. And what does madame say to it?"

"Contessa Muralto remains Contessa Muralto. I have broken completely with her and with my old life. I wish to make my position clear to you. I have come here as an emigrant, poor, and accompanied by a woman who is my true wife, but can never be lawfully recognized as such."

"H'm! H'm! - that is grave, very grave," said Judge Elkinson. The roguish twinkle in his eyes vanished and he assumed the severe, inexorable expression of the judge.

Then, as simply as possible and with the trusting uprightness that would make the strongest appeal to his kind heart, I recounted the vicissitudes of my lot. Mutely he listened to my story, obviously interested and touched, wondering what to make of this cage.

"And now?" he finally asked. "What do you expect now? I know that a deep sensibility to what we here call the tender passion is one of your national characteristics. But after all you are no longer a boy, and you have enough sense and experience of life to know that your present position does not offer you much chance of success, not even in this country."

"I do not expect or desire success in the American sense of the word. A frugal, existence is all I want. I shall endeavor to obtain that. By giving lessons, for example."

"And had you hoped to be in any degree supported by me in that direction?" asked the careful and practical American.

"No! - I did not come to you for that. I have not the slightest intention of burdening my old acquaintances by presuming on our former relations."

"Good!" said Elkinson honestly.

"I know them too well for that," said I, perhaps a bit scornfully.

"You know what it would signify for them, don't you? You can easily put yourself in their position. You defy public opinion for the sake of a woman, but you can't expect that your former friends should do it for your sake."

"If I had thought that they were friends, I should perhaps expect it. But I know that they are not friends, only acquaintances, and I demand nothing of them."

The judge looked at me a while, not without kindliness. He seemed to feel a certain respect for my stoicism.

"Good!" he said again. "But what can I do for you then? What is your object in calling on me?"

"To make you happier than you are."

"That is indeed very generous. For after all I did not get the impression that I was the unhappier of us two. And if you would have me continue to believe in your mental balance, you must give me a more plausible reason."

"Is it so unlikely that I should increase my own happiness by means of yours?"

"Aha! Of what kind of happiness are we talking?"

"Of the most desirable, that can alone be attained by straining all our energies to their utmost capacity, their utmost efficiency."

"Ho capito! - accord! - now for the explanation. What slumbering qualities in me would you rouse to action?"

"Your qualities as a leader of men. The qualities that I lack."

"And which in yourself then?"

"Those of the thinker. Of the original thinker."

Elkinson glanced at me with a look, sharp, cold and penetrating as a dissecting-knife. He thought he understood what it was that he had to deal with.

"A system?" he asked gruffly.

"On the contrary - the release from a system. The shattering of inhuman, un-Christian morals. The breaking through a wall of horrible institutions."

"Which?"

"First of all, that which everyone condemns and everyone nevertheless maintains - the remuneration of the rich simply because he is rich, even though he does nothing to deserve remuneration. The morally and lawfully tolerated unlimited squandering of the products of common labor by irresponsible persons. The exploiting of the weaker, approved and even accounted honorable, without control, by means of craft, through the agency of countless middle men. The tenant-farmer, the laborer; the property owner, the tenant-farmer. The manufactory, the factory hands; the shareholder, the manufacturer. The landlord, the lessee; the lessee, the sub-lessee; the sub-lessee, the lodger. The speculator again exploits all the others, while the waster of finance exploits the speculator, and thus ad infinitum. The system, in one word, of mutual ruthless exploitation and of irresponsible, no less ruthless, squandering. A system in which what each holds in view as the crowning ideal is to do nothing himself, to squander without measure or care, and to have as many as possible work for his own personal profit, without asking who they are and how they live. A system that slowly but surely must demoralize and impoverish every nation to the core, even the richest and the strongest. A system that gives peace to none and can bring none to the highest possible grade of development and happiness. A system by which at least ninety per cent of the national wealth is lost without a trace. A system under which no art, no science, no higher element in man can attain to perfect bloom. A system that is further removed from the original desires and sentiments of humanity than any other that has ever been maintained by large masses of men - a system that no one with any consideration can approve or wish to preserve, that is only maintained because we know or believe in nothing better, and that is doomed to disappear because of its suicidal character. A system that can only be declared lasting and necessary by him who thinks that men are not capable of education and development and, with open eyes, shall ever seek their own ruin."

Elkinson remained silent a while after I had finished speaking. The expression in his eyes was serener now.

"As a criticism nothing new," he said, nodding his head. "But what new remedy do you propose? - Government aid?"

"First morals, then laws," said I; "no Government initiative; perhaps, if necessary, Government assistance. Begin with the most powerful public opinion, the group instinct."

"And how? - orations? - pamphlets? - meetings? and addresses? - That seems to me nothing exactly new either, nor has it proved effectual. Is one deformity like the social democracy not enough?"

"More than enough. The dead child with two heads has itself made its own name impossible. Use that name no more, for the mother who has borne the child is ashamed of it and will hear of it no more. Give the potion another label and another color if you would make men take it, or better, give it no color. And talk as little as possible, but do, act, carry out. Make of the deed your shepherd's staff and of facts your milestones and your guideposts. Let your shepherd dog not bark, but bite, and see to it that the flock find something to graze on."

"Clearer! clearer! - no Eastern metaphors, American facts."

"Very well! Judge Elkinson is acquainted with the psychology of the mass and he knows the individuals of which it is composed. He has governed a state, organized and conducted commercial undertakings, instituted laws and seen them carried out. He knows thousands of individuals, their worth and their abilities. He enjoys the universal confidence, and possesses great influence. His name alone guarantees the help of thousands, and of the very best moreover. Let him form a group, with better group-ideas, with better group-ethics, better morals, better customs, and higher standards of right and wrong, good and evil, than the group in which he now lives and works."

"Clearer still and more concrete if you please. How do you imagine the beginning?"

"As every group began always. As every business man forms his business, every general his army. Select a staff of the most capable and tell them what is essential for them to know. Formulate the plan so that in the course marked out the chief idea cannot be missed, without frightening off any one of the great herd by peculiar, unusual or doubtful terms, theories or visions of the future. And then organize, practically, systematically, always aiming directly at the concrete reality without troubling yourself in the least about abstractions. And see that your herd is fed and sheltered and stabled as quickly as possible, and that it find gratification of its instincts in the course once marked out. And on the way - heed it well, on the way, not beforehand - teach them to comprehend the object of the fight and what they shall gain. Teach them first to follow and to find gratification in following, and then they will gradually go of their own accord, if it agrees with them, and be less and less in need of guidance. Promise as little as possible, but show and prove by the result, and predict nothing that you cannot immediately prove."

"Thus a non-political organization? An ethical corporation?"

"A business proposition, judge, a business proposition. But a great and holy business. A business for making money, for accumulating as much and as quickly as possible. The herd must eat, must have a good time, must have abundance and must have its future assured. What kind of business is indifferent. Every kind that is possible. If the group only learns that it can obtain enough and much more even than before - much greater wealth and much more happiness and content - by no longer pilfering one another and squandering, but by intelligent mutual agreement and by restriction of personal boundless liberty for the sake of the whole common welfare."

"And your own part in this affair? How do you imagine that?"

"As the part of a match at a forest fire. For myself full of profound satisfaction, for the outer world absolutely obscure. I shall come to talk with you now and then. Judge Elkinson is the man, the benefactor of his people, the liberator of mankind."

"And for you - nothing? No money, no glory, no honor?"

"This disinterestedness seems incredible to you. But it is a natural outcome of our different functions. Every different function involves different passions and desires. Practical work involves a love of glory and honor. We are so organized that we find enjoyment only in what our own peculiar endowment can yield. A very sensible organization which you may take as an example. My work is contemplative, speculative and affords enjoyment through the satisfaction of correct discoveries and clear vision. In practical life I am unhappy, with money, honor, glory and all. But you, Judge Elkinson, have need of me for this very quality. Humanity must not only act organizedly but also think organizedly. No greater folly than to imagine that the safe way for the herd shall be found by its own blind instinct, or that as a mass it can itself think out what it must do. No greater nonsense than the work of these sages who sling a few formulas at the masses, and then, with the aid of these uncomprehended and incorrectly interpreted terms and abstractions, would let them find the way alone. Humanity would and must think, and advance by the light of contemplation and reflection, but it must think organizedly, so that each in this great thinking process exercises his own peculiar function - the scholar, the business-man, the statesman, the artist, the poet. And only when this organization for the good of all is completed, is there a chance that every member of the herd will participate more and more in the thinking functions, and thus also in the delights of the others, that we obtain a world of free men and majors, a truly mature and full-grown humanity, the flaming ideal in which the poor anarchistic moths now still scorch their wings."

"My dear Mr. Muralto, in a way I really feel that you are placing me in the position of Dr. Faustus, to whom every imaginable glory was held out, all that human ambition could desire, if he would but sign his name. You will pardon the comparison, I hope."

"Certainly, but you will probably have something more to do than sign your name. And I will gladly give you every occasion to search your deepest conscience whether I should be counted among the good or the bad demons."

"Until now, my friend, I considered myself capable of getting on without guiding spirits."

"But after all that was only an opinion, as all other opinions very open to criticism."

"That is possible! - At any rate I am very grateful to you for the most interesting conference. I hope that we may continue it another time."

"I gave you my address. I shall be at your disposal there at any moment."

"Much obliged! - I feel myself, honored by your confidence and by the high opinion you seem to entertain of me. Once more - many thanks."

With these ceremonious courtesies we parted from one another.

Then I went back to my little house where Elsje awaited me. I had the dissatisfied and well-nigh angry feeling of one who

Frederik van Eeden

has not been able to do himself and his ideas justice. The process of realizing our ideas is always full of surprises and disappointments, like the performing of a play or the developing of a photograph.

Elsje awaited me, with everything in readiness that the little house could offer of comfort and of cheer - and best of all, with eager interest in that which stirred my heart so deeply. She knew that this was my first stroke in the campaign and she participated in it, with all her soul, as I gratefully read by her looks and her attitude when I came home.

"How was it?" she asked.

"So, so! dearest. - I did what I could. But I do not know whether I said just what I should have to make the most impression. It isn't enough to say the right thing, but one must say it in such a way and so often that it makes an impression and takes effect. You can never do that all at once. But nevertheless I am not dissatisfied with my first attack."

And I told her how my words had been received.

"You dear, good man! You do your best so faithfully. If only they knew what I know, how good you are, and how sincere your intentions."

One usually attaches little value to a loving woman's judgment upon the man she loves. But the perfect faith of a pure spirit is not alone a wondrous comfort and consolation, but also a mighty creative power for the good. And it is not confusing and blinding, but calming and beneficial to see oneself reflected in a clear glass, in a favorable light.

XXX

I shall never admit that the plan of my campaign was unpracticable or ill contrived. I remain firmly convinced that the main idea was correct and will be of service to future combatants. But it had one fault which I could not be aware of and which could only reveal itself in the practice. It is not impossible to inoculate men like Elkinson with an original and to them new idea, and even to impress it. On them in such a manner that they come to conceive of it as their own idea and are driven to action by it.

But then this operation must be performed as skilfully and carefully as a botanical or surgical grafting, so that the idea becomes one with their own nature, and continues to grow, nourished by their own life. Now in my case the grafting did not succeed - just as the first botanical graftings did not succeed - because I was not sufficiently experienced and practised in it and had not yet found the right method. Still this does not prove the impossibility of the principle.

One can never remind oneself too often that no one, not even the most sagacious, broadest mind, is led to assume different fundamental ideas solely by reasonable arguments. The element of faith is always indispensable, even in purely scientific questions.

Frederik van Eeden

What I said to Judge Elkinson would have been entirely sufficient to convince him and to stir his powers into action, had it been told him in the same words but under more favorable circumstances; or if he had heard it oftener, from different persons and in different words.

The unfavorable, hampering circumstance was that because of my poverty and my illegitimate marriage I now stood outside the circle of Elkinson's social intercourse. I had foreseen this to be sure, but thought nevertheless that he would confer with me in secret and private interviews often enough to afford me the opportunity of keeping in contact with him and in the end convincing him. I did indeed see him now and then too, once also he came to me and evinced as much interest, kindliness and broad mindedness as could be expected of a man in his position. But illogical as it may seem, the influence of my words was much slighter because we no longer stood on an equal footing. Had he, as formerly, met me everywhere in the distinguished circles, had he there, in club or salon, parried on the same conversations with me, and above all, had he not gained the impression that I spoke intentionally and with the purpose of rousing him to action, he would then, I am sure, have assimilated these same ideas and seemingly on his own initiative would have commenced to act upon them.

But the arguments that upon the lips of a man of position and distinction are convincing lose their persuasive power when spoken by an erratic or eccentric, even though they may be exactly as logical, because the element of faith and of trust are wanting.

Thus the release from social convention, which liberated my spirit and gave me the courage to honestly assert and maintain myself, at the same time had a crippling effect upon my powers. When the knight had buckled his coat of mail he could no longer move his arms.

I did not stop at this first attempt, but continued working restlessly, trying to provide a living for us and seeking a fertile ground for the seed of my thoughts. I tried to find pupils to take lessons in languages and strove to gain admission to the editors of magazines and newspapers. I composed short articles in which I endeavored to make ideas of great importance and value interesting and readable. Urged by necessity I even attempted to write short stories, which were complete failures however, and caused me miserable hours of struggle and inward shame. For purposely manufactured art is just as insipid, unworthy and humiliating as true art is sacred and exalting. The last is divine worship, the first waste of time.

I also tried to engage the interest of other influential persons besides Judge Elkinson. But I had rightly selected him as the most available, and with all the others met with less success. I had used up my best powder at the first onslaught. Now I ran great danger of being looked upon as one of the many harmless, but troublesome and tiresome fools, who are called "cranks" over there, and who seem to flourish in America. People who go about everywhere and pursue everyone with an infallible system, an ingenious invention, a gigantic scheme. They have calculated everything and only want a millionaire or an influential person to realize their idea - to reform the world and make it happy or to amass fabulous riches.

Once counted in that category and my chance was lost, that I knew. People would warn one another against me and no one in this hastily-living world would have even one minute to spare to listen to me.

Every day of the campaign on which I had so bravely

entered, I saw more distinctly the fatal difficulty I was facing. In order to be able to carry out anything I should have to "make a name," as it is called. And making a name, the forming of a centre of suggestive influence working, not through essential worth but through idle sound, - this is in conflict with a contemplative nature and a lover of reality as I am. The man of action will make a name, he will work for it unashamed, he finds unadulterated pleasure in being honored and celebrated and renowned. For in his capacity the power of a name, a personality, is indispensable. Wisely he has been equipped with the suitable instincts for this.

But I myself had an insurmountable horror of anything that would tend to bring my own personality, my most transitory, spectral unimportant being into the limelight. To see my name printed or to hear it discussed was quite indifferent to me, even very disagreeable. I should be willing to bear it for Christ's sake, if I realized that I could only thus serve him and that he demanded it of me. But it was impossible for me to exert myself to that end. It is harder for the Original than for anyone else to act contrary to his natural disposition. To uphold the important truths whereof I knew myself to be the sole and responsible supporter, I was always ready to make any sacrifice. But to fight for my person, my career, my name, did not attract me in the least and thus also rarely met with success.

So for days, weeks, and months I worked without the slightest result. A pupil, sent to me by Elkinson, stayed away after a few weeks without paying me - perhaps because he may have heard something about my illegitimate marriage. Some journalists who had known me in former days received me with superficial friendliness and promised to do something for me. But they did nothing - speedily absorbed again in their own interests. Of Elkinson, I heard that he had been brought into consideration for the presidential candidacy;

sufficient reason for him to forget hundreds of conversations with a Muralto, shipwrecked through his own folly.

Just as prosperity again begets prosperity, so also does misery grow like a snowball rolling down hill. The great, tremendous, busy world about me rushed restlessly onward in the fog - striving, seeking, building up and demolishing, urged on by uncomprehended impulses - and considered we no more than any of the thousand lost creatures that are crushed under its blind and heavy tread, cruel as the machine that catches the careless worker in its wheels. And yet I knew that this tremendous structure was the obedient tool of the same power that had entrusted me with its most precious gifts, that had urged me on my way, that was responsible for my strength and for my weakness.

And in proportion as the want that reigned in my little house grew more and more real and the struggle for existence more and more anxious, in the same proportion this humble home also began to grow dearer to me. I was approaching the age when a man, even though not yet tired and worn out, still, more than ever before, longs for a resting place, a small intimate sphere of quiet and rest, of cherishing love and peace, a home. What had formerly been my home had always remained inwardly strange to me. It afforded me every comfort and physical ease, but my heart found no happiness there. And now I had more than I had ever expected to find. I found the true domestic happiness more beautiful, more sublime and holy than I had imagined - but its beauty was touched with anguish and its joy with anxious sorrow because it was so transitory.

We needed so little - a couple of tidy rooms with few ugly things and one or two objects of beauty, a small garden plot with flowers, some sunlight by day, some lamplight cheer at night, enough to eat, and quiet and serenity for study - and all the hours spent together were completely satisfying in their measure of glory and every minute of separation became endurable through the prospect of finding each other again.

Elsje had the child-like power of enjoyment, that in a trifle - an opening flower, a new piece of furniture, an ornament or decoration, a song, a few fine lines of poetry - can find gratification and delight for hours and days. She had the pure taste that, above all, fears overloading and over-excitement, and takes pleasure only in what is simple and what is truly enjoyed.

How little I would have needed to make her life a constant joy. But even that little I was not able to give. The poverty from which I had wished to teach men to escape, the poverty falsely, proclaimed as Jesus' friend and the bride of the devout, - in truth Christ's fiercest enemy and a horror and terror to every truly devout man - this poverty slunk into my house and with a grim laugh of scorn revenged herself upon me who had dared assail her sacredness and sublimity. And she struck the most beautiful and the dearest that life had offered me, she menaced my greatest treasure, won but so shortly and at such great sacrifice.

It seemed as though Elsje's dauntless efforts to prepare a comforting home for me, her unfailing patience and brave cheerfulness consumed her physical being all the more. I saw the battle that she was waging, and it tortured me with a thousand variations of pain. Her keeping up when she was well-nigh powerless with exhaustion. Her increased tenderness when she saw me yield under the heavy pressure of care, whereby I noticed that she felt herself responsible for my suffering, as it was for her sake that I had given up my life of prosperity.

Then at the time of our greatest troubles, came that which Elsje had expected and longed for as the highest blessing - maternity.

I too had desired the child and had longed for it with fervent tenderness, picturing to myself how I could now bestow all the interest and fatherly devotion without self-constraint, from natural instinct, from overpowering love. How I should love this child and delight in the sight of its development day by day. Recalling with bitter sorrow how vaguely and distantly the lovely blossoming of Lucia's children had passed by me, because I had not participated with my entire being in their growth and their development, I now hoped after all to be father in the full sense of the word, and with clear perception and unabating interest to delight in this lovely miracle. Surely no child before it had yet breathed the air, has ever been an fervently loved, as tenderly discussed, as devoutly looked forward to as this.

But a dark foreboding dwelt in me with relentless certainty. I knew that calamity threatened, my dreams betokened it and it became daily clearer what form this calamity would take. The glad promise had a diabolically mocking sound, the subtle perceptive faculty of my insensible being felt the falseness of the sweet announcement. Toward Elsje as she tranquilly sat by my side sewing at tiny garments and absorbed in the sweet prospect of her child, toward Elsje I could feign hopefulness and enter into her sweet phantasies - but myself I could not deceive. I knew that a picture of happiness was teasingly held out to me that my eyes would never behold. I knew that the genuineness of my conviction, the strength of my faith, would be submitted to the severest test, to the keenest torture.

Then too, through Elsje's peculiar condition, which makes certain spiritual longings speak so loudly, it became clear to

Frederik van Eeden

me what she had so carefully hidden from me.

She always questioned me about my dreams what and whom I had seen, where I had been. And once the words escaped her:

"Oh, I wish that I could dream like you!"

"Why, Elsje? What would you do?"

"I should try to go to Holland," she said softly.

Then I understood her. It was homesickness that had taken hold upon her.

"Do you long to be back in Holland?"

She nodded mutely, but immediately added in a livelier tone:

"But I don't want you to mind that, my dear husband, as long as you consider your work here is not yet accomplished. I am patient and can very well wait a while. But there is a possibility after all, isn't there, - when our child is a little bigger - that we go back to live in Holland?"

"If my endeavors meet with no better success than they have so far, Elsje, we can just as well live in Holland."

Then no longer restraining herself, she said:

"I should have thought it so lovely if my baby had been born in Holland, amid the green pastures in a bright pretty little Dutch house, under the lovely Dutch clouds, near our sea. And then I could already early have shown him all the beautiful things that we have only in Holland - our quaint little town, and the paintings in the museum, and the peasant houses, and the dunes. Here everything is so big, so hard, and so ugly -"

I promised to remain here no longer than I considered strictly necessary. But I knew that her wish could not be fulfilled. Even had I had the money, she would not have had the strength at the time to take the trip. But her mind was constantly occupied with Holland and her child in Dutch environment. And her growing aversion to the food in the strange country, her desire for the diet of the land where she had been brought up, wrought fatally upon her system.

One day when I had again returned home discouraged after a useless attempt to induce a learned society to apply and test its sociological and biological knowledge in a practical direction, she said:

"Dearest husband, is it stupid of me to think that Jesus who has drawn and led you hither, could now so easily also move others to listen to you, and to translate your thoughts into deeds?"

"No, Elsje. For if I assume that Christ has influenced me in particular, for his purpose, then I can also think that he influences others for that purpose. But yet such a thought seems like superstition. That is to say like the regarding of things divine in a human way. Yes, if Christ went to work as a man, then we might be surprised that he did not act as we should.

"But though he is a thinking, feeling being, that loves us, still he acts toward us individuals with the exalted greatness and seeming ruthlessness of a natural force, of a divine power. He can love us and know us, better than we know the cells of our own body, and yet take no account of our little worries, because he knows how insignificant they are. And he always

Frederik van Eeden

acts through great, universal things, instincts and impulses, that must serve for all, but under which the individual must often suffer. His laws are good, good for us all, but not perfect, any more than human laws. Cannot all impulses degenerate? Are not all our tendencies full of danger? Is not our body full of defects? Must we not help and improve continuously? And nevertheless is not everything again compiled with an ingenuity incomprehensible to us? Think what it means to heal a slight wound or, a thousand times more wonderful still, to give birth to a new human being!"

"But new plants and animals are born too, and the construction of a plant or an animal is just as ingenious. Is that all the work of Jesus? Let me say Jesus instead of Christ, I love that name better."

"Yes, there is perhaps something more intimate in this name. When in my dream I asked my father about Christ, he pointed out to me the beautiful markings on the wings of a butterfly. And with this in mind I began to suspect what Jesus is. It is really so simple, so perfectly obvious. One or the other: either this butterfly decoration originated accidentally, or it was made with intention, feeling and thoughtful consideration. For centuries God, the Supreme Omnipotence, has been held responsible for it. And when the scholars finally could no longer believe in so many contradictions and so many imperfections in an almighty, perfect Being, then they tried their best to prove that the beautiful markings of the butterfly had originated quite accidentally; which is even more foolish than to think that an etching by Rembrandt or a statue by Phidias is an accidental formation. And absolutely to prove the contrary is impossible. One can merely speak of extreme improbability. But I know nothing more improbable than this - that a butterfly, a flower or a human being should be the accidental product of blind forces, supposing that one may speak of blind or unconscious forces. That the sun and the stars revolve around the earth, that the Egyptian hieroglyphics are accidental scratches on the granite - all this is even a great deal less improbable. But then they must also be living, thinking, feeling and reasoning beings that have created butterfly, flower and man and are still constantly creating and changing them, with infinite skill, with incomprehensible ingenuity, but nevertheless with ever-recurring imperfection. And probably beings who are by no means always in harmony with one another, that fight and struggle among them, supplanting and replacing one another, whose desires, endeavors, joys and sorrows are far beyond the comprehension of insignificant individuals as we - but whose expressions of life we nevertheless clearly discern as separate entities, as races and species struggling side by side, sometimes with, sometimes sharply opposite to one another. The being that has created us, whose spirit, mind, will and sensibility binds us together, as does our body its cells, into one great unity, outwardly imperceptible, but perfectly evident to our inner sensibility, is the Spirit of Humanity, the Primal Reason, the Genitive Soul of Mankind - Christ."

"Thus every species of animal and plant then must have its Jesus?"

"Certainly, every species must have its genitive Soul, - and every cell in every individual has its own. How these entities are connected and how they are separated from one another - that the biologists will learn gradually. They are scarcely at the beginning of their knowledge."

"But God the Supreme Omnipotence nevertheless just calmly tolerates all this struggle, this suffering and this imperfection."

"Certainly - for it is."

Frederik van Eeden

"Why? Wherefore? Isn't that just as unsatisfactory?"

"Dearest wife, the difficulty is ever merely transferred; this will continue so, until we possess higher insight. I shall not pretend that as Milton I can justify God's ways before mankind, nor yet that as Dante I can say everything there in to be said concerning God and the Universe, nor even that as Spinoza, Hegel or Schopenhauer I can build up a complete system. That is unscientific, all true science is assuming and computing. Of the highest Power we know next to nothing: but nevertheless enough for our life. We know that his laws obtain everywhere as far as our perception reaches, and we know that He works equally in the living and in the apparently not living, in the smallest and in the greatest, and that our life rests on faith in him, that our peace lies in His will. But of Jesus we know much more, for, scientifically, we see his expressions of life and we feel his effect upon our spirit. And that is over and above sufficient to comfort us in all our suffering and all our troubles. But future generations will know much more, will go much more surely, will lead much more beautiful lives and die much happier."

"Didn't you tell me, dear, that Emmy, your first love, did not seem to know Jesus, but Lucia did? And yet you loved Emmy so and have seen her in your dreams and she has brought you to Jesus and to me. But Lucia has always remained a stranger to you. How is that?"

"Yes, it is so, Elsje. And I see no contradiction in it. Emmy lived in a dead, false Protestantism, but she was designed for something better. Lucia lived in the warm, living faith of the Middle Ages, which, however, we are outgrowing. The Middle Ages knew Jesus and lived in him fervently, truly and really, as is manifest in their entire nature. Their inner sensibility of him was much stronger than ours, but their knowledge, their definite realization of him was much more faulty. Lucia's piety belongs to an earlier phase - never can it reconcile itself to ours. She is a perfect blossom on a more ancient branch of humanity. But she can never be perfectly mated with any who, as we, belongs to a more modern generation. My love for Emmy was not as deep and as strong as my love for you, Elsje. Never. It was a much more superficial, personal sentiment, not encouraged by return, not sufficiently powerful to stream out further. I never learned to love mankind through Emmy, as I did through you. And that Emmy in my dreams as it were reserved me for herself, and then brought me to Elsje, so that my power of love has attained to perfect, glorious development, that I shall never be able to regard otherwise than as the greatest blessing, the greatest privilege that Jesus ever let me experience."

"And do you believe, dearest, even though now your work should remain entirely useless here, that humanity shall nevertheless be benefitted by our love?"

"I believe it. But it goes beyond my responsibility and beyond my care. Our responsibility goes no further than our comprehension. I am simply obedient to what I recognize as my noblest and highest inclinations. I act according to the beat of my knowledge. The responsibility I leave to Him, who gave us our impulses and our faculty of judging, whose wisdom and sensibility are so far exalted above ours as a human body is exalted above the most ingenious machine invented by man. But though now I am powerless to exert a direct influence, I shall not give it up and shall not rest. I shall write down everything and testify of Him. And He in His own way and in His own time, will bring it all into regard and into practice."

"Perhaps through our child," said my poor wife; and my firmness forsook me.

XXXI

The child of our love lived only one day.

When, a hundred years earlier, it befell my brother Lessing that he lost his only-born after a single day of life, he bitterly reviled Christ in his sorrow. With cutting sarcasm be lauded the wisdom of this child, who would not enter life until he was dragged into it with tongs of iron, - and the same night departed again.

My brother Lessing was a devout man, but yet not sufficiently devout to revere the beauty, the majesty and greatness of Human Being amid the suffering he had to undergo. The true, living Christ had also called him to testify, and he did not in his testimony spare the Bible-Jesus, the artificial product of human fancy. But the belief in the future Glory of Mankind for which the suffering of the individual is not too high a price, afforded him no solace and did not reconcile him to the bitterness of life.

I will not laud my strength. I was as weak in my overwhelming sorrow as one might expect of a poor mortal. As long as my wife survived her child, my love for her gave me the strength outwardly to show nothing that might resemble bitterness or despair. When she too was taken from me, there was nothing or no one to force me to a display of cheerfulness and resignation, and for a while I was a crushed, beaten and broken creature, a faded, falling leaf.

But the knowledge, the spiritual, intellectual knowledge, could not forsake me even though all sensibility had been dulled and stifled by excess of grief. As long as we contemplate ourselves with the scientific eye, from the height of our inmost consciousness, so long too there is something that exists above pain, old age and death. He who accurately observes himself in suffering and old age, is thereby exalted above time and sorrow, for that which contemplates is always more and higher than that which is contemplated. And so in the midst of ray wretchedness I knew that gladness and eternal youth dwelt within me through this tiny spark of contemplative power.

I knew and never forgot that the Eternal in which we live does not take anxious account of a little more or less of suffering and does not spare his creatures.

It suffers thousands of seeds to perish in order that one of them may attain perfect growth. I knew that the pain I felt was the after effect of a craving now grown useless and that I should no longer be sensible of it as soon as I considered what had been attained, and desisted from the unessential and unattainable.

And I saw no reason to doubt of the supremacy of blessedness and joy above all sorrow, because I, insignificant individual, in a few short years of life had been made to suffer the utmost that I could endure.

I was weak, weak as all human beings, but an inconceivable spark of knowledge shone out like a bright tiny star above all my dark infirmities. And it is upon this little twinkling star, dear reader, that I would fix your attention, and not upon my frailties.

What else is it but weakness, miserable, lamentable weakness, that is spread out before us in the bitter invective speeches against Life by those who are called pessimists, by Schopenhauer, Wagner, Ibsen, dragged along as they were in the ebb of life toward the middle of this century?

I was born at the shifting of the tide and I know that the rising waters are bearing me upon them. I know full well that pure blessedness is not yet in Human Being, but that it must be created and that the first condition for its advent is the faith and the will, the courage and the strength of the Originals. Wherever true being obtains there is pure blessedness, and it is our part to attain this true being - but the first essential for it is the foreseeing conviction. For willing is creating and each of us, building in eternity, follows his own plan.

My optimism is truly not the hiding myself from inevitable grief, for with towering waves the sea of sorrow has pounded against my beacon towers. The fires were not extinguished and beamed out above it all.

But not a moment longer than I can help it do I allow myself to dwell on the dark, the gloomy and melancholy side of life. Nor shall I try to thrill your heart, dear reader, with scenes of melancholy, sad as the things may be that I have to tell you. The worst of all demoniacal aberrations is a passion for wallowing in the mire of dreariness, of melancholy. Guard yourself, guard yourself against the dismal lime rods that threaten the free flight of your thoughts.

Elsje and I had frequently spoken of dying, but only when a vigorous mood permitted us to do so without sadness or apprehension. For the worst thing about death is not the actual dying, but the breath of horror that it sometimes casts upon our sensibilities.

That our age permits so few to live beautifully is sad, but it is far worse that it gives to so few the opportunity and the courage to die worthily. Our generation ill understands how to lives but it knows even less how to die. Most die, not the quite unappalling death of the hero, but the horrible Philistine's death, as Goethe called it.

To die beautifully and worthily had been the dearest wish of both of us, after that of a long life in happy unison. And Elsje attained this desire as nearly as our wretched circumstances allowed.

"It is good after all now," she said when she felt the certainty of what was about to take place, "that our darling baby did not live. For it would have been so hard for you, poor, dear man, to care for the child alone and at the same time continue with your work."

Eagerly she questioned me every morning about my dreams and it pleased her exceedingly when I could honestly say that despite my anxieties my dreams had been of a serene, refreshing splendor. And she always wanted to know more of this wonderful state, that must be so like what we shall experience after this body's decay and is so difficult to describe and to comprehend.

"I think the worst," she said, "is that perhaps we shall never be certain, when we see each other again, whether it is not a delusive image, a product of our own imagination, instead of the other's actual being. For then we no longer, as now, have our senses and thus nothing to convince us that what we perceive is the same as what we perceived in life."

"I can't say much in answer to that, dearest, except this - that even in the brief moments of perception during sleep, I have felt assurance. Self-deception may indeed be possible, but there is also infinite, quiet time for consideration, observation, recollection, which in my sleep is always wanting. And there must also be amalgamation, dissolution of personality, perception through the medium of still living beings - a multitude of conditions and faculties now still wholly incomprehensible to us."

"That sounds sad to me: dissolution of the personality. For it will be for you, for you as you are now, for your own personal nature, your dear voice, your gentle eyes that I shall long for ever and ever, and for that above everything."

"I only know, Elsje, that nothing has been lost or can be lost of all our impressions, of all the most beautiful and precious things we have experienced. Nothing perishes, and surely least of all that which is the constituent element of all that is: feeling. All feeling is eternal, and the least that we experience is lastingly recorded in the memory of the Almighty. I can say nothing more nor be more explicit about it, we must comfort ourselves with this main thought."

"If you are comforted and brave, dearest husband, I am too."

"I am, for even if I must live on ten or twenty solitary years after our separation, I have my work and my study, and I also have my nights in which I shall call you. And you'll surely want to come when I call you?

"Oh, dearest, whether I will want to? If I know that it can comfort you! Whether I will want to?"

And her dim eyes smiled at the extreme superfluence of my question.

"And when you have your gloomy moments again, dear, will you forgive me then that I induced you to cause and to experience so much sorrow? - I know of course that you never think bitterly of me, and that you forgive me everything in your joyous, vigorous times, when your real, true nature dominates. But there are periods of dejection too. Will you not think bitterly of me then?"

"Rather ask me, Elsje, whether I will forgive Christ that he induced me to cause you so much suffering, that he did not point out my way to me sooner and more distinctly, and left you to pine and wait so long. Christ is the Mighty, the Strong, the Wise, who governs us and who bears the greatest responsibility. We two are poor, blind, little toilers who have helped one another to the best of our abilities. For each other we have only gratitude!"

"Yes!" said Elsje, contented; "for each other only gratitude."

And to the last moments of her life she was absorbed and comforted in the thought that I would still have the nights, in which I would call her and find strength and encouragement for the lonely day.

"To forgive Jesus," she said another time, "is really absurd, isn't it? For I would love him at least just as much as you, if only I might think of him as human."

"Everything we say, Elsje, is absurd. But what we feel is not absurd. When we have returned to the Source of Life, to the Genitive-soul of humanity, only then I think shall we realize how absurd were our words, but how true our feeling."

The last words I heard from her, in her anxious care for me, were a whispered: "Will you call me!" and once more when her voice had grown toneless her lips formed the word: "Call!"

Then the blossom withered, and fell. But the mighty stem had grown richer through the beautiful bloom of her love-breathing life.

XXXII

After Elsje's death I had no more peace in the new country. It seemed as though her homesickness had passed on to me. My dreams spoke night after night of Holland, only Holland, and of the place where I had found my wife. Her supernatural being seemed to drive me toward the land of her longing.

A long time I resisted this desire, unwilling to give up the work that I had begun with go much sacrifice and carried through with so much anguish.

Then I received a strange communication. I heard through a business agent of my family in Italy, with whom I had remained in touch, that my mother had died and had left her fortune to my children; and that my daughter Emilia, having attained her majority, was determined not to accept the money but to give it to me. My children were all married or independent, and the whole family was scattered. Lucia was an abbess in a religious institution.

Then I could no longer resist the secret craving which did not cease night or day and so distinctly appeared to me like a warning from my dead wife, and I went back to this little town, where I bought my present house and the small nursery garden, which still furnishes me daily occupation.

Frederik van Eeden

What I received from my daughter was not much, but sufficient for maintaining my simple, provincial life here. Gradually I succeeded in accustoming the petty provincials to my strange ways, and now my life is as endurable as any that I could still have hoped to find on earth.

Only by this strange communication and Emilia's friendly act was I aroused from the dark stupor into which Elsje's death had plunged me. I would not perhaps have had the power to rouse myself to an interest in life and in my work, would perhaps have fallen ill and died without once seeing Elsje in my dreams. For my despair and my homesickness had also dimmed the clarity of my dreamlife. I slept little and badly, the tortured soul could not separate itself sufficiently from the restless body to attain to reintegration and transcendental perception.

Emilia's act saved me. And then I made the comforting observation, that with the recovery from a period of deep affliction the power of enjoyment is extraordinarily heightened. I saw my daughter again in Paris, where we had agreed to meet before I should go to Holland, and the one single day there was marked by a wondrous indescribable joy.

It overcame me quite suddenly - during the journey from America - that I felt the dark melancholy giving way. And then too came the clear perception during the night, brief but intense, in which I for the first time summoned the beloved dead, heard her soft, loving voice, and saw her eyes.

In Paris the reunion with the only one of my children who had remained true to me - the gentle devoted girl who wanted to continue to understand and to help her father - was an exquisite joy.

It is impossible to put into words what takes place in the soul at such a time, and the effect is so strange that, even while experiencing it, I was filled with continual devout wonder.

The connection between the spiritual body and waking body must then suddenly be supplied and firmly restored again, and the weakness of this spiritual joint that was caused by melancholy all at once relieved.

All that I saw that day was joy, was well-nigh bliss. And above all - it signified so much! With everything I saw, I felt the existence of infinite prospects of joy and beauty that were indicated by it, only just briefly indicated - but unmistakable.

There was a large exposition - one of these banal world fairs which I had often railed at. But now with my thousand-fold heightened sensibility of joy and beauty, I saw it all as a distinct dawning and precursor of untold approaching glory.

The wide, sunny avenues with the gilded statues gleaming in the clear sunlight, the temples and galleries white and stately, the thousands and thousands of people assembled from every land, the joyous festive aspect, the music on all sides, the odor of dust, of linden-blossoms, of faintly perfumed clothes - ah! how powerless is this summary to picture the indescribable, the beautiful joy whereof all this seemed to me to be a fleeting proclaimer. I could look about me where I would - at an Eastern façade, at a group of musicians, at a leafy row of sunlit trees, at the sweet, pretty, well-dressed girl who walked by my side and who was my daughter - everything betokened gladness, strange, subtle, unknown joy, intense splendor, secret expectation of great, never-suspected mysteries and wonders.

On this happy day these two truths were firmly rooted in my

soul: First, that humanity is on its upward course, that the wound of God is healing, that a new common welfare, surpassing all imagination, is in store, even on this earth, with a glory beyond measure or example. And secondly, that our power of enjoyment continues to grow under the weight of our mortal body and that there is nothing improbable in the expectation of the ancient believers that we shall only then really know what true blessedness is when we are forever delivered from this burden.

Even as all faculties, all organs, are developed by opposition, provided it is not overpowering, so also the power of loving and of being blessed is developed under the outward opposition of the mortal, physical life, provided the spirit retains the once acquired knowledge and is able to endure the tribulations and with prudence to conquer them.

This advantage I did not lose again in my later solitary life. My old age, monotonous and inwardly lonely though it may be, is joyous and happy, full of bright expectation, full of gentle resignation.

A few times I again had the great outward pleasure of having my daughter visit me and of being able to speak with her openly and honestly about my life, about her mother, about Elsje, my eternally beloved, true wife. I could speak to no one else of this. But Emilia always listened attentively and reverently, and I do not doubt but that it taught her something and that it broadened and cleared her mind.

Aside from these few eminently happy days, I do not despise the most trifling daily pleasures - nevertheless I leave my little city but seldom. I find pleasure in the beauties of my little town and this low land at all seasons, in the working and cultivating of my little plot of land, in the freshly plowed earth with its sweet smell, in the eager interest in the thriving of my plants, and also in the small domestic joys.

An old faithful servant from "The Toelast" has, after the death of Jan Baars, gone over into my employ, and she cooks deliciously and cares for me as for her own child. And the long, solemn, solitary evenings in my quiet house with my books, papers, memories and a little music are never too long for me.

What I mind most are the meetings of the board of directors of the orphanage, but I shall tell of that another time. It is not a heavy affliction, however.

The nights have, as formerly, continued to be my greatest solace. The years now pass swiftly and fleetingly, for in age one measures the flight of time with a larger scale. I now reckon its flight almost solely by the milestones of my dreams, by the times when I could summon my beloved and was sensible of her presence.

In this connection I shall recount one more dream - it was in the late morning hours between seven and eight o'clock. The dream began with a conversation concerning the life after death, in which I tried to convince some one that there would be a fusion of units, not a personal continuation of life, but an absorbing of our individual being into the universal being with complete retention of our memory and our experience. This was clearer to me than ever before.

Then all at once came the thought: I have not yet seen my beloved, she is waiting, I must go quickly to greet her. Thereupon the consciousness that I was dreaming and was in E—and that I should find her there. I went out of doors and saw the blue sky and a magnificent landscape. Then I passed into the state of ecstasy. Following one upon the other in rapid succession, the most glorious spectacles unfolded

Frederik van Eeden

themselves and I did nothing but utter cries of rapture and fervid thanks. I saw an entrancing mountain landscape, clearly and sharply outlined, the crevices in the rocks, the rough stony ledges lit up by the sun, the mountain pastures o'erspread with golden radiance. And then all at once there lay before me a fair green valley, with low shrubs, a clear, gently-flowing, winding stream, quiet houses and a few tall-stemmed tropical trees. An indescribable, deeply-significant calm and stillness reigned there. The land was populated and thickly settled, but enwrapped in a universal breathless consecration of peace and joy. I saw light-blue peacocks quietly strutting about in the sun, their images reflected by the water. The colors, the pure atmosphere, the pretty, quiet house, the solemn silence, the presence, felt but not seen, of thousands of peaceful, happy human beings, the light horizon with the mighty sun-lit mountain chain - all this was too beautiful for words.

I called my beloved that she should come and look too. I did not see her, but I heard her dear voice saying:

"What a quantity of flowers!"

Then I felt the desire to pray, and facing toward the direction whence the light came, I for the first time no longer saw the dark cloud which I had always seen there until Elsje's death and which after that time only gradually dissolved. And for the first time in the dream-world I saw the disc of the sun.

Then I spoke to Christ, passionately and eloquently as I had never done before and surely would never be able to do in the day-time. Gratitude and love I gave utterance to.

"My father and my mother thou art, and I love thee despite all I have suffered for thee. I am willing to suffer for thee, and I feel no bitterness for the grief I have suffered. I forgive thee, I forgive thee, and I know that thou forgivest me all my follies and my weaknesses - for between us there shall no longer be any question of forgiveness, but only of gratitude, even as between myself and my beloved. For we cannot conceive thee and therefore cannot love thee sufficiently, and we only love thee in each other, even as we know each other. But I know that the love for my beloved is love for thee and that in her I love thee. And I feel no regret and am happy and thankful, content to have followed thee and served thee, firmly believing that I shall grow in power till I shall recognize and attain fitness for eternal blessedness. I ask for nothing, but I long for thee and for thy Glory, and I shall leave behind a glowing trail of gratitude so that the others may find thee by it."

As I said this, I saw light mists draw away from the face of the sun, and it began to shine with blinding radiance. This seemed such a gracious revelation to me that I could only cry: Ah! Ah! in my transport. Then I felt that I would weep or faint from joy, but that I did not want, and I awoke!

That morning I was refreshed and well fortified against trouble.

The only thing I still fear is a weakening of the mind in my declining years, so that I should have to drift about for years as a hopeless wreck. I have a theory that one can prevent this by sagacious prudence and by exertion and exercise of the contemplative power.

But this theory has yet to be proved. And my example alone would not be sufficient for that.

As long as I retain my clearness of mind, I have plenty of work in elaborating these ideas and conceptions which so far I have only briefly indicated.

Frederik van Eeden

In the first place?

- - -

The E—Journal in its issue of June 12th, 1908, published the following account:

"To-day a sad accident occurred outside the harbor within eight of our town. On the yacht 'Elsje,' belonging to Mr. Muralto, a fire started, presumably caused by the upsetting of an alcohol lamp. The entire vessel was speedily ablaze. Mr. Muralto, despite his great age a strong swimmer, jumped overboard, endeavoring to carry his companion, a skipper's lad who could not swim, to the haven on some planks. But the strong current pulled both out to sea. The boy was picked up by a home-sailing sloop, Mr. Muralto was drowned. As the deemed was universally respected and loved for his benevolence and unassuming manner, his death arouses universal sympathy in our town."

Choose from Thousands of 1stWorldLibrary Classics By

A. M. Barnard
Ada Leverson
Adolphus William Ward
Aesop
Agatha Christie
Alexander Aaronsohn
Alexander Kielland
Alexandre Dumas
Alfred Gatty
Alfred Ollivant
Alice Duer Miller
Alice Turner Curtis
Alice Dunbar
Allen Chapman
Alleyne Ireland
Ambrose Bierce
Amelia E. Barr
Amory H. Bradford
Andrew Lang
Andrew McFarland Davis
Andy Adams
Angela Brazil
Anna Alice Chapin
Anna Sewell
Annie Besant
Annie Hamilton Donnell
Annie Payson Call
Annie Roe Carr
Annonaymous
Anton Chekhov
Archibald Lee Fletcher
Arnold Bennett
Arthur C. Benson
Arthur Conan Doyle
Arthur M. Winfield
Arthur Ransome
Arthur Schnitzler
Arthur Train
Atticus
B.H. Baden-Powell
B. M. Bower
B. C. Chatterjee
Baroness Emmuska Orczy
Baroness Orczy
Basil King
Bayard Taylor
Ben Macomber
Bertha Muzzy Bower
Bjornstjerne Bjornson

Booth Tarkington
Boyd Cable
Bram Stoker
C. Collodi
C. E. Orr
C. M. Ingleby
Carolyn Wells
Catherine Parr Traill
Charles A. Eastman
Charles Amory Beach
Charles Dickens
Charles Dudley Warner
Charles Farrar Browne
Charles Ives
Charles Kingsley
Charles Klein
Charles Hanson Towne
Charles Lathrop Pack
Charles Romyn Dake
Charles Whibley
Charles Willing Beale
Charlotte M. Braeme
Charlotte M. Yonge
Charlotte Perkins Stetson
Clair W. Hayes
Clarence Day Jr.
Clarence E. Mulford
Clemence Housman
Confucius
Coningsby Dawson
Cornelis DeWitt Wilcox
Cyril Burleigh
D. H. Lawrence
Daniel Defoe
David Garnett
Dinah Craik
Don Carlos Janes
Donald Keyhoe
Dorothy Kilner
Dougan Clark
Douglas Fairbanks
E. Nesbit
E. P. Roe
E. Phillips Oppenheim
E. S. Brooks
Earl Barnes
Edgar Rice Burroughs
Edith Van Dyne
Edith Wharton

Edward Everett Hale
Edward J. O'Biren
Edward S. Ellis
Edwin L. Arnold
Eleanor Atkins
Eleanor Hallowell Abbott
Eliot Gregory
Elizabeth Gaskell
Elizabeth McCracken
Elizabeth Von Arnim
Ellem Key
Emerson Hough
Emilie F. Carlen
Emily Bronte
Emily Dickinson
Enid Bagnold
Enilor Macartney Lane
Erasmus W. Jones
Ernie Howard Pie
Ethel May Dell
Ethel Turner
Ethel Watts Mumford
Eugene Sue
Eugenie Foa
Eugene Wood
Eustace Hale Ball
Evelyn Everett-green
Everard Cotes
F. H. Cheley
F. J. Cross
F. Marion Crawford
Fannie E. Newberry
Federick Austin Ogg
Ferdinand Ossendowski
Fergus Hume
Florence A. Kilpatrick
Fremont B. Deering
Francis Bacon
Francis Darwin
Frances Hodgson Burnett
Frances Parkinson Keyes
Frank Gee Patchin
Frank Harris
Frank Jewett Mather
Frank L. Packard
Frank V. Webster
Frederic Stewart Isham
Frederick Trevor Hill
Frederick Winslow Taylor

Friedrich Kerst
Friedrich Nietzsche
Fyodor Dostoyevsky
G.A. Henty
G.K. Chesterton
Gabrielle E. Jackson
Garrett P. Serviss
Gaston Leroux
George A. Warren
George Ade
Geroge Bernard Shaw
George Cary Eggleston
George Durston
George Ebers
George Eliot
George Gissing
George MacDonald
George Meredith
George Orwell
George Sylvester Viereck
George Tucker
George W. Cable
George Wharton James
Gertrude Atherton
Gordon Casserly
Grace E. King
Grace Gallatin
Grace Greenwood
Grant Allen
Guillermo A. Sherwell
Gulielma Zollinger
Gustav Flaubert
H. A. Cody
H. B. Irving
H.C. Bailey
H. G. Wells
H. H. Munro
H. Irving Hancock
H. R. Naylor
H. Rider Haggard
H. W. C. Davis
Haldeman Julius
Hall Caine
Hamilton Wright Mabie
Hans Christian Andersen
Harold Avery
Harold McGrath
Harriet Beecher Stowe
Harry Castlemon
Harry Coghill
Harry Houidini

Hayden Carruth
Helent Hunt Jackson
Helen Nicolay
Hendrik Conscience
Hendy David Thoreau
Henri Barbusse
Henrik Ibsen
Henry Adams
Henry Ford
Henry Frost
Henry James
Henry Jones Ford
Henry Seton Merriman
Henry W Longfellow
Herbert A. Giles
Herbert Carter
Herbert N. Casson
Herman Hesse
Hildegard G. Frey
Homer
Honore De Balzac
Horace B. Day
Horace Walpole
Horatio Alger Jr.
Howard Pyle
Howard R. Garis
Hugh Lofting
Hugh Walpole
Humphry Ward
Ian Maclaren
Inez Haynes Gillmore
Irving Bacheller
Isabel Cecilia Williams
Isabel Hornibrook
Israel Abrahams
Ivan Turgenev
J.G.Austin
J. Henri Fabre
J. M. Barrie
J. M. Walsh
J. Macdonald Oxley
J. R. Miller
J. S. Fletcher
J. S. Knowles
J. Storer Clouston
J. W. Duffield
Jack London
Jacob Abbott
James Allen
James Andrews
James Baldwin

James Branch Cabell
James DeMille
James Joyce
James Lane Allen
James Lane Allen
James Oliver Curwood
James Oppenheim
James Otis
James R. Driscoll
Jane Abbott
Jane Austen
Jane L. Stewart
Janet Aldridge
Jens Peter Jacobsen
Jerome K. Jerome
Jessie Graham Flower
John Buchan
John Burroughs
John Cournos
John F. Kennedy
John Gay
John Glasworthy
John Habberton
John Joy Bell
John Kendrick Bangs
John Milton
John Philip Sousa
John Taintor Foote
Jonas Lauritz Idemil Lie
Jonathan Swift
Joseph A. Altsheler
Joseph Carey
Joseph Conrad
Joseph E. Badger Jr
Joseph Hergesheimer
Joseph Jacobs
Jules Vernes
Julian Hawthrone
Julie A Lippmann
Justin Huntly McCarthy
Kakuzo Okakura
Karle Wilson Baker
Kate Chopin
Kenneth Grahame
Kenneth McGaffey
Kate Langley Bosher
Kate Langley Bosher
Katherine Cecil Thurston
Katherine Stokes
L. A. Abbot
L. T. Meade

L. Frank Baum
Latta Griswold
Laura Dent Crane
Laura Lee Hope
Laurence Housman
Lawrence Beasley
Leo Tolstoy
Leonid Andreyev
Lewis Carroll
Lewis Sperry Chafer
Lilian Bell
Lloyd Osbourne
Louis Hughes
Louis Joseph Vance
Louis Tracy
Louisa May Alcott
Lucy Fitch Perkins
Lucy Maud Montgomery
Luther Benson
Lydia Miller Middleton
Lyndon Orr
M. Corvus
M. H. Adams
Margaret E. Sangster
Margret Howth
Margaret Vandercook
Margaret W. Hungerford
Margret Penrose
Maria Edgeworth
Maria Thompson Daviess
Mariano Azuela
Marion Polk Angellotti
Mark Overton
Mark Twain
Mary Austin
Mary Catherine Crowley
Mary Cole
Mary Hastings Bradley
Mary Roberts Rinehart
Mary Rowlandson
M. Wollstonecraft Shelley
Maud Lindsay
Max Beerbohm
Myra Kelly
Nathaniel Hawthrone
Nicolo Machiavelli
O. F. Walton
Oscar Wilde

Owen Johnson
P.G. Wodehouse
Paul and Mabel Thorne
Paul G. Tomlinson
Paul Severing
Percy Brebner
Percy Keese Fitzhugh
Peter B. Kyne
Plato
Quincy Allen
R. Derby Holmes
R. L. Stevenson
R. S. Ball
Rabindranath Tagore
Rahul Alvares
Ralph Bonehill
Ralph Henry Barbour
Ralph Victor
Ralph Waldo Emmerson
Rene Descartes
Ray Cummings
Rex Beach
Rex E. Beach
Richard Harding Davis
Richard Jefferies
Richard Le Gallienne
Robert Barr
Robert Frost
Robert Gordon Anderson
Robert L. Drake
Robert Lansing
Robert Lynd
Robert Michael Ballantyne
Robert W. Chambers
Rosa Nouchette Carey
Rudyard Kipling
Saint Augustine
Samuel B. Allison
Samuel Hopkins Adams
Sarah Bernhardt
Sarah C. Hallowell
Selma Lagerlof
Sherwood Anderson
Sigmund Freud
Standish O'Grady
Stanley Weyman
Stella Benson
Stella M. Francis

Stephen Crane
Stewart Edward White
Stijn Streuvels
Swami Abhedananda
Swami Parmananda
T. S. Ackland
T. S. Arthur
The Princess Der Ling
Thomas A. Janvier
Thomas A Kempis
Thomas Anderton
Thomas Bailey Aldrich
Thomas Bulfinch
Thomas De Quincey
Thomas Dixon
Thomas H. Huxley
Thomas Hardy
Thomas More
Thornton W. Burgess
U. S. Grant
Upton Sinclair
Valentine Williams
Various Authors
Vaughan Kester
Victor Appleton
Victor G. Durham
Victoria Cross
Virginia Woolf
Wadsworth Camp
Walter Camp
Walter Scott
Washington Irving
Wilbur Lawton
Wilkie Collins
Willa Cather
Willard F. Baker
William Dean Howells
William le Queux
W. Makepeace Thackeray
William W. Walter
William Shakespeare
Winston Churchill
Yei Theodora Ozaki
Yogi Ramacharaka
Young E. Allison
Zane Grey